THE JAIMINIGṚHYASŪTRA

सामवेदीयं

जैमिनिगृह्यसूत्रम्

कतिपयस्थलेषु संस्कृत
व्याख्योपेतम्

श्रीमता कैलेन्डमहोदयेन

आङ्ग्लभाषानुवादेन भूमिकया च सह सम्पादितम्

मोतीलाल बनारसीदास पब्लिशर्स प्रा० लि०
दिल्ली

THE JAIMINIGṚHYASŪTRA

BELONGING TO THE SĀMAVEDA

With Extracts from the Commentary

Edited with an introduction and translated
into English by

W. CALAND

PROFESSOR OF SANSKRIT IN THE UNIVERSITY OF UTRECHT

MOTILAL BANARSIDASS PUBLISHERS PVT. LTD.
DELHI

First Edition: Lahore, 1922 (Punjab Sanskrit Series No. 2)
Reprinted: Delhi, 1984, 1991

Also available at:
MOTILAL BANARSIDASS
41 U.A., Bungalow Road, Jawahar Nagar, Delhi 110 007
120 Royapettah High Road, Mylapore, Madras 600 004
16 St. Mark's Road, Bangalore 560 001
Ashok Rajpath, Patna 880 004
Chowk, Varanasi 221 001

PRINTED IN INDIA
BY JAINENDRA PRAKASH JAIN AT SHRI JAINENDRA PRESS, A-45 NARAINA INDUSTRIAL AREA, PHASE I, NEW DELHI 110 028 AND PUBLISHED BY NARENDRA PRAKASH JAIN FOR MOTILAL BANARSIDASS PUBLISHERS PVT. LTD., BUNGALOW ROAD, JAWAHAR NAGAR, DELHI 110 007

INTRODUCTION.

Remarks on the literature of the Sâmaveda in general.

According to Hindu tradition the Sāmaveda comprised once no less than a thousand "schools or branches" (*śâkhâs*). But, as in these schools the holy texts were studied at forbidden times, Indra is said to have destroyed them with his thunderbolt. So only few of them are now a days extant. In the first place the śākhā of the Rāṇāyanīyas, which is subdivided into seven parts: Rāṇāyanīyas, Śātyamugras, Kālopas, Mahākālopas, Lāṅgalāyanas, Śārdúlas and Kauthumas. According to some authorities the Kauthumas fall into six subdivisions: Kauthumas, Āsurāyaṇas, Vātāyanas, Prāñcadvainabhṛts, Prācīnayogyas and Naigamīyas (cp. Mahīdāsa on Caraṇavyūha, p. 44 ed. of Benares). Besides this tradition others tell us, that the Rāṇāyanīyas comprised nine schools: Rāṇāyanīyas, Śāṭyāyanīyas, Sātyamudgalas, Khalvalas, Mahākhalvalas, Lāṅgalas, Kauthumas, Gautamas and Jaiminīyas. Further tradition informs us, that at present of all these śākhās only three are left over: the Kauthumas in Gurjara (Guzerat), the Jaiminīyas in Karṇāṭaka (the present Karnatik) and the Rāṇāyanīyas in Mahārāṣṭra (the country of the Marāṭhas). To our knowledge have come the text books of these three śākhās, if not wholly complete.

As the Vulgata of the Sāmasaṃhitā is considered that of the Kauthumas, while eight Brāhmaṇas are handed down as belonging to this śākhā: 1. The Tāṇḍyamahābrāhmaṇa or Pañcaviṃśa brāhmaṇa (ed. in the Bibl. Indica); 2. The Ṣaḍviṃśabrāhmaṇa (edited by H. F. Eelsingh: Ṣaḍviṃśabrāhmaṇam vijñāpanabhāṣyasahitam, Leiden, Brill 1908 and by Jibananda Vidyasagara, Calcutta 1881); 3. The Sāmavidhānabrāhmaṇa (edited by Burnell, London 1873 and by Satyavrata in the journal Uṣā, Calcutta 1895, translated into German by Sten Konow, Halle, 1893); 4. The Ārṣeyabrāhmaṇa (ed. by Burnell, Mangalore 1876, and by Satyavrata in "Uṣā", Calcutta 1892); 5. The Devatādhyāyabrāhmaṇa (ed. by Burnell, Mangalore 1873 and by Vidyasagara together with the Ṣaḍviṃśa); 6. The Upaniṣadbrāhmaṇa, of which the first two prapāṭhakas contain the Mantrabrāhmaṇa (ed. by Satyavrata in "Uṣā" 1890); the last eight prapāṭhakas comprising the Chāndogya-upaniṣad (ed. by Röer in the Bibl. Indica and by Böhtlingk with a german translation, Leipsic 1889); 7. The Saṃhitopaniṣad (ed. by Burnell, Mangalore 1877); 8. The Vaṃśabrāhmaṇa (ed. by Burnell, Mangalore 1873 and in the "Uṣā" 1892).

The following Sūtras are dependent on the Saṃhitā and the Brāhmaṇas of the Kauthumas: 1. The Maśakakalpasûtra or Ārṣeyakalpa (ed. by W. Caland, Brockhaus, Leipsic 1908); 2. The Kṣudrasûtra, being an appendix to the ārṣeyakalpa (printed after this text); 3. The Śrautasûtra of Lāṭyāyana (ed. in the Bibl. Indica); 4. The Gṛhyasûtra of Gobhila (ed. in the Bibl. Indica and with German translation by Fr. Knauer, Dorpat 1884; English transl. by H. Oldenberg in Sacred Books of the East, vol. XXX); 5. The Śrādhakalpa of Gobhila or Vasiṣṭha (ed. in the Bibl. Indica as an appendix to Gobhila); 6. The Karmapradīpa or Chandogyagṛhyapariśiṣṭa (ed. by Jiv. Vidyasagara in Dharmaśāstra saṃgraha and elsewhere); 7. The Gṛhyāsaṃgraha (ed. by Bloomfield in the Journal of the German Oriental Society, vol. 35, and in the Bibl. Ind. and the "Uṣā"). There are many texts more as the Puṣpasûtra, the Pañcavidhasútra (both ed. by Simon), the Nidānasûtra etc., most of which have been edited. For a complete survey of these texts see: "Die Jaiminīya Saṃhitā" ed. by W. Caland, Breslau 1907, page 14.

Thus for the texts of the Kauthumas.

Whether the Rāṇāyanīyas are a śākhā or a caraṇa, i. e. whether, besides an independent tradition of the sûtras they possess a separate recension also of the Saṃhitā, is not yet ascertained: the Audgātraprayoga of Sāyaṇa, who, as we know, adhered to the Sútra of Drāhyāyaṇa, shows in the musical notation of the Sāmaveda divergencies, although slight, from the Vulgata. For the rest are at present considered as Rāṇāyanīya texts the following: 1. The Drāhyāyaṇaśrautasûtra (edited partly by Reuter, London, Luzac 1904); 2. The Khādiragṛhyasútra (ed. with the comm. of Rudraskanda at Mysore 1913, and translated H. Oldenberg in the Sacred Books of the East, vol. XXIX); 3. The Gautamapitṛmedhasútra (ed. by W. Caland together with the Pitṛmedhasútras of Baudhāyana and Hiraṇyakeśin, Leipsic 1896); 4. The Gautamasmṛti (ed. with Telugu comm. by Chentral Rao Pantalu, Madras 1890). But it is at far from certain, that all these texts belong to the Rāṇāyanīyas. Āśārka in his commentary on the Karmapradīpa informs us that the Gobhilasûtra contains the domestic ritual followed not only by the Kauthumas but also by the Rāṇāyanīyas. In agreement with this statement is the fact, that Hemādri in his Śrāddhakalpa thrice (pag. 1424, 1460, 1468) designates Gobhila as the Rāṇāyanīyasūtrakṛt. If we accept these statements, the Khādirasūtra cannot be also the Sūtra of the Rāṇāyanīyas. Now, in Southern India there is said to exist a Khādiragṛhyasûtra of the Śārdûlas (see Report on a search for Skt. mss. in the Bombay Presidency 1891–1895, by A. V. Kathavate, Bombay, 1901, No. 79), who also are a śākhā of the Sāmaveda, and this Sûtra of the Śārdûlasāmagas agrees, as I am informed, with the exception of a few various readings, with the text of our Khādirasūtra. That at the time of Hemādri there existed a living tradition of the Śārdûlaśākhā is seen also from his Śrāddhakalpa, where (on page 1078), he mentions those parts of the Veda that are to be recited by the Śārdûlaśākhins during the feeding of the Brāhmaṇas. It is, therefore, possible that at least the Khādirasûtra contained originally the domestic ritual of the Śārdûlas. But there is still another tradition current about this Khādirasūtra. In the Gṛhyaratna edited at Mysore in 1881 with the commentary called Kaṇṭhabhûṣaṇa, we find several times cited a Gautamagṛhyasûtra, and all the passages here attributed to Gautama are to be found in our Khādirasûtra. Besides, we possess, as has been noted above, a Pitṛmedhasūtra of the Gautamas, a Gautamadharmasûtra (ed. by Stenzler, London 1876) and a Gautamasmṛti. All these may have been the books of the Gautamas, who also formed a subdivision of the Sāmaveda.

Of the third greater śākhā belonging to the Sāmaveda, the Jaiminīyas, until a few years ago but one single book was known, viz. the Talavakāra or Kena Upaniṣad. A. C. Burnell, who during his sojourn in Southern India published many Sāmaveda texts, brought to Europe a collection of other texts belonging to this śākhā. Of these texts are now published: 1. The Jaiminīyasaṃhitā (Die Jaiminīyasaṃhitā mit einer Einleitung über die Sāmaveda literatur by W. Caland, Breslau 1907); 2. The Jaiminīyabrāhmaṇa partly; of this important and extensive Brāhmaṇa copies procured by Burnell are to be found at the India Office in London. Several miner parts have been published by H. Örtel in the Journal of the American Oriental Society. As the manuscript materials, however, were inadequate to give a complete edition of this book, the writer of this Introduction published large extracts from it (Das Jaiminīyabrāhmaṇa in Auswahl, Text, Ülbsersetzung, Indices; Amsterdam, 1919); 3. The Jaiminīya-upaniṣadbrāhmaṇa (properly: the Gāyatryupaniṣad, being a part of the great Brāhmaṇa; ed. by Örtel, New Haven 1894 as Vol. XVI of the J. A. O. S.); 4. The Ārṣeyabrāhmaṇa (the Jaiminīya text of the Ārṣeya brāhmaṇa of the Sāmveda ed. by Burnell, Mangalore 1878); 5. The Jaiminīyaśrautasútra (edited with a Dutch translation under the title: "Bijdrage tot de Kennis von het vedische ritueel" by D. Gaastra, Brill, Leiden 1906); 6. and lastly The Jaiminigṛhyasútra, on which text see below. Besides these texts, now printed, the India Office possesses also copies of the Gānas of the Jaiminīyas, brought to Europe also by Burnell. But until the key to its musical notations is found, an edition of these books can hardly be expected.

Remarks on the Jaiminigṛhyasûtra.

In his Introduction to the Ṛktantravyākaraṇa (page XLIX) Burnell informed us, that a copy of the Gṛhyasûtra of the Jaiminīyas with a commentary by Śrīnivāsa had just (in the year 1879) come into his possession. This Manuscript was presented to the India office, and through the kindness of Dr. F. W. Thomas, Chief Librarian of the India Office, I was allowed to make use of it. The Mss. is in excellent condition, in Grantha characters. On the title page we read in Burneli's handwriting:

"A. C. Burnell, 1879.

I. Jaiminigṛhyasûtra with C. by Çrīnivāsa. The author refers to previous Kārikās and Vṛttis.

2. Vinatānanda, a prayoga to the same.

Both from Tinavelly MSS. 1. about 200 years old.
2 recent."

The Manuscript is registered as B 464, written neatly on blue paper on 73 folia, 19 c. m × 24 c. m, in Grantha. Each Sútra is followed by its bhāṣya.

In two Reports ("Report on a search for Skt. and Tamil mss. for the year 1896/97 by Śeṣagiri Śāstrī No. 1, Madras 1898" and in a ditto for the year 1893/94) I found two more mss. of this text mentioned under No. 24 of the no, 1 and under no. 65 of no. 2. The first of these two is a copy of an original from Trichinopoly, on paper in Nāgāri comprising 48 pages of 15 lines each. This copy contains the continuous text of the Sûtra alone. The second of the two Madras mss. gives the commentary called Subodhinī composed by Śrīnivāsin Adhvarin; this is a copy of a Telugu original on paper, 100 pages of 20 lines each.

On these three mss. so based the text as given below:

B. designates the ms. of Burnell at the India Office.

M^1 designates the first Madras ms. (text only).

M^2 designates the second Madras ms. (Subodhinī).

The text is given by me continuously, just as found in M^1, without division into Sūtras. To facilitate understanding the sentences are separated by a small daṇḍa above the line. In indicating the close of a sentence the commentary was mostly, but not always, my guide.—Of the commentary only extracts are presented, but I do not believe that anything deserving mention has been omitted. Against ordinary use Śrīnivāsa comments also on the mantras. These vyākhyās have been received into the extracts only for those mantras, which do not occur in any printed text, or when they occur only in the Mantrabrāhmaṇa of the Kauthumas. I regret to state that I was not able to give a wholly faultless text as the text of the commentary as handed down only in one ms.(B) complete, M^2 treating of the second part only the śrāddha, the aṣṭakāritual, the gṛhavidhi, and the anaśnatsaṃhitākalpa.

A few remarks must be made concerning the relation of the commentary to the text as handed down in M[1]. It is only in the first part (the first Adhyāya) that Śrīnivāsa follows this text closely. As to the second part, the commentary disagrees in two respects the texts of M[1]. First there is no trace that to Śrīnivāsa were known the adbhutaśānti (II. 7) and the grahahoma (II. 9). Consequently these two chapters were the most difficult to reconstruct. In the second place the disposition of the materials in the Subodhinī differs in some respects from the one in the text of M[1]. After treating Khaṇḍa 3 the Subodhinī continues: *itah param âhitâgneh śarîranâśe ityâdi* (cp. p. 29, l. 12 of the text) *dahanâdisâpiṇḍyânta-vidhâyakasûtrâṇy ante vyâkhyâsyâmaḥ*. Then follows immediately the exposition of kh. 6 (gṛhakarma) as fourth kh. and after it the anaśnatsaṃhitākalpa (kh. 8). No numbering of khaṇḍas is given further on, at the end we read only *ity anaśnatsaṃhitâkalpaḥ*. Then follows, in agreement with what had been stated by Śrīnivāsa (see above), the treatment of khaṇda 4, introduced by the words, *atha dahanapatalo vyâkhyâyate*. Having then treated from khaṇda 4 unto p. 29, l. 17 (unto: *madhye śarîram*, these included) Śrīnivāsa deviates again from the text as given by M[1], as he begins communicating some passages from the Jaiminīyabrāhmaṇa (viz. I. 46–48, cp. the extracts of the commentary on page 65) and explaining them (*atha âhitâgneḥ kramasaṃskâra ucyate*). As the Sūtra itself (p. 30, l. 1–2) refers to this passage of the Brāhmaṇa with the words *tasya nâsikayoh sruvan nidadhyâd ity etenânuvakena* this passages cannot have formed a part of the Sútra proper. After treating this matter, and lending with the words: *ity āhitāgnidahanakalpaḥ*, Śrīnivāsa continues explaining the text, first the passage p. 29, l. 17—unto p. 30, l. 9 (unto *anavekṣamāṇaḥ*, incl.); this part and indicated: *iti dvitiyaḥ paṭalaḥ*. Then follows the exposition of p. 30, l. 9—p. 31, l. 9. At the end we read: *iti dahane tṛtiyaḥ paṭalaḥ*.

On the relation of the Jaiminigṛhyasûtra to the other txts of the Jaiminīyas the following may be said. From various facts it is clear, that our sūtra is a genuine text of the Jaiminīyas and that it attaches itself to the other bocks of this śākhā.

While in the list of Veda-teachers, to whom at the utsarga ceremony libations of water are to be presented, the Rāṇāyanīyas begin with Rāṇāyani and end with Jaimini (cp. Simon, Beiträge zur Kenntniss der Vedischen Schuler, p. 27, rem. 1, and Subrahmaṇyavidvān, Gobhilagṛhyaprakāśikā, p. 113), the Jaiminigṛhya mentions Jaimini Talvakāra in the first place (cp. the text, p. 14, l. 11).

The Vrātikavrata prepares the student for the study of the Vratas, i. e. of those parvans of the Saṃhitā, which begin with the vrataparvan; thus the commentary, and cp. Jaim. gṛhs. p. 15, l. 8. This statement agrees with the sequence of the Sāmans as handed down by the Jaiminīyas, this śākhā beginning the Āraṇyaka with the vrataparvan, in contrast with the tradition of the Kauthuma-Rāṇāyanīyas who begin with the arkaparvan, cp. Jaim. ārṣ. br. p. 23 and Ārṣeyabrāhmaṇa (Kauth.) p. 62, both cited according to Burnell., edition of these texts.

The Aupaniṣada vrata prepares for the study of the Upaniṣada, which according to Śrīnivāsa, comprises ten adhyāyas. This statement seems not to agree with other facts, as the Jaiminīya upaniṣad brāhmaṇa, edited by Örtel comprises not ten adhyāyas, but twelve anuvākās. On the other hand the assertion of Śrīnivāsa, does agree with a communication made by Burnell to Max Müller (see Sacred Books of the East, vol. I, p. Xc.): "The Kena upaniṣad comprises the 135–145 Khaṇḍas or the tenth anuvāka" (that is, of the Jaiminīya brāhmaṇa).

Most conclusive, however, is the fact that our Sûtra refers repeatedly to the Jaiminīyasaṃhitā, indicating by their pratīka the verses, that are to be taken from this Saṃhitā and thus presupposing it as known to its readers (or auditors ?). So e. g. the puruṣasûkta according to the Subodhinī (see p. 44, l. 15) has seven verses, whereas the Kauthuma recension knows only five. This is in harmony with the Saṃhitā, where the seven verses of this sûkta are handed down in II. 3. 6–II. 4. 2.

The Jaiminīyabrāhmaṇa also is supposed to be familiar to those, who accept the domestic ritual of our Sûtra as their own. This is clearly seen from Jaim. gṛhs. II. 4 (p. 29, l. 12), where the author refers to the 48th. and 46th. anuvāka of the first book of the Brāhmaṇa (see J. A. O. S., vol. XIX, p. 106, 103).

There is one point of linguistic character, where our Sûtra harmonizes with the tradition of the Jaiminīyas, viz. the use of the Tamil-malayālam ḷ instead of Sanskṛt ḍ; this ḷ occurs twice : in *Kâraḷi* (p. 14, l. 12) and in *iḷopahavana.*

That Hindu tradition itself knew our Sūtra to be that of Jaimini is proved by a citation (this is the only passage, where I found the Jaiminigṛhya cited) found in the unpublished Bhāṣya of Sāyaṇa on the Darśapûraṇamasasûtra of Baudhāyana. Sāyaṇa here says : *talavakârakalpe jaiminiś cāha: âhitâgneś cet pûrvaṃ jâyâ mriyeta tâṃ nirmanthyena dahet saṃtapanena veti.* The passage occurs Jaim. gṛhs. II. 5 (beg.).

About the relation of the Jaiminigṛhyasûtra to the other Gṛhyasūtras of the Sāmaveda we remark that our Sûtra, as is to be expected, has a closer affinity to the Sûtras of the Sāmaveda (Gobhila and Khādira) than to the Sūtras of any other Veda. Whereas Gobhila and Khādira differ from one another principally in the distribution of the materials, the Khādira, moreover, being more concise than the Gobhilasûtra, the Jaiminisútra as compared with them, has a totally independent character. It is true that many a sentence of the Jaiminisûtra agrees verbally with the Gobhilasûtra: compare Gobh. I. 1. 9 with Jaim. 1. 2—3 (we remark the ungrammatical *prâcyaḥ* in Jaim.); Gobh. I. 1. 10 with Jaim. 1. 3; Gobh. I. 5. 15 with Jaim. 1. 9—10; Gobh. I. 5. 18 with Jaim. 1. 11—12; Gobh. IV. 5. 4 with Jaim. 2. 3; Gobh. IV. 5. 5 with Jaim. 2. 3 (here Khādira and Jaim. agree, in opposition to Gobhila, as both texts reckon the *parisamūhana and bhūmyâlambhana* to the paribhāṣās); Gobh. III. 3. 2—5 with Jaim. 14. 7—8; Gobh. III. 2. 51 with Jaim. 14. 15; Gobh. III. 3. 9—10 with Jaim. 14. 16—17; Gobh. III. 1. 29 with Jaim. 15. 4—5; Gobh. III. 2. 11 with Jaim. 15. 5; Gobh. III. 2. 12 with Jaim. ib.; Gobh. III. 2. 1—4 with Jaim. 15. 10—11; Gobh. III. 2. 6 with Jaim. 15. 11; Gobh. III. 2. 5, 18, 19 with Jaim. 15. 12; Gobh. III. 2. 29 with Jaim. 15. 16—17; Gobh. III. 2. 52 with Jaim. 16. 5; Gobh. III. 5. 3 with Jaim. 18. 4; Gobh. III. 5. 11, 12, 14 with Jaim. 18. 4—5; Gobh. III. 5. 32—34 with Jaim. 18. 4—6; Gobh. III. 5. 13 with Jaim. 18. 6; Gobh. III. 5. 31 with Jaim. 18. 6; Gobh. III. 5. 7—10 with Jaim. 18. 7—9; Gobh. III. 5. 21—22 with Jaim. 18. 10—12; Gobh. II. 1. 21 with Jaim. 20. 5. Some of these sûtra-sentences are found also in the Khādirasûtra, but usually in a more or less (different wording. So our Jaiminisûtra stands nearer to the Gobhila–than to the Khādirasûtra. This fact does not necessarily compel us to suppose, that it is caused by direct influence of the one on the other Sûtra, as it is more probable that the Sāmavedins from older times possessed a common stock of ritual prescriptions, from which each of them drew.

Whilst the Gobhila and Khādira sūtras stand very near to one another and especially have this fact in common, that both of them acknowledge the Mantrabrāhmaṇa as their authority for the mantras, citing the mantra taken from this source by its pratīka, the Jaiminisútra in this respect also stands by itself. Many a mantra given by the Mantrabrāhmaṇa is found in the Jaiminisútra also, but it is here given always sakalapāṭhena and, as is seen from the list of mantras at the end of this edition, never wholly agreeing. Not a few times do we find a mantra in the Jaiminisútra occuring also in the Mantrabrāhmaṇa, but in a wording agreeing more closely with the recension of the texts of the Black or White Yajurveda. Further it is to be remarked, that our Jaimini text contains some mantras, which as yet are known only from the Kāṭhakagṛhyasútra.

We may close this Introduction with a few remarks concerning the relation of our Sūtra to some texts outside the Sāmaveda. In the second part of our Sūtra we met with some whole chapters, which, mutatis mutandis, are found also in other texts. So the last four chapters occur also in texts of the Baudhāyanīyas. The gṛhavidhi (II. 6) is found almost verbally agreeing in Baudh. gṛhyapariśiṣṭa (I. 16); the adbhutaśānti (II. 7) occurs, somewhat longer, in Baudh. gṛhyasûtra III. 9, the mantras, as is to be expected, differing; the anaśnatsaṃhitākalpa (II. 8) has its counterpart and perhaps its origin in Baudh. dharmasûtra III. 9., whilst finally the grahavidhi agrees nearly verbally with Baudh. gṛhyapariśiṣṭa I. 15. I, for my part, am inclined to believe—we cannot prove it with absolute certainly—that we must admit the possibility of the Jaiminisûtra having borrowed these parts from Baudhāyana. On the whole, the texts of the Baudhāyanīyas have become very popular in Southern India and have influenced apparently also other texts of the Sāmaveda, especially the still unpublished Pariśiṣṭa, the contents of which are given by Winternitz in his Catalogue of South Indian Manuscripts, London 1902, page 120.

TABLE OF CONTENTS

THE RULES OF DOMESTIC CEREMONIES OF THE JAIMINÎYAS.

I. 1.

General outline of gṛhya-sacrifices.

Now, being about to carry forward the fire (to the place where he is to perform the domestic ritual, he should prepare with sand or clay) a piece of ground sloping towards the north-east (measuring a square cubit); having sprinkled over with water this sthaṇḍila, he should in its centre (with a grass stalk) make the mark by drawing one line from west to east and another touching the first, at its west side, from south to north; then three lines in the middle from west to east.[1] Having sprinkled it over (with water), he should establish thereon the fire with the formula: "Bhûḥ, bhuvaḥ, svah". This making the mark must at all times be performed (when a fire is established for ritual purposes).

Now we shall explain the sacrifices of cooked food. They are huta (i. e. consisting of a simple burnt-offering), ahuta (devoid of any burnt-offering), prahuta (preceded by a burnt-offering), and prāśita (i. e. where food is eaten). The burnt-offerings are performed in one single fire (not in three, as is the case with the Vedic ritual).

Regularly prescribed are (here) the wearing of the upper garment above the left shoulder and beneath the right arm-pit, and the sipping of water.

These offerings follow the rite of the new and full-moon sacrifices (i. e. the now following description must be completed according to this rite), or they are self-dependent.

---

1. The mark thus resembles a trident, the points of which are directed toward the west.

To the south of the fire and near it he places a vessel (filled with rice etc., destined as sacrificial fee for the officiating priest) and a sacrificial ladle filled with water; to the north of the fire the fuel and Kuśa grass.

After being sprinkled once with the formula: "On the instigation of god Sāvitṛ I sprinkle thee with the arms of the Aśvins with the hands of Pûṣan," and twice without muttering the formula, the fuel and grass have been put down ready. The fuel should be of palāśa or khadira wood. If he cannot obtain this wood, he should take the fuel from any tree with the exception of Vibhîtaka, tilvaka, bādhaka, nimba, rājavṛíkṣa, śalmali, aralu, dadhittha, kovidāra and śleṣmâtaka.[1] If kuśa grass cannot be obtained, any kind of grass is allowed with the exception of śûka-grass, saccharum reed, uśîra[2], balbaja, mutava, nala and śuṇṭha. The flowers (used for ornamenting the fire-stead) should be white. If he cannot obtain these, fragrant flowers of any other colour are to be used, with the exception of japārûpā, kākuttha, caṇḍī and kuraṇḍaka.

There are four normal substitutes of the clarified melted butter (the "ghee", destined for the offerings) viz. fresh butter (?), milk (?), sour coagulated milk, and fresh milk.

Behind the fire should take place the rinsing of the mouth. Thrice he should rinse the mouth, twice wipe (his lips with the base of the thumb of the right hand).

Once he should touch water: having sprinkled his feet, he should touch with water the head and the organs of sense in the head (i. e. eyes, nose, ears).

Having touched water he mutters, sitting down behind the fire on which fuel has been put, whilst touching

1 Cp. Gobh. I. 5. 15; these kinds of wood are used in abhicâra-rites.

2 Uncertain; cp. Gobh. I. 5. 18.

the earth, the formula: "Here we partake of the earth; here the prosperous, here the auspicious. Repel the adversaries, obtain thee another one's wealth," and if it is night, the same formula, but closing with : "another one's riches."

With the triplet, beginning: "Let us prepare this song"[1] he should wipe with his wet hand around the fire, or thrice with the first of these three verses.

Having seized a prastara (i. e. a bundle of darbha grass taken from the barhis), he strews (this grass) round (the fire) at every quarter of the sky, beginning in the south-east, (first from east to west, then from west to north, from north to east, from east to south), covering the roots (of one layer) with the tips (of the next). Or he strews the grass first at the west side and lays down two rows of grass in easterly direction at the southern and northern ends of the westerly row, so that they join before the fire and form a triangle. At the point, where these last two rows are connected (i. e. at the east side, before the fire) the tips of the southern blades of grass lie above those of the northern.

I. 2.

From the prastara he takes two (grass-stalks as) "purifiers," measuring a span, even, with unbroken tips, and which do not bear a young shoot in them. Holding them between thumb and ring-finger, he cuts them (to obtain the required length) with any other instrument than his fingernails, muttering the formula : "You two are purifiers, sacred to Viṣṇu." Three times he should stroke them upward with water, muttering the formula: "Through the mind of Viṣṇu you are purified": once with this formula, twice silently. Holding (in his left hand) the "purifiers" above a vessel, he pours in it (with the right hand) the ghee (destined for the

1 Jaim. S. I. I. 7. 4-6.

sacrifice). Then he thrusts some burning coals out of the fire in northerly direction, puts (the vessel with the ghee) thereon, holds two flaming young stalks of darbha grass above it, throws the two stalks into (the fire), moves thrice a burning grass stalk from left to right around the vessel, removes it from the fire in northerly direction, thrusts the burning coals back into the fire and purifies thrice with the northward-pointed purifiers the ghee, the sacrificial substance (destined for the chief oblation), the praṇita-water, and the sacrificial ladle, muttering (each time) the formula:" "May the god Savitṛ purify thee with unimpaired purifier, with the rays of the good Sun."[1] Of the ghee (the purifying takes place) whilst moving the two purifiers back (only, and not forward through the ghee). This purifying is performed once with the formula, twice silently.

Having carried the pranîta-water to the north of the fire, having covered it with dûrvâ-grass, having put down the prastara (i. e. the bundle of grass) to the south of the fire, having put the two purifiers above the bundle of grass, he mutters the virûpâkṣa formula: Om ! heat, lustre, truth, all-soul, firmness, righteousness, vitality, renunciation, Brahmā, brahman ; to these I resort, may these favour me. Bhûḥ, bhuvaḥ, svaḥ, om ! The great all-soul I ascend. Thou art the one with deformed eyes[2], of shining teeth (?) Thy couch is on the leaf[3], thy dwelling is in the atmosphere, golden is thy shed. There those hearts of the Gods are deposited inside an iron jar[4]. Strong (art thou) and bestowing strength. Protect us, do not neglect us. In truth, thou hast twelve sons; these, performing for thee year

1 The translation of the following words fall out in a European language.

2 Rudra is meant.

3 Cp. TS. IV. 5. 9. m.

4 The commentator cites TS. IV. 5. 9. p.

after year a desire-granting sacrifice, again practise chastity[1]. Thou art the brāhmin[2] of the Gods, I am the brāhmin of men : the brāhmin resorts to the brāhmin : to thee I resort. When I mutter the formula, do not obstruct my muttering, when I offer, do not obstruct my offering, when I perform a sacrificial action, do not obstruct my action. To thee I resort. Instigated by thee I will perform here the sacrificial action. May this thrive for me. Obeisance to the God of the deformed eyes, to the one of shining teeth, to the son of Brahman, to the Highest, the Best, the unfailing, the Lord of sacrificial action !"

I. 3.

He should pour the contents of the sruva-ladle into the praṇîta-water, hold the sruva above the fire (to expel all evil influence), sweep it clean by means of darbha-grass stalks, throw these stalks after sprinkling them into the fire, bend his right knee, sprinkle the ghee after having removed from it anything unfit for sacrifice that might have fallen into it, e. g. a wood fretter, a tryambakâfly, a bee, an ant, up to five[3], purify it (with the two "purifiers") and then make the offering. He lays around (the fire) the (three) enclosing pegs, touching each other with their extremities : the middle and thickest one on the west-, the longest one on the south-[4], the smallest one on the north side.

On the south side of the fire he pours a pail of water with the formula : "Aditi, give thy consent", on the west

1. Rudra-S'iva being considered as the Time, the Year, his twelve sons are the months. At the end of each year they again begin their sacrifice, introduced by the dīkṣā, of which chastity is a factor.

2. i. e. the purohita ?

3. After he has removed some unclean animal five times, he need not need it further.

4. The second madhyama is incomprehensible and probably interpolated, cp. Hir. gṛhyas. I 2. 1-4.

side with: "Anumati, give thy consent", on the north side with: "Sarasvatī, give thy consent." Then from left to right he thrice pours water around the fire, the first time with the formula: "God Savitṛ speed the sacrifice, speed the lord of the sacrifice unto good fortune. May the heavenly, thought-cleansing Gandharva cleanse our thought. May the Lord of speech render our voice palatable", the second and third time silently.

Having taken a piece of fuel and having by means of the ladle drawn ghee, he anoints the stick and puts it on the fire with the formula: "This fuel is thy self, Jâtavedas! Thereby thou shalt grow and be inflamed. Inflame us and make us grow; through offspring, cattle, holy lustre, and through the enjoyment of food make us increase. Svâhâ!

The two âghâras he pours out in thought[1], uninterrupted, crossways; the first with the formula: "To Prajâpati. Svâhâ!" approaching the sruva on the inside of the northern junction of the pegs; the second with the formula: "To Indra. Svâhâ!" approaching the sruva on the inside of the southern junction[2].

Having poured out the āghāras, he offers the two portions of ghee, in the northern part of the fire with the formula: "To Agni, Svāhā!", in the southern part with the formula: "To Soma. Svāhā!"

Between them is the space for the (chief) oblations (of the caru): "Bhûḥ, Svāhā! Bhuvaḥ, Svāhā! Svaḥ, Svāhā! Bhûḥ Bhuvah Svah. Svāhā!" (after these four) on the day of full-moon: "To Agni; to Agni and Soma", on the day of new-moon: "To Agni; to Indra and Agni."

1. Thinking only, not speaking, the accompanying formula.

2. The first āghāra is poured out in south-eastern, the second in north-western direction.

In pouring out the oblations he avoids to pour out a subsequent one on the place of a previous one, in north-eastern direction, backward of the spot where the oblation to Agni sviṣṭakṛt is performed.[1]

Regularly prescribed is (the oblation to) Agni sviṣṭakṛt towards the east[2] at the end (of each sacrifice), except at a vapā-offering and a ghee-offering.[3]

After the oblation to Agni sviṣṭakṛt he does not (as is done otherwise, see the next sentence) again pour ghee (on what is left of the caru).

He "spreads under" once in the sruva (i. e. he first pours some ghee into the ladle), cuts twice from the sacrificial substance (the caru), pours once ghee over (the cuttings in the sruva), and pours again some ghee (on what is left of the caru).

With the thumb and the two fingers (next to the thumb), which are joined at the fleshy side, he cuts off twice from the sacrificial substance. For descendant of the Ṛṣi Jamadagni he pours twice ghee over the cuttings and then pours again ghee over what is left of the sacrificial substance. For this is the fivefold cutting off.[4] Or (instead of thumb and two fingers) he may use (to cut off the portions to be offered) either his (fore-) finger or a bunch of grass.

This is everywhere the mode of sacrificing.

---

1. The oblation to Agni sv., then, closes the others in the north-east.

2. Towards the north-east, cp. Hir. I. 3. 7.

3. The oblation to Agni sv. falls out if the chief oblation is performed with ghee, cp. Gobh. I. 9. 26. Khād. 1. 3. 12; as to the vapāhoma, according to the comm. on our Sūtra, the lājāhoma is meant.

4. Once "spreading under", twice cutting off, twice pouring over the ghee.

I. 4.

He then takes the prastara together with the purifiers and anoints its points in the sruva with the formula: "Anoint thee in the sky," its middle part in the ghee with the formula : "Anoint thee in the atmosphere", its roots in the sacrificial substance with the formula : "Anoint thee on the earth."

Having torn a grass stalk out of the prastara with the formula : "For long life thee," he throws the prastara into the fire, with the formula : "For Agni, for Anumati. Svāhā !" The grass stalk he throws after it with the formula : "Fetter my enemy and burn him. Svāhā !"

He puts on the fire sticks of fuel anointed with ghee with the formula : "For prosperity. Svāhā !" and taking hold of the earth he should touch the vital organs in his head.

Having touched water he performs the twelve prāyaścitta oblations : "For intuition. Svāha ! (1). For desire. Svāhā ! (2). For prospering. Svāhā ! (3). By the verse make the chaunt to prosper, by the gāyatra the rathantara, the bṛhat that has the gāyatra as its track. Svāhā ! (4). This god Jātavedas is borne upwards by the rays ; the sun, for all to see. Svāhā ! (5). The radiant splendour of the gods has arisen, the eye of Mitra, Varuṇa, and Agni ; it has filled the earth, the sky, the atmosphere : the sun, the soul of all that moves and stands. Svāhā ! (6). Out of the darkness, gazing on the higher light, we have come to the god among the gods, to Sûrya, the highest light. Svāhā ! (7). Prajāpati, none other than thou has encompassed all these beings ; for what we sacrifice unto thee, be that ours ; may we be the lords of wealth. Svāhā ! (8) Bhûḥ. Svāhā ! (9) Bhuvaḥ. Svāhā ! (10). Svaḥ. Svāhā ! (11). Bhûḥ, Bhuvaḥ, Svaḥ ! Svāhā !" (12).

Having brought the strewn darbha-grass and having put this on the praṇîta-water and on the sruva, he pours the water out (of the sruva into the praṇîta ?), whilst muttering the formula : "Thou art the real ; be real for me. Thou art the all ; be all for me. Thou art full ; be full for me. Thou art imperishable ; perish not for me."

He then pours out the praṇîta-water successively in the direction of the quarters : in the easterly direction with the formula : "May the gods, the priests, cleanse themselves' ; in the southern direction–whilst wearing his upper-garment on the right shoulder and beneath the left arm-pit-with the formula : "May the months, the Fathers, cleanse themselves", in the western direction–having again shifted his garment above the left shoulder and beneath the right arm-pit, and having touched water—with the formula : "May the house, the cattle cleanse themselvss; in the northern direction with the formula : "May the waters, the plants, the trees cleanse themselves"; in the upward direction with the formula : "May the sacrifice, the year, the lord of the sacrifice cleanse himself." Having poured out (the rest of the) water (on the earth) with the verse : "To the ocean I send you, the imperishable (waters); go back to your source. May I not suffer loss in my offspring, may my sap not be shed", he should wipe his eyes with thumb and ringfinger with the verse : "The sweet of thee, Sarasvatî, that is in the waters, in the cows, in the horses, therewith, O Sarasvatî with your swift horses, anoint my face."

Having thrown the darbha grass and the pegs into the fire, and having averted all evil, by singing the Vāmadevya chaunt he should thrice sprinkle water around the fire, besprinkling at the same time the (rest of the) sacrificial substance, from left to right ; the closing words of the formula (cp. I. 3) he should alter in this way : "...thou hast given thy consent :...thou hast sped."

The full vessel put down near the fire (cp. I.) is the sacrificial fee.

At the sacrifices of cooked food the sacrificial fee is either in accordance with the faith (śraddhâ) (of the performer), or it consists in the full vessel.

I. 5.

The ceremony to secure the birth of a male child.

The ceremony to secure the birth of a male child takes place in the third month (of the pregnancy), except in the case of a woman who has a child.[1]

Having boiled a mess of rice in ghee, or having consecrated by the sacrificial formula, as is done with a sthâlî pāka, a portion of ghee mixed with coagulated milk, he should offer it with the puruṣasūkta.[2]

Having shaped two beans and a barley corn into the male organ of procreation, he should give it her to eat together with a drop of sour milk with the formula (which should be muttered by the pregnant woman): "Prajāpati, the male, the overlord, may he give me a long living glorious son. May I together with my husband bring forth living children."

Then having fastened a nyagrodha shoot, which has fruits, with two threads, one white, one red, she should bear it on her throat.

This they, say, is a sure means to get a son.

A garment is the sacrificial fee.

---

1 In this case, according to the comm., the pumsavana should be performed in the fourth month (?)

2 For this sūkta (consisting of 7 verses) see Jaim. S. II. 3. 6–4. 2 (page. 58 of the edition).

I. 6.

The Śraddha preceding every sacrament.

Now we shall explain the śrāddha which on the day previous (to any festivity) must be performed in honour of the glad-faced Fathers (the Manes).

It finds place in the fortnight of the waxing moon, under a propitious nakṣatra.

On the preceding day or on the day itself having dressed food he invites clean and learned brāhmins.

Being clean, and having put on a white, not wet garment, wearing his uppergarment above the left shoulder and beneath the right arm-pit, having sipped water, he offers bali-offerings consisting of four white substances: thick sour milk, unhusked rice, perfume, white flowers, having spread darbha grass on the fire place with the tips to the east, saying: "To Agni obeisance! To Soma, obeisance! To Prajāpati, obeisance! To the allgods, obeisance! To the seers, obeisance! To the Bhûtas, obeisance! To the Manes, obeisance! To all the gods, obeisance!" To the brāhmins he gives food fit for offering, together with thick sour milk, or, according to another view, together with food and eatables such as beans, fish, flesh. Then he takes the following four substances: rice, barley, flowers and mustard, and together with these a jar filled with water, saying to the brāhmins: "Compose your mind, be propitious," and then with the syllable om: "Let the glad-faced Manes be pleased." In the same way the others should answer, conformably to each wish.

I. 7.

The parting of the hair.

The parting of the pregnant wife's hair he should perform in the 4th., 6th. or 8th. month, during the bright half of the moon, under an auspicious nakṣatra, when the moon stands in conjunction with hasta or with a subsequent nakṣatra[1].

After he has boiled a sthālīpāka (a mess of rice) mixed with sesamum and mudga beans, he should sacrifice, while she standing behind lays her hand on his shoulder, with the "great words" and with the verse addressed to Prajāpati[2]. After he has made her sit down to the west of the fire on a splendid seat or on a mattress of erakā grass covered over with a new garment, he should by means of the white-spotted part of a porcupine's quill that has three white spots, part her hair right over the nose up to the head (i. e. beginning at the forehead and ending at the top of the head) with the formula: "For outbreathing thee; for inbreathing thee; for throughbreathing thee." Having adorned the tips of her hair on the right side with wreath and in the same way on the left side, he should fill a vessel of white brass with water mixed with gold dust, and, while causing her to look at this water, ask her: "Him, Bhûḥ, bhuvaḥ, svaḥ! What do you see?" The other answers: "Children, cattle and good luck for me, long life for my husband." A garment or a piece of gold is the sacrificial fee.

I. 8.

The ceremony for the new born child.

When a boy has been born the ceremony of the new born child takes place. Before the sucking he should grind to powder some rice and barley by means of a piece of gold and cause the child to eat (of this powder) with the formula: "Here is food, here sap, here nectar together with breath;

1, If a naksatra as phalgunī, asâḍhâ or prosthapadâ covers more than one day, then on uttrâ phalgunī etc.

2. See I. 4, middle.

thy mother is the earth, thy father the sky." Live a hundred autumns, look a hundred autumns." Then he speaks over h m the verse : "From limb to limb thou art produced, out of the heart thou art born. Thou, verily, art the self, called son, so live a hundred autumns, see a hundred autumns. He then consigns him : "To the day I consign thee ; let the day consign thee to the night ; let the night consign thee to day and night together ; let day and night consign thee to the half-months ; let the half months consign thee to the months ; let the months consign thee to the seasons ; let the seasons consign thee to the year ; let the year consign thee to old age, to death."—Then he says : "Who art thou ? Who of many art thou ?" (and): "Enter upon the month that belongs to the Lord of days, N. N."[1] Then he gives him the secret name with the formula : "Veda art thou", he then kisses him on the head with the formula : "Be a stone, be an axe, be insuperable gold; with the cattle's himkâra I kiss thee." In the same way he kisses the head of his sons after returning from a journey.

During ten days he should sacrifice into a fire mustard seed mixed with rice husks, with the two verses : "To Ṣaṇḍa, to Marka, to Upavîra. Let Ṣauṇḍikera, Ulûkhala, Malimluca, Duṇâṣi, Cyavana vanish hence. Svâhâ.—Let Âlikhat, Vilikhat, Animiṣ, Kimvadanta, Upaśruti, Kumbhin, the foe of Aryaman, Pâtrapâṇi, Nipuṇahan, Antrîmukha, Sarṣapâruṇa vanish hence. Svâhâ."[2]

1. Read probably: Katamo' sīty âhâbaspatyam mâsam praviśa, cp. Gobh. II. 8. 14. If this is right, the words N. N. should be replaced by the name of the child derivated from the name of the naksatra under which it is born.

2. Cp. Pâraskara I. 16. 23.

During a period of ten days husband and wife are impure on account of the childbirth. At the end of this period after having bathed she rises (from the childbed).

I. 9.

The giving of the name.

Next the giving of the name. It takes place in the first half of the month under an auspicious nakṣatra, or on the twelfth day. The father or the teacher (âcârya) should give the name. The father should sit down with the child on his lap, after having wrapped it in a new garment. He should give him a two- or three- or foursyllabic name, beginning with a sonant, with a semivowel in it, derived from the name of the nakṣatra (with which the birth has coincided) of the deity (which presides over this nakṣatra), (or) derived from the (i. e. the father's) name, containing no taddhita (suffix), ending in ā for a female child ; or the name may be appropriate.—(On this occasion) and on all occasions when a sacrifice on behalf of the boy is performed, he sacrifices to the nakṣatra, to the deity of the nakṣatra and to the weekday (of the birth). Moreover he sacrifices to the following eight deities : to Agni, to Dhanvantari, to Prajāpati, to Indra, to the Vasus, to the Rudras, to the Ādityas, to the Allgods. If these are well honored with sacrifice, all the deities are propitious.

I. 10.

The first feeding with solid food.

Now the (first) feeding with solid food. Having fed in the first half of the month under an auspicious nakṣatra a number of brahmins, he should cause the child to partake of food fit for sacrifices, whilst muttering the verse : "Lord of food, give us food painless and strong, bring forward the giver, bestow vigour on us : on men and animals.

I. 11.

The tonsure of the child's head.

In the third year (after the day of the birth) he should shape the twisted hair (of his son) (i. e. he should perform the cūḍākarman), according to some authorities in the third year reckoned from the beginning of pregnancy. During the northern course of the sun, in the first half the month, under an auspicious nakṣatra having caused a number of brahmins to pronounce their blessing, he should in the afternoon carry forward the fire and put down to the south of the fire four vessels : two filled with rice and barley on both sides (i. e. the vessel with rice to the west, the one filled with barley to the east), between these two other vessels, one filled with sesamum, one filled with beans.

While the boy, who has sipped water, touches him from behind, he should sacrifice (four times ghee) with the "great words" and a fifth time with the Virūpākṣa formula (see I. 2).

They pour out the water decocted[1] from the various kinds of herbs—the rice, barley, sesamum and beans (above mentioned) are the "various kinds of herbs."—Then he takes up the razor with the verse : "Hither has come Savitṛ with the razor, approved of by the Allgods, by the Maruts ; may he, Viśvakarman, be propitious unto us ; do ye protect us ever with prosperity." He takes the water with the verse : "Come, Vāyu, with the hot water ; may Aditi shave the hair." With the verse : "May the waters moisten thee for life, for old age, for splendour" he should moisten the hair near the right ear. In this (hair) he puts three darbha blades or a single one. He should hold (the hair and the blade in his left hand) with the verse : "Prajāpati hold

1. Translation uncertain, cp. the critical notes and Gobh. III. 4. 11.

again and again, for good shaving." Having touched with a mirror thrice (the hairs and the grass blades) in upward direction, he should shave off (some hair together with parts of the blades) by means of the razor, muttering (the three mantras): "With the razor, wherewith the creator has shaved (the head) of Bṛhaspati, of Agni, of Indra, for the sake of long life, therewith I shave thy (head), for the sake of long life, of glory, and of welfare."—With the razor, wherewith Prajāpati has shaved (the head) for the Maruts householders, therewith I shave thy (head) for the sake of long life, of glory, and of welfare.—With the razor wherewith this one may go about further, and may long see the sun, therewith I shave thy (head) for the sake of long life, of glory, and of welfare." In the same way the back and the left side of the head. At each mantra he should deposit the hair and the rest of the darbha blades on bull's dung, which should not be put on the bare ground ; if the boy belongs to the brahmin caste, this bull's dung should be put to the east, if he belongs to the two other castes, behind. He then should hand over the razor to the barber with the mantra : "When thou shearest with the...razor,[1] O barber, make the limbs clean ; do not injure the life, the splendour, O barber." (The barber then shaves the hair) according to the custom of the Gotra or family (of the boy).

After the boy has been washed, he (i. e. the father or the ācārya) should perform the prāyáscitta offerings (cp.I.4). By the......act, and without mantras the ritual is performed for a female child. If it is performed with the mantras, the sacrifice (of the principal oblations) should be performed afterwards.

---

1. The words are corrupt from Ath. S. etc.; read: marcayatâ instead of mamlâ vaptrâ.

Then he takes hold of his (i. e. the boy's) head and mutters the verse : "The threefold age of Kaśyapa, Jamadagni's threefold age, the threefold age that belongs to the gods, may that threefold age belong to thee."

The hair he should bury in a cornfield or in a cow-shed. The person who arranges the hair should take the full vessels. A cow constitutes the sacrificial fee.

I. 12.

The initiation of the student.

In the 7th year he should initiate a brahmin--in the 5th, one that is desirous of spiritual lustre, in the 9th, one that is desirous of attaining long life–, in the 11th a kṣatriya, in the 12th a vaiśya. He should not perform the initiation after he has passed his 16th year. "For (in this case) he becomes of shattered testicles[1], equal to a śûdra" it is said in holy tradition).

Then (viz. when he has reached this age) they bring him (to his spiritual teacher) after he has bathed, has been adorned, his eyes have been anointed, and the barber has made his toilette.

He should put on him a new garment with one of the three following verses, according to his caste : "We clothe, O **Soma**, this (boy) with the holy word, for the sake of great **learning**, so that it (i. e. the garment) may lead him to old age[2] and he may long watch over **learning**. Live thou a hundred autumns, see thou a hundred autumns.–We clothe, O **Indra**, this (boy) with the holy word, for the sake of great **power**, so that it may lead him to old age and he may long watch over **power**. Live thou a hundred

1. Translation uncertain, see the commentary.

2. The mantra here and Hir. I. 4. 9 is corrupt, cp. AV. XIX. 24, 2 and Kâth. gṛhyas.

autumns, see thou a hundred autumns.--We clothe, O Poṣa, this (boy) with the holy word, for the sake of great wealth, so that it may lead him to old age and he may long watch over wealth. Live thou a hundred autumns, see thou a hundred autumns."

Now the teacher, having made him sit down to the west of the fire with his face directed toward the east, and wearing his upper garment above the left shoulder and beneath the right arm-pit[1], makes him rinse his mouth. Then he makes him stand up, strews northward pointed darbha grass to the north of the fire, puts on this grass an unbroken stone, and causes him to step with his right foot on this stone with the verse: "Mount here on the stone, like the stone be thou firm; press away thy enemy, but let not thy enemy[2] slay thee."

Now the teacher causes him to sit down to the west of the fire with his face turned to the east, and himself sits to the left (of the boy) and sacrifices, whilst the boy takes hold of him, with the "great words" and the oblations to the Vedas, pouring after each formula the dregs of each oblation into the mouth of the boy: "Bhûh, the Ṛk-verses. Svāhā! Bhuvaḥ. the Yajus-formulae, Svāhā! Svaḥ, the Sāman-chaunts. Svāhā!"

When the boy has swallowed the dregs and rinsed his mouth, the teacher causes him to stand up, and leads him around the fire, turning his right side to it, with the formula: "Obeisance to the Wind, obeisance be made to Agni, obeisance to Earth, obeisance to the Plants, obeisance I make to you, to the unseen Great One" (and he addresses the boy

1. The meaning may be also: "after he has hung the sacred thread" (the yajnopavíta) on him.

2. Dviṣato is corrupt, we expect dviṣan.

with the words): "Study thou, who art going to study" (to which the boy answers): "Imparter, So-and-so, impart to So-and-so the Veda."

Now the teacher causes him to stand to the west of the fire with his face turned toward the east, whilst he himself stands before him with his face turned toward the west. Then they join their open hands together, the teacher holding his own above those of the boy. The hands of the teacher are now filled by some other person with water, so that the water trickling down, fills the hands of the other (i. e. the boy). He (i. e. the boy) directs him: "I have come hither for studentship; initiate me." "Who by name art thou?" Answering: "So-and-so" he (the boy) should mention his own name. Now the teacher mutters: "Him! Bhûḥ, bhuvaḥ, svaḥ! With him who comes hither we have come together. Drive ye thoroughly away death[1]. May we walk unhurt; may this one walk in bliss." He then seizes with his right hand his (i. e. the boy's) right hand, with the formula: "Indra has seized thy hand, Dhātṛ has seized thy hand, Pūṣan has seized thy hand, Savitṛ has seized thy hand, Aryaman has seized thy hand. Thou art Mitra by rights; Agni is thy teacher." Having touched (the place of) his navel, he mutters: "Thou art the knot of the breaths; do not loosen thyself; make not an opening to death, thou that art free from (premature) death."[2] Having gradually passed with his hand along his right shoulder, he mutters, whilst touching (the place of) his heart: "In my will be thy heart; after my will shall thy will follow; in my word thou shalt rejoice with all thy will; let Bṛhaspati join thee to me."

He now consigns him: "To Agni I consign thee. To Vāyu I consign thee. To god Savitṛ I consign thee.

1. Only the reading mṛtyum instead of martyam gives a good sense.

2. This must be the meaning of the corrupt tradition.

To the Waters I consign thee. To the Plants I consign thee. To all the Gods I consign thee. To all the Beings I consign thee, for the sake of security."

Now he directs him : "A student art thou. Put fuel on (the fire). Drink water (as thy only beverage). Do the service. Do not sleep in the day-time."

He (i. e. the student) puts pieces of fuel anointed with ghee on the fire with the following mantras, one after each svāhā : "To Agni, to the great Jātavedas, I have brought a piece of wood. As thou, Agni, art inflamed through the piece of wood, thus may I prosper through long life, splendour, vigour, gift, insight, wisdom, offspring, cattle, holy lustre, the enjoyment of food, and riches. Svāhā.—The insight that dwells with the Apsaras, the mind that dwells with the Gandharvas, the divine insight and that which is born from men : May that insight, the fragrant one, rejoice me. Svāhā.—Bhûḥ, svāhā.—Bhuvaḥ, svāhā.—Svaḥ, svāhā.-Bhûḥ, bhuvaḥ, svaḥ, Svāhā. '

He (i. e. the student) ties a girdle round himself with the verses : "Here protecting me from evil words, purifying my kind as a purifier, bringing strength to exhalation and inhalation, has come to me the sisterly goddess, this blessed girdle.—A protector of right, a defender of mortification, slaying the goblins, overpowering the foes : do thou, O blessed girdle, surround me from all sides ; may we, that wear thee, not perish." The girdle consists of muñja-grass for a brahmin, of mûrvā-grass for a kṣatriya, of tāmala-bark mixed with muñja-grass for a vaiṣya, or for all of muñja-grass.

Now as for the garments : the under-garment consists (for all!) of linen or hemp ; the uppergarment for a brahmin is made of the skin of an antelope, for a kṣatriya of the ruru-deer, for a Vaiṣya of a goat, or for all of the antelope.

With the formula : "Evil averting art thou" he should give the staff, reaching up to the nose, of palāśa-wood for a brahmin, of bilva-wood for one who is desirous of spiritual lustre, of nyagrodha-wood for a kṣatriya, of udumbara-wood for a Vaiśya, or for all of palāśa-wood.

He should beg food first of his mother, then of other friendly disposed women. He should beg, if he is a brahmin, with the word 'Lady' at the beginning : "Lady, give alms"; with this word in the middle, if he is a Kṣatriya : "Give, Lady, alms"; with this word at the end, if he is a Vaiśya : "Give alms, Lady" not emphasizing (i. e. speaking nearly inaudibly) the last syllalle of the word **bhikṣam** (alms) and of the word "give" (**dehi**). Or all may beg with the word "Lady" at the beginning.

When something abnormal (something to be atoned for) occurs between the act of assuming the garment and of begging alms), he should cause him to sip water with the formula : "You are living, bestow life on him. Waters are ye by name, immortal ones are ye by name ; svadhā are ye be name ; of you, being such, may I partake ; receive me into favour ; be auspicious to me. Obeisance to you, do not hurt me."

The begged food is brought to the teacher.

After three days, or on the same day, he (i. e. the teacher) should recite to the student the verse addressed to Savitṛ, to the west of the fire : first by verse quarters, then by versehalves, then entire. When the pupil has learned the verse and has (by learning the first verse of the Ṛgveda, the first chaunt of the Sāmaveda, the first formula of the Yajurveda) begun the (study of the) Vedas, he puts on the fire sticks of wood anointed with ghee, with the formula : "Agni, lord of the observances, I shall keep the observance, may I be equal to it, may I succeed in it. Svāhā ! Vāyu, lord of the observances etc...Svāhā ! Âditya, lord of the observances etc...Svāhā ! Lord of the observances, ruling over the observances, etc...Svāhā !" This instruction in the performance of the observances is everywhere practised (where an occasion presents itself). At the close of the period during which the observances are kept, he should alter the formula, so as to say (in stead of : "I shall keep,... may I be equal,...may I succeed): "I have kept,...I have been equal,...I have succeeded."

Then he instructs him (i. e. the student): "Be a student of the Veda, subject to the teacher, subdued, lying on the ground, bearing the staff, the girdle, the antelope-hide, the matted hair abstaining from women, falsehood, honey, meat, perfume, garlands." During three days he eats no pungent or saline food.

After the lapse of the three days he should leave the village in eastern or northern direction go to a palāṣa tree, anoint it with "the great words," sacrifice a mess of boiled rice (at the foot of the tree), throw away his sacred thread, his staff, etc., and return (to the village).[1] The sacrificial fee consists of a cow.

I. 13.

The twilight devotion.

In the evening and the morning he should, being pure, at the brink of the water (i. e. on a shore, a bank) with a purifier (i. e. a grass stalk) in his hand, wash himself with water with the three verses, beginning : "You, waters, are",[2] with the four verses, beginning : "May this gladdening one cross"[3]; the vāmadevya chaunt[4] (comes) at the end.

1. **Afterwards** he should take another staff etc.
2. Known to the student of this sūtra from the Jaim. S'rautasūtra (k.12).
3. Jaim. S. I. 3. 4. 4. 7.
4. Chanted on Jaim. S. I. 2. 1. 6. 5.

Sitting on a pure spot on darbha grass, holding, darbha grass in his hand, directed toward the west, restraining his speech, he should meditate on the evening twilight until the appearance of the stars. When the stars have appeared, he should, after having thrice restrained his breath, repeat the verse addressed to Savitṛ a thousand times or a hundred times, (but) at least ten times. He then addresses to the fire the verse beginning: "Agni, be thou our nearest"[1]; to Varuṇa the verse beginning: "Thou art Varuṇa and Mitra."[2] In the same way in the morning, but now directed toward the east, and he addresses to the **Sun** the verse beginning: "Out of the darkness"[3] and to **Mitra** the verse beginning: "To Mitra, to Aryaman."[4] If the sun should rise or set while he is sleeping, he should repeat mentally the verse addressed to Savitṛ during the rest of that (day or night). This is the atonement in this case.

I. 14.

The opening of the annual course of study.

On the day of full-moon of Śrāvaṇa or Prauṣṭhapada, under the nakṣatra Hasta, the opening ceremony of the annual term of Veda-study (is performed). Having thrice restrained his breath and having sipped water, all (the students) mutter the "fore-muttering": "May it be ours in common, may it enjoy us in common, may it be efficacious to us in common; may no hatred spring up between us; may it be efficacious to all of us." To them he (i. e. the teacher) should recite the verse addressed to Savitṛ in the way as described in the upanayana (ch. 12) and mentally the Savitṛ-chaunt[5] and the one composed on the verse:

1. Jaim. S. I. 2. 4. 9. 2.
2. Jaim. S. III. 54. 6.
3. Jaim. br. II. 68.
4. Jaim. S. I. 2. 2. 3. 3.
5. Found at the end of the âraṇya-gâna of the Jaiminîyas.

"Soma the King."[1] When they have learned the chandas part (of the Sāmaveda, i. e. its first part, containing the three parvans of the agni-, indra-, and pavamāna-verse), beginning at the beginning and as much as is suitable (i. e. at least one verse with its chaunt), he[2] sacrifices nine offerings of entire barley-corns and thick sour milk: to the Ṛṣis (who have "seen" the diverse verses and chaunts that have been learnt) (1); to the Deities (to which the versees are addressed) (2); to the Metre (of these verses) (3); to the verses (4); to the Formulae (contained in brāhmaṇa and sûtra) (5); to the chaunts (6); with the verse, beginning: "The verse, the chaunt, we revere"[3] (7); with the verse, beginning: "The Lord of the seat, the wonderful"[4] (8) and with the verse, beginning: "The one who gives insight"[5] (9). Then he (i. e. each student ?) gratifies (with a libation of water) the first six already mentioned groups (the Ṛṣis, the Deities, etc.), then his (present ?) teacher, and then the following thirteen (ancient) Teachers: Talavakāra, Sātyamugra, Rāṇāyani, Durvāsas, Bhāguri, Gauruṇḍi, Gaurgulavi, Bhagavat Aupamanyava, Kāradi, Sāvarṇi, Gārgya, Vārṣagaṇya and Daivantya.[6] Having muttered the two verses, beginning: "Him who possesses grain"[7] and: "To Dadhikrāvan"[8] over the rest of the sacrificial substance,

1. The bârhaspatya-sâman, composed on Jaim. S. I. 1.-10. 1.
2. Probably each student is meant. But the sense of this passage is not absolutely clear; it seems, however, impossible to take, as the commentator does, adhītya in the sense of adhyāpya.
3. Jaim. S. I. 2. 3. 6. 10.
4. Jaim. S. I. 2. 1. 6. 7.
5. Jaim. S. III. 28. 6.
6. This list contains nearly the same names as the one of the Kauthumas, see Caraṇavyûha ed. of Benares, page 45, and Simon, Beitraege zur Kenntniss der Ved. Schulen page 28.
7. Jaim. S. I. 2. 1. 10. 7.
8. Jaim. S. I. 2. 3. 5. 7.

they eat the remnants and study during the forenoon.[1] When the study of the part sacred to Agni (of the sāmaveda ārcika) has been completed, a he-goat is given as fee; after the part sacred to Indra, a ram; after the part sacred to Pavamāna Soma, a cow.

He (i. e. the newly initiated pupil) should entertain (his teacher) and his fellow students, who have come together.

On the day sacred to Savitṛ, and at the leaving off (the studying the Veda) they wait[2], one night together with the two adjoining days (i. e. the preceeding and the following days)[3]. He should not eat meat, should avoid śrâddhas, should not shave the hair on his body, should not have intercourse with women; his wife however, he may approach when she has her monthly periods. These observances belong to the rainy season and the autumn, according to some authorities they last (only) half a month.

I. 15.

The ending of the term of study.

On the day of the full-moon of Taiṣa they leave off (studying the Veda). Having left off studying with the formula: "May the Metres, that increase each by four syllables, repose duly in the Vedas; may they think of us propitiously", they should, paying attention to the prescriptions of studying and not-studying and to the observances, study at discretion (?) the Veda. Thenceforward (i. e. from Taiṣa full-moon on), however, they, shold not study if clouds rise.

1. Translation uncertain.

2. Viz. they do not continue their study, cp. Oldenberg's note on Gobh. III. 3. 9.

3. Cp. Oldenberg on Gobh. III. 3. 10 and 16.

I. 16.

The observances (I. 16–18).

The gaudânika-[1], vrâtika-[2], and aupaniṣada-observances[3] last one year each. During these, at the evening and at daybreak, water should be touched: he should not take food in the morning, before he has touched water, and the evening, after he has touched water, he should not take food before he has put the piece of fuel on the fire. He should put fuel on, that he has taken from the forest.

The Âditya observance[4] lasts a year. During this period he should wear one garment, should not-mount a yoked chariot, should not interpose on umbrella between himself and the sun, nor a seat and couch or sandals between himself and the earth; he should not descend (for bathing) farther than knee-deep, except at the injunction of his teacher. During the period of the vrātika observances he (i. e. the teacher) should communicate (to him) the vrataparvan (and the arka-and dvandva-parvans), during the period of the ādityavrātaka, the śukriyas, during the aupaniṣada period the upaniṣad.

---

1. The vrata undertaken with the formula (cp. I. 12): "Agni, lord of observances, I will undertake the Gaudánika observance" etc., and introducing the study of the parvans of the pûrvârcika, called after agni, indra and pavamâna.

2. The vrata introducing the study of the three parvans of the áraṇyaka, called successively: vrata-, arka-and dvandvaparvan. (see the edition of the Jaim. S'., pages 23-28).—It is remarkable tha the Gobhila-and Khádira-sûtras call this vrata equally vrátika, although in their recension of the Sámaveda these parvans have the sequence: arka, dvandva, vrata. Thence follows that the sequence preserved by the Jaiminíyas was the original one.

3. Introducing the study of the upaniṣad, which contains ten adhyáyas: the bráhmaṇa, the vams'abráhmaṇa the upaniṣad-bráhmana (or gâyatrasyopaniṣad), the Kena upaniṣed, and the árṣeya brahmana.

4. Introducing the study of the s'ukriyaparvan (see edition of the Jaim. S. page 28).

I. 17.

To the study of the mahānāmnī (verses and their chaunts) are consecrated twelve, nine, six, or three years; these are the various possibilities; according to some authorities, one year, in case the mahānāmnīs have already been studied by his (i. e. the student's) father. During a year he should practise continence, wearing one garment, but the observances (in case he devotes to this part of the Veda one year only) are enhanced. He should stand in the daytime and sit at night. According to some his food and clothing should be dark. But because of the objection to the colour, he should rather[1] put on a white, not a dark (garment). At the study of all (the mahānāmnīs) he should touch water, for it is said that "the śakvarī-verses are the water."[2] He should not cross a river in a boat, but if his life is in danger (viz. if he would cross the river swimming), he (may cross by means of a boat, but) should touch water before (ascending) and after (disembarking). Or he may, (before ascending and after disembarking) give drink to (some) cows, for it is said "that the śukriya-verses are the cows."[3] He should not interpose an umbrella between himself and the rain, but walk in the rain. If he acts thus, Parjanya will send rain according to his wish.

At the close of this period of self-restraint he fasts one day and one night. Having gone to the forest and having filled a brass vessel with water in which a blyxa octandra (a plant growing in water) has been mixed, he, (i. e. the teacher) causes him (the student) to sit down near him, and having embraced him he should cause (the student), who keeps his eyes shut, to sing after him the three stotra-verses (i. e. the mahānāmnīs) together with the parts called purîsha.[4] The

1. Reading s'uklam tveva instead of s'uklam caiva.
2. Jaim. br. III. 114: apo vai mahânâmnyas.
3. Jaim. br. l. c.: pas'avo vai mahânâmnyas.
4. See the edition of the Jaim. S. page 60.

teacher then should get up and encircle from left to right the face of the student with a new garment. During the rest of the day the student (having returned home) should stand, holding a vessel filled with water in his hand. During the (following) night he should sit (holding the vessel with water) restraining his speech. On the following morning he (the teacher with the pupil) should go into the forest, put fuel on the fire, bring near a calf and unloosen the garment (from the student's eyes). He (the student) should then raise the brass vessel (with water, which he still bears in his hand) and look at it with the formula: "At the waters I look down", with the formula: "At the sun I look", he should look at the sun, with the formula: "At the light I look", at the fire, with the formula: "At the calf I look", at the calf; having poured out the water with the verse beginning: "Some meet"[1] he should (having returned home) take the garment, the brass vessel and the calf to his teacher. From a sthālīpāka he makes burnt oblations to Viśvāmitra and Indra, and to the mahānāmnī-verses. He then should entertain his teacher and his retinue with food. A cow is the fee.

I. 18.

The study of the Veda lasts twelve years; reckoned from the birth onward, according to some authorities (in which case, if he is a brahmin, the study is extended over six years only); or until he has learnt the Veda. Constantly he has to add fuel to the fire in the evening, and to go out seeking alms evening and morning. He should avoid two three-stringed objects: a three-stringed amulet and three-stringed shoes.

In the sixteenth year the godāna (finds place), that means: "the cutting of the beard." The mantras are the

1. Jaim. S. II. 1. 6.

same as those used for the tonsure (I. 11). The undertaking of the observances is the same as that of the initiation (I. 12). Here, however, no new garment is prescribed. He causes to shave off all the hair of his body and to cut his nails, according to Audgāhamani with the exception of his toplock. When he has been shaved, he should bathe. With the formula: "Thou art the skin (the bark) of the trees. O cleansing one, cleanse me. I bring thee near for the sake of long life, of lustre" he rubs himself with paste prepared from (the bark of) trees. With the formula: "Thou art the perfume of the trees. O sweet-scented one, make me sweet-scented among gods and men. I bring thee near for the sake of long life, of lustre" he rubs, after having bathed, his body with ointment. With the formula: "Thou art the flower of the trees. O sweet-scented one, make me (etc. as above)", he fastens a garland on (his head). With the formula: "Thou art a mirror (ādarśa); may both gods and men look (ādṛśyāsan, sic !) at me. Thou art shining, may I shine among gods and men" he should look at himself in the mirror. Having taken away the wreath he (i. e. the teacher) should give him directions (to put fuel on the fire etc.). The ordinances (to which the student is subjected) during the years (of the study following after the godāna) are treated. A cow is the fee.

I. 19.

The bath taken at the end of studentship.

After he has studied the Veda and observed the observances, a brāhmin, being about to take the (absolving) bath, gets ready the (following) requisites: a new garment, a mat of erakā-grass, paste for the bath, ointment, flowers, collyrium, a mirror, two new garments, a three-stringed amulet, a bamboo staff and two white shoes. A fully equipped barber stands near on the north side.

Having spread out the mat of erakā grass and covered it with the new garment with the fringe toward the north, he (the teacher) should cause him (i. e. the student) to sit down with his face directed toward the east and should throw his staff into the water with the formula: "Thou art the thunderbolt destined for the enemies." The girdle he should make him loosen with the verse beginning: "Unloose the highest."[1] The girdle also he should throw into the water. The mantras (for the shaving) are the same as those of the shaving (I. 18); the shaving also takes place. He shaves (on this occasion) first his head, then his beard, then his other limbs successively; he (the student or the teacher?) should bury the hair of his head, the hair of his beard and his nail-clippings at the root of an aśvattha or udumbara-tree. With luke-warm water, holding a piece of gold between (the water and the body) he (i. e. the teacher) should bathe him with the verse: "Be thou propitious and most favourable to us, and gracious, O Sarasvatī; let us not be separated from sight of thee."[2]

He should take the bath under the nakṣatra Rohiṇi, this nakṣatra belongs to Prajāpati, if he wishes to get offspring. He should take the bath under the nakṣhatra Mṛgaśiras, this nakṣatra belongs to Soma, if he wishes that a Soma-sacrifice may fall to his share.[3] He should take the bath under the nakṣatra Tishya, this nakṣatra belongs to Bṛhaspati, and Bṛhaspati is the Brahman (the holy Word, the Veda), if he wishes to get spiritual lustre. He should take the bath under the nakṣatra Hasta, this nakṣatra belongs to Savitṛ, if he wishes to be impelled by Savitr. He should take the bath under the nakṣatra Anūrādhās, this nakṣatra

1. Jaim. S'. II. 5 1.
2. Only the reading samdrs'ah of Ath. V. gives good sense.
3. If he wishes afterwards to be chosen as priest at a Soma-sacrifice.

belongs to Mitra, if he wishes to be dear to his friends (**mitra**). He should take the bath under the nakṣatra Śravaṇa, this nakṣatra belongs to Viṣṇu, and Viṣṇu is the sacrifice, if he wishes that a sacrifice may fall to his share.[1]

He (i. e. the teacher) should invest him with the new garment with the verse : "We clothe, O Soma this boy" etc.[2] Then he should salve his eyes, first the left and then the right, with the verse beginning : "With glory me."[3]

The three-stringed amulet, which must be made of palāśa-wood if he is desirous of averting evil, he (i. e. the student) fastens to his neck with the formula : "Thou art the one averting evil", of bilva-wood, if he is desirous of spiritual lustre with the formula : "May I become possessed of spiritual lustre," of arka-wood, if he is desirous of getting food with the formula : "May I eat food."

With the formula : "Thou art the Gandharva Viśvāvasu ; protect thou me, guard thou me" he takes the bamboo staff.

He should put on the two shoes with the formula : "You are the leaders, lead me." First he fastens on the right one.

The observances for him are the following : he should not wish for sport with a girl that has not reached the age of puberty, he should not run while it is raining, nor take his shoes in his own hand, nor gather fruits of the trees himself, nor go toward evening to another village, neither go alone nor together with Śûdras, not look into a well, not climb a tree nor a bridge, nor be seated without inteposing (something between himself and the ground), not eat food which has been brought in at the western door ; nor (pre-

1. For similar prescriptions cp. Baudh. s'rs. XVII. 39.
2. Cp. I. 12 (page 14).
3. Jaim. S'. II. 2. 12.

pared) food that has turned sour, nor food which has been cooked twice (i. e. has been warmed) or which has been kept over for the night, except such as is prepared of vegetables, meat, barley, rice, flour, parched rice, juice of sugar-cane, coagulated milk, honey, and ghee. He should not laugh if there is no cause for mirth, not bathe naked, not speak harsh words, avoid scandal and quarrels.

According to Âruṇi Gautama there are three kinds of Snātakas: the Snātaka by knowledge, the Snātaka by the completion of his observances, and the Snātaka by knowledge **and** by the completion of his observances. Of these the last ranks foremost, the first two are equal (to each-other).

(The Arghya reception on Madhuparka)

When he has taken the (absolving) bath (and has become a "Snātaka") he should address his teacher: "Your honour should bring me the madhuparka" (i. e. the mixture of ghee, curds, and honey). He or another person, competent to replace the teacher should bring to him, who is seated with his face turned toward the east, the madhuparka: the bed of grass (to sit down upon), the water for washing the feet, the arghya water, and the water for sipping, each separately. He seats himself on the bed of grass. He washes his feet with the water destined for this use with the formula: "In me may fortune rest": when it is a śûdra who washes his feet, the left foot should be washed first; then the right foot with the formula: "In me may rest the pādyā virāj."[1] With the verse beginning: "In me may lustre"[2] he should accept the arghya water; the water offered him for sipping he should sip. Underneath the wooden vessel (in which the madhuparka is now to be given), a

1. See the remark of Professor Oldenberg in sacred B. of the East XXIX, page 97.

2. Jaim. S'. II. 1. 4.

bushel of grass is held ; the two bushels of grass (viz. this one and the other one, mentioned in the following sentence) are (beforehand) tied together at their topparts[1]; one bushel of grass lies above the vessel ; between these two bushels curds and honey are put together in the vessel. If he adds curds, the madhuparka is a dadhimantha, if water : a udamantha, if milk : a payasya. This madhuparka he should accept with the formula : "On the impulse of god Savitṛ (I accept thee with the arms of the Aṣvins with the hands of Pûṣan)". Having put it down on the ground and having mixed[2] the contents[2] with his thumb and ring-finger, he should thrice eat of it with the formula : "For the sake of glory, of fortune, of food, of holy lustre (I take) thee to me."

The rest of it he should give to a brahmin, having seized the vessel at the left side[3], or to a non-brahmin, but then after first having sprinkled it with water, or he may bury (the remains) in a hole. Any other person then holding a knife in his hand, speaks, looking at the cow, (which now is brought near) : "The cow, the cow, the cow !" To this (cow) he addresses the formula : "The cow will become a milch-cow[4]" (and the verse): "The mother of the Rudras, the daughter of the Vasus, the sister of the Âdityas, the navel of immortality—to the people who understand me I will say : do not kill the guiltless cow, which is Aditi.—Let it drink water, let it eat grass." Immediately after this verse he should say : "Om ! Let it loose", but if it is to be killed : "Slaughter it."

1. According to Baudháyana the madhuparka is given Kûrcábhyám parigṛhya.

2. This probably is the meaning of avaghṛsya, which usually signifies: to rub off.

3. Translation doubtful.

4. The s'rautasutra also has the reading havyá in stead of the only possible bhavyâ.

Now there are six persons, to whom the arghya reception is due : an officiating priest at a Vedic sacrifice, a teacher, a Snātaka, a King who has received the royal consecration, a dear friend, and a learned brahmin. For these he should kill the guest-cow. He should sprinkle her with water with the formula : "For the guest (I sprinkle thee)."

I. 20.

The wedding (I. 20-22).

Having taken the (absolving) bath he (should return home and) attend upon his parents, being subject to them. With their permission he should take for his wife a girl, who has reached the age of puberty, who is his equal in birth, who should belong to a different gotra (from her husband's), who should not be related to his mother in the seventh degree, who should be younger than himself who is older.

The messenger (who is to ask the girl in his name) he dismisses with the verse : "May be free from thorns, and straight, the paths by which our friends go a wooing for us ; may Aryaman, may Bhaga lead us all, may our domestic state be well regulated, ye gods !"

On the fire, when it is being brought near on the occasion of the taking of the hand (i. e. at the wedding proper), he speaks the verse : "May Agni come hither the first of the deities ; may he release the offspring of this (woman) from the fetter of death. May this king Varuṇa grant, that this woman shall not weep over distress (falling to her lot) through her sons." To the fire, when it has been kindled, he addresses, standing before it and looking at it, the verse : "May Agni gārhapatya protect this woman, may he lead her offspring to long life. With fertile womb may she be the mother of living children ; may she experience delight in her sons."

Before the fire a brahmin, restraining his speech, should stand turned to the west, holding a vessel filled with water ; to the south of the fire the mother (of the bride) should stand holding in a winnowing basket roasted grain mixed with śamî leaves, in the absence of the mother any female person who can replace her (i. e. the mother's sister or the mother's mother). To the west of the fire he should put down a mat of erakâ reed, or a bundle of grass, or something else of that kind, after having rolled it up, so that, when (at the moment the bridegroom and the bride are going to take their seat upon it) it is pushed forward, it reaches up to the western part of the grass strewn (around the fire).

Now he gives her the two garments after having sprinkled them and having spoken over them the verse : "The goddesses, who spun, who wove, who spread out and who drew out the end on both sides, may these goddesses clothe thee with long life. Put this grament on, living long."

Then he should address her : "Strike on this erakâ mat with your right foot (so that the mat lies as indicated above). (The bride does so) with the formula : "May the path leading to the husband be successful for me." If she should not mutter, he (the groom) himself should mutter, changing it : "for her." (instead of "for me"). On the southern (i. e. right) part of the mat he causes the bride to sit down, the bridegroom himself takes place on the northern (left) part. They should touch one another (putting, for a moment, their hand on each other's shoulder). He himself (sitting on the mat) should offer the following burnt oblations speaking loudly, whilst the bride takes hold of him. Having sacrificed with "the great words" (i. e. bhûḥ, svâhâ! bhuvaḥ, svâhâ ! svaḥ, svâhâ ; bhūr bhuvaḥ svaḥ, svâhâ !) he sacrifices seven offerings, pouring the residue of the ghee after the oblation with the first verse on the head of the bride: "Thou who liest down athwart, thinking: "it is I who keep all things asunder", thee with a stream of ghee we propitiate completely. To samrādhā, Svāhā ![1] (1). May no lament arise at night in thy house, may the weeping (females) take their abode apart from thee, mayest thou not beat thy breast with loose hair, mayest thou, with thy husband living, shine in thy husband's world, beholding thy offspring, with well-willing mind. Svāhā ! (2). May Anumati approve today our sacrifice among the gods, and may Agni the oblation-carrier bring this about ; may he prosper. Svāhā ! (3). May heaven protect thy back, Vāyu thy thighs, and the two Aśvins thy breast, may Savitṛ protect thy suckling sons. Until the garment is put on (thy sons) may Bṛhaspati guard (them) and the All-gods afterwards. Svāhā ! (4). Taking childlessness, death of sons, evil, and distress (from thee) as a wreath from the head, I fasten it to thy foes as a fetter. Svāhā ! (5). Whichever evil was in all thy limbs, that I have removed by the offerings made with a ladle full of ghee. Svāhā ! (6) (and the last or seventh) with the verse beginning: "O Prajāpati."[2]

I. 21.

Now he seizes with his right hand her right hand–her open hand with the fingers extended, if he wishes male, her fingers (only), if he wishes female children, her hand together with the thumb, if he wishes both—with the verses: "I seize thy hand that we may be blessed with good-fortunes, that with me as a husband thou mayest live to old age.[3] Bhaga, Aryaman, Savitṛ, Purandhi, the gods, have given thee to me that we may rule our house.—Soma gave

1. The mantra is corrupt, cp. e. g. Hir. I. 2. 18.
2. See I. 4.
3. The correct reading would be yathásah.

her to the Gandharva ; the Gandharva gave her to Agni ; Agni gave welfare and riches and this one to me.—Soma acquired thee first as his wife, after him the Gandharva acquired thee. Thy third husband is Agni, the fourth am I, (thy) human (husband)."

Then he should make her step upon a stone after the manner described in the chapter on initiation (I. 8), changing the masculine gender into the feminine.

Whilst being regarded by the bride on the north-eastern part of the fire he murmurs the verses : "Be not of evil eye, not bringing death to me, thy husband ; bring luck to the cattle[1], be kindly disposed and full of lustre. Give birth to living children, love the gods, be friendly. Bring luck to our two-and four-footed ones.—May Prajāpati generate progeny for us, may Aryaman unite us to reach old age, enter, not ill-omened, the world of thy husband. Bring luck to our two-and four-footed ones.—Lead her, O Pūṣan, to us, the highly blessed one, into whom men pour their sperm, her, who may willingly part her thighs, into whom we willingly may introduce the member.—Yonder am I, this one art thou; the Sāman am I, the Ṛc art thou ; the mind am I, the word art thou, the Heaven am I, the Earth art thou. Come, let us join together, let us unite our sperm to generate a male child. Be devoted to me, occupy one couch with me, thou So-and-so." Here he should instead of "So-and-so" put in her name.

Thereupon the pair should walk around the fire, whilst the bridegroom mutters the formula : "Thou art food[2], strength by name is thy mother ; come thou to me **with** progeny, **with** wealth."

1. Thus according to the MSS. of the text.

2. in stands according to the comm. for it (nom. of ish)

After the circumambulation her brother or another person who is a friend of hers should pour with his joined hands out of the winnowing basket into her joined hands roasted grain sprinkled with ghee, "picking out" again and again (i. e. not all the grain at once, but at several times) Having "spread under" and poured over (the roasted grain) some ghee, the other one (i. e. the bride) should sacrifice it in the fire with the three verses: "This young girl going from her parents to the world of her husband, has sacrificed away her dīkṣa[1]. Svāhā.—This woman, strewing grains into the fire, prays: "May my husband live long, may my relations be prosperous." Svāhā.—To the god Aryaman the girl has sacrificed,[2] to Agni; may he, the god Aryaman, loosen her from here, not from thence.[3] Svāhā! After each oblation he mutters, four times (i. e. after each of these three, and after the fourth one, mentioned beneath) the verse: "May we find our way with thee through all hostile powers, as through streams of water." Without mantra the person who holds the roasted grain (the mother etc. cp. I. 20) should pour out as a fourth oblation (the rest of the grain in the winnowing basket) for (the obtaining of) a (special) wish (i. e. in order that the bride may see fulfilled any wish, on which she has to fix her thought).[4] The right neb of the winnowing basket they call "the wish."[5]

On the north-eastern part of the fire he causes her to step forward seven steps[6], each with one of the following

1. The dīksa in the sacrifice of Soma comprises also the abstinence of sexual intercourse.
2. The verb in the plural, the subject in the singular, corrupt from AV. XIV. 2. 52.
3. Viz. from her future state as a housewife.
4. Cp. Kaus su. 76. 18.
5. For this passage cp. S'ānkh. I. 14. 4, As'v. I. 7. 14, P'ar. I. 7. 5.
6. Probably the groom follows her and puts his right foot on each trace of the right foot of the bride.

formulae: "One for sap; may Viṣṇu go after thee.—Two for juice; may Viṣṇu go after thee.—Three for prosperity; may Viṣṇu go after thee.—Four for comfort; may Viṣṇu go after thee.—Five for progeny; may Viṣṇu go after thee.—Six for the seasons; may Viṣṇu go after thee.—Be a friend of seven steps."

At the seventh (step), having caused her to stand directed to the east, they[1] should sprinkle her out of the vessel filled with water with the three verses, beginning: "Ye waters are beneficent."[2]

The lookers-on he addresses with the verse: "This woman wears auspicious ornaments. Come up to her and behold her. Having brought luck to her, go away back to your houses."

Then he should make her look on the pole-star, the star arundhatī (i. e. alkor of ursa major), and the seven seers (ursa major), when she declares: "Let me see (them)." To the pole-star she addresses looking at it, the formula: "Thou art the pole-star (dhruva, firm), may I become firm (i. e. fixed) in the house of my husband So-and-so", uttering the name of her husband (instead of "So-and-so"), and at the end of the formula her own name in the nominative case. On arundhatī she looks with the formula: "Arundhatī, may I be held fast[3] by my husband So-and-so," uttering the name of her husband and at the end of lhe formula her own name.

I. 22.

When she departs (to the house of her husband), he speaks over her the verse; "May Pūṣan lead thee thence,

1. Viz. the person who holds the water (I. 20) together with the bridegroom and the person who has held the grain.

2. See I. 13 big.

3. Instead of aruddhā we expect ruddhā, see Gobh. II. 3. 11.

grasping thy hand ; may the Aśvins carry thee forth in a chariot ; go to the house, that thou mayest be a housewife ; having control thou shalt speak unto the council."

When she has reached her own house, (some women) of good disposition, that possess beautiful progeny and have reached old age together (with their respective husbands), make her descend with the verse : "May here succeed for thee by progeny what is dear (to you). Watch thou over this house for housewife-ship ; unite yourself with this one, your husband ; then, being not deficient, thou shalt speak to the council."[1]

Thereupon he makes her sit down on a bull's hide with the hairy side turned upwards, with the verse : "Here may cows sit down, here horses, here men. Here may also Pūṣan with a thousand sacrificial gifts sit down." Having placed a boy in her lap he should throw sweetmeats[2] or fruits (in its hands). Having removed the boy he should, whilst the wife holds on to him from behind, sacrifice with the following eight formulae, each concluded with the word Svāhā ! : "Here is steadiness. Here is independant steadiness. Here is delight. Here take delight. In me the steadiness. In me the independant steadiness. In me the joy. In me rejoice."

During a period of three days and nights they should abstain from saline or pungent food and from sexual intercourse, sleeping on the ground and lying together without approaching one another. After the lapse of the three days they should cohabit.[3] In the night[4] (following on the three-day period) (begins) the ritual work of the married pair.

1. The text is corrupt, cp. RV. X. 85. 27.
2. Thus the comm.; the precise meaning is unknown.
3. Apparently the "some" of Gobh. II. 5. 7 are the Jaiminîyas.
4. The following is the caturthikarman: the ritual of the fourth night.

He should sacrifice the expiatory oblations with the formulae: "Expiating Agni! Thou art the expiation of the gods. I, a brahmin, entreat thee, desirous of protection. The substance, which dwells in her that brings death to progeny, remove from her. Svāhā.—Expiatory Vāyu! Thou art the expiation of the gods. I, a brahmin, entreat thee, desirous of protection. The substance, which dwells in her that brings death to cattle, remove from her. Svāhā.—Expiatory Sûrya! Thou art the expiation of the gods. I, a brahmin, entreat thee, desirous of protection. The substance, which dwells in her that brings death to the husband, remove from her. Svāhā.—Expiatory Candra! Thou art the expiation of the gods. I, a brahmin, entreat thee, desirous of protection. The substance, which dwells in her that brings destruction to the house, remove from her. Svāhā.—Expiatory Agni, Vāyu, Sûrya, Candra, you are the expiation of the gods. I, a brahmin, entreat you, desirous of protection. The substance, which dwells in her that brings destruction to fame, remove ye from her. Svāhā."

Having sacrificed from a sthālīpāka to Agni and Prajāpati and having poured together into a wooden vessel the remnants of each oblation, he should address her with the words: "Anoint thy vital canals." First (she anoints) the navel, then the organs of sense which are above (viz. eyes, nose, ears, mouth), then those beneath (the navel).

After the three days have passed, the cohabitation takes place, after the husband has muttered the three following verses: "May Viṣṇu make the womb ready; may Tvaṣṭṛ frame the shape (of the child), may Prajāpati pour forth the sperm, may Dhātṛ give thee conception.—Give conception, Sinīvālī, give conception, Sarasvatī; may the two Aśvins, the gods wreathed with lotus, give conception to thee.—The embryo, which the Aśvins with golden fire-drill produce : that embryo I put into thee, for giving birth in the tenth month."

The cohabitation takes place in this manner after each menstrual period.

After the burnt oblations he should give a cow to his teacher, in default of the teacher he should give a cow to (some) brahmins.

I. 23.

The regular evening-and morning-sacrifices.

At the evening-and morning-sacrifice he offers first an oblation of ghee to Agni, a second to Prajāpati; thus also in the morning, but then instead of Agni : to Sûrya.

The Vaiśvadeva.

Of his evening-and morning-food he puts aside two great portions[1] destined for the bali-offerings, and sacrifices into the fire from the foremost portion : "To Agni. Svāhā ! To Soma. Svāhā ! To Dhanvantari. Svāhā ! To Heaven and Earth. Svāhā ! To the All-gods. Svāhā ! To all the Deities. Svāhā ! To Prajāpati. Svāhā !" The last one only mentally (i. e. he thinks only : "To Prajāpati. Svāhā").

Then to the north of the fire he offers (on the ground) a bali-sacrifice with the verse : "The gladdening, trembling, increase-bringing ones, that follow on the track of the wind : to these I, desirous of food, offer a bali-sacrifice. May much nutritive food fall to my share." In the same way if (someone) hungers.[2]

On the place where he collects his revenues (his rice, barley, etc.) he offers a bali-sacrifice with the formula : "To Death's abode." Of the rest bali-offerings are made sun-

1. Possibly dhrâjim was the original reading.

2. This is not clear to me. During a sacrifice the Brahman-priest has his seat to the south of the fire.

wise, with the formula : "To the house-deities I offer a bali ; may they accept this from me, may they protect me, may they guard me, may they preserve me. To these obeisance, to these Svāhā," first near the water-jar, then in the middle of the house, in the north-eastern part, near the bed, on the threshold, near the enclosure, and near the place where the Brahman has his seat.[1] The remains he should pour out for Dhanvantari.

At all the house-rites[2] a benediction must be said (by one or more brahmins who must then be entertained with food). This (benediction) is called the great means of appeasement (i. e. of averting evil).

I. 24.

The sacrifice of the first fruits.

When he is about to undertake the sacrifice of the first fruits, he should first perform a sacrifice with the old fruits to Agni, Dhanvantari, Prajāpati and Indra, they offer three oblations of the first fruits, in autumn of rice, in spring of barley, in the rainy season of millet. On these occasions a mess of the corns boiled whole, is offered successively to Indra and Agni, to the Allgods, to Heaven and Earth.[3] Or one mess only is offered.[4] The "spreading under" and the sprinkling of ghee have been dealt with (and should take place here). Twice he cuts of a fragment from the sacrificial substance, then he should partake of it after having muttered the verse : "From the good ye have led us to the better, ye gods ! Through thee, the nourishment, may

1. This is not clear to me. During a sacrifice the Brahman-priest has his seat to the south of the fire.

2. Perhaps read gṛhyeṣu in stead of gṛheṣu.

3. All is based on the s'rauta-ritual, see e. g. Āp. VI. 29. 3, 7, 10.

4. This means probably that of the first fruits a caru is offered to Agni, Dhanvantari, Prajāpati, Indra, and Indra and Agni and so on.

we obtain thee. Thus enter into us, O Poticn, being refreshment, for the good of our children and ourselves, pleasant." Of the barley he should partake with the verse: "This barley, mixed with honey, they have ploughed through Sarasvatī under Manu. Indra was lord of the plough, the hundredfold wise one ; ploughers were the Maruts, the exuberant givers." Of the millet he should partake with the verse : "May Agni partake first, for he knows how the sacrificial substance is ; may he, the friend of all human tribes, make the herbs blessed for us."

II. 1.

The s'râddha (II. 1–2).

When thy are going to perform a śrāddha, they should bathe, put on clean garments, strew the house with sesamum, and prepare the food, sprinkling it with "substances fit for oblation"; during all the acts they should use the left hand, wear the sacred thread (or the upper garment) on the right shoulder and beneath the left arm-pit. All that he gives, he should give after sprinkling it with "substances fit for oblation." The expression : "substances fit for oblation" means : sesamum.

Having brought tooth-sticks, water and unguents proper for bathing, water for washing the feet, which has been drawn first of all[1], he causes to sit down (some, at least three) brahmins, spotless in three respects (i. e. knowledge, birth, and behaviour) with the verse : "May my Fathers come to their share, called by the Virāj, from the oceanic water. Live ye upon this undiminished (share), delight ye at free will in that which is given by me." Then he should give to the brahmins darbha grass cut off near the root,

1. Translation uncertain.

having made (from this grass) layers wound from right to left[1], with the formula: "Here, Father, So-and-so is a seat for thee and for those who come here with thee; for these also is the seat." In the same way for his grandfather and great grandfather. Then he should give them water mixed with sesamum (pouring it out) through a strainer, perfumes and flowers.

Having cut off a portion of the food and having sprinkled it with ghee, he takes the grass for strewing around the fire etc., asks the brahmins' permission to sacrifice into the fire, carries it forward in south-eastern direction and strews the grass shaking it around the fire three times from left to right, wearing his sacred thread (or his upper-garment) on his right shoulder and beneath his left arm-pit. He should sprinkle water around the fire three times from left to right and three times from right to left. The fuel and the enclosing pegs are of udumbara-wood, as also the ladle. Having made and consecrated by mantras the two purifyers, and having "purified" with them the food, he throws the purifyers into the fire and sacrifices by means of the ladle (from the food): "To Agni, who carries the oblaticn to the Manes. Svadhā! Obeisance! Svāhā!—To soma, who is accompanied by the Fathers. Svadhā! Obeisance! Svāhā." Then having shifted his sacred thread (or his upper-garment) to the left shoulder, and having touched water, he throws the ladle into the fire with the formula: "To Yama, who is accompanied by the Angiras. Svāhā!" Having performed the namaskāra according to the deities[2], he should sprinkle (again) water around the fire in the same way as before.

1. This refers to the manner in which the thread holding the grass, has been slung around it.

2. He has to mutter: "I make an obeisance to my Father. I make an obeisance to my grandfather" etc.

Then he puts a big portion of food with condiments in (different) vessels and pours milk or ghee upon it with the verse: "In the raw ones (i. e. the cows) the boiled nectar has entered; delight ye at free will in that which is given by me." The big portions he assigns with the verses: "This, ye Fathers, is your share, given in the vessels, the nectar, full of svadhā. Live ye upon this undiminished (share), delight at free will in that which is given by me.—The immortal Word, the immortal Waters, the (immortal) Food: this is the threefold, one-law-ed immortality of the Word.[1] Delight ye at free will in these three given by me; may here, ye gods, be weal for us.—This sacrifice to the Fathers is the highest: what is given in the vessels, what is destined for the Fathers, O Agni. Word and Mind, ye Fathers, are your offering.[1] Delight ye at free will in what has been given by the Aśvins.—The Fathers here on the earth, those in the atmosphere, and those of the ocean, those that have reached the Word, that have become immortal, may these all delight in this sacrificial substance.—Here is strength (food) for you and here Svadhā, eat ye and drink it[1], and may this (portion) not be diminished for you. Take with you the Svadhā: the spring of nectar; enjoy the Svadhā, ye Fathers, that is here.—The strength (food) and the deity that is here, ye Fathers, upon that may we live a hundred years. Make ye my life full of light and devoid of old age." There upon he puts these (vessels with food) down near the brahmins and assigns them with his thumb, muttering: "To So-and-so. Svadhā. To So-and-so. Svadhā."

While thy eat he speaks over them the verse: What by me (is bestowed) against or with my will, on an imperfect brahmin or on a non-brahmin[1], what food drops into

1. The text of these verses being more or less corrupt, I have followed the recension of the Kâthakagṛhyasûtra.

terrific Nirṛti, by which our Fathers and the deities are gladdened–may Vāyu purify all that ; by it, being purified, may the deities rejoice, in it may the Fathers rejoice."

Having chanted the Âśvasāman, composed on the verse beginning: "The ocean roared,"[1] and having asked if (their meal) is finished, he should, wearing his sacred thread (or his uppergarment) upon his left shoulder, make them rinse their mouths. Then he says: "May you be pleased", circumambulates them, turning his right side toward them, and while they depart, mutters over them the verse: "What a black bird and a beast of prey, what an unclean person, have eaten of the food prepared by me with mantras, may Savitṛ Vaiśvānara purify that ; by it, being purified may the deities rejoice ; in it may the Fathers rejoice themselves."

II. 2.

Having begged for the rest (of the food, to do with it as he pleases) he should return (from the spot to where he has accompanied the departing brahmins). He smears with bull's dung a quadrangular spot, directed toward the south-east, and in the middle of it by means of a piece of wood scratches a line with the formula: "Driven away are the asuras, the rākṣasas, the piśācas, who dwell among the Fathers", and lays down to the south of this square a fire-brand with the verse: "Whatsoever asuras roam about at will assuming various shapes, being large-bodied or small-bodied (?), may Agni expel them from this space." Having strewn darbha-grass along the line, he makes him (i. e. his father) rinse his mouth by means of a vessel filled with water (from which he pours out some quantity): "Father So-and-so, rinse thy mouth, and may these that accompany

1. Jaim. S. I. 3. 6. 5.

thee here also rinse their mouths." In the same way for his grandfather and great-grandfather. On these places (where he has poured out the water, for each of the three ancestors a little more to the south) he lays down little balls of boiled rice, addressing each of his ancestors by his name, with that part of the hand which is sacred to the Manes[1], with the formula: "This is for thee, Father So-and-so, and for those who accompany thee. Svadhā. Obeisance." In the same way for his grandfather and great-grandfather. If he does not know their names, then with the formulae: "Father, this is for thee. Grandfather, this is for thee. Great-grandfather, this is for thee." If he does not know his kinsmen (nor their names)[2], then with the formulae: "This is for the Fathers, who dwell on the earth. This is for the Grandfathers who dwell in the atmosphere. This is for the Great-grandfathers who dwell in the heaven." With the formula: "Here, ye Fathers, regale yourselves; like bulls come hither, each to your own share" he should turn round to the north and sit down, holding his breath as long as possible. Then he (turns back and) having muttered the formula: "The Fathers have regaled themselves; like bulls they are come hither, each to his own share", he makes them rinse their mouths in the same way as described above, he loosens the tuck of his garment[3], performs obeisance to each of the deities[4], and assigns garments to them: a knot of wool or a cloth consisting of the fringe of his garment, with the formulae: "Here is a garment for you, O Fathers; give ye a house to us, O Fathers; give fruit to the womb, O Fathers: a boy wreathed with lotus, that here may be a male child." He gives ointment and

1. The part between thumb and fore-finger.
2. Cp. Âp. s'rs. I. 9. 6.
3. See Eggeling in Sacred Books of the East, vol. XII, page 368, note 2.
4. He has to say: "Obeisance to my Father So-and-so" etc.

collyrium with the formula: "Anoint thee, So and-so!" and "Anoint thy eyes, So-and-so!" He should give perfumes and flowers. He then addresses them with the following six formulae of obeisance: "Obeisance to your sap, ye Fathers! Obeisance to your lustre, ye Fathers! Obeisance to your life, ye Fathers! Obeisance to your terror, ye Fathers! Obeisance to your strength, ye Fathers! Obeisance to your wrath, ye Fathers! and to your Svadhā. Obeisance to you, ye Fathers!" With the verse: "Ye waters, who carry food, nectar, ghee, milk, kīlāla[1] and parisrut[1], are Svadhā; satiate my Fathers" he pours out water, and speaks over it the verse: "May it not diminish for me; may great liberality fall to my share; may the Brahmins delight in the food I offer repeatedly. May what I give (to the Brahmins) become for me in the highest abode Nectar-water of a thousand streams.—May Gods and Fathers subsist here upon this liberality of mine. Live ye upon this undiminished (share), delight at free will in that which is given by me." He then circumambulates, turning toward it his right side, (the spot where the ancestors have been regaled) with the verse: "They who are common and benevolent, the living amongst the living, mine: may their prosperity fall to my lot in this world through a hundred years."

The rice balls may be eaten by a sick person, by one who is desirous of food, or they may be thrown into the fire or the water, or given to a goat, a cow, or a brahmin. Of the rest (i. e. either the rice from which the rice balls have been taken, or the rest of the food eaten by the brahmins) he may eat, but he should not eat his fill.

---

1. Kinds of spirituous liquor, 0 Surā.

II. 3.

The Aṣṭakás.

On each of the three dark halves of the months following on the Âgrahayaṇī-fullmoonday fall the Aṣṭakās: the Aṣṭakā of vegetables, the Aṣṭakā of meat, and the Aṣṭakā of flour-cakes. The sacrificial substance is vegetables, flesh, flour-cakes, and (for all) a mess of boiled rice. Of these substances he should sacrifice into the fire in the manner prescribed for a sthālīpāka, with the formulae: "To the Aṣṭakā. Svāhā ! To the Aṣṭakā par excellence. Svāhā ! To the favourable Aṣṭakā. Svāhā ! To the Saṃvatsara, to the Parivatsara, to the Idāvatsara, to the Idvatsara, to the Âvatsara make ye (the offering) with obeisance. Through thee may we, undecayed, unbeaten, long enjoy the favour of these (years), which are worthy of sacrifice. Svāhā !"[1]. Having poured out the burnt-oblations, he should respectfully address (the fire ?) with the formula: "Come, thou good Fortune (or: "O Bhaga); come, thou good Fortune; come, thou good Fortune."

At the middle Aṣṭakā he should have a cow slaughtered. He should sprinkle her with the formula: "To the Aṣṭakā agreeable I sprinkle thee." Of this (cow) he should take out[2] the left flank, the left apaghanī[3] and the left buttock.

On the next day he performs the anvaṣṭakya-śrāddha (i. e. the śrāddha on the day after the aṣṭakā), or it may take place on the same day. Having made sit down (some)

---

1. According to the comm. this last mantra consists of five separate mantras: "To the Saṃvatsara make ye offering" (etc.) (1). "To the Parivatsara make ye offering" (etc.) (2). etc. etc. This is not wholly certain.
2. Probably these parts are reserved for the anvaṣṭakya, cp. the following.
3. Perhaps the thigh, see Gobh. IV. 1. 5.

Brahmins (at least three), who are worthy to partake of the sacrificial substances, he should satiate them, carry forward to the south (out of this fire) six fires, and dig near each of these fires one trench, a span long, three fingers broad, one finger deep. In these trenches he deposits the balls of boiled rice, addressing his ancestors each with his name, with that part of the hand which is sacred to the Manes[1]. The marrow he lays down for the male ascendants, the ribs (etc.) for the female ones.

Some adhvaryus[2] teach about this subject, that the middle rice ball (offered at the anvaṣṭakya-śrāddha) should be eaten by the wife of one who is desirous of offspring; thus also (the middle rice ball) of an (ordinary) śrāddha, or the sthālīpāka.[3]

II. 4.

The funeral ceremonies (II. 4–5).

When the corpse of one who had consecrated and during his lifetime maintained the three sacred fires has gone lost, he (viz. the son) should fetch 360 palāśa-stems and shape these on the skin of a black antelope into a human frame: for the head he lays down 40, for the neck 10, for the two arms 100, for the fingers again 10, for the breast 30, for the belly 20, for the thighs 100, for the organ of generation 10, for the knees and the legs 30, for the toes 10. "So many are the bones of a man", says the sacred tradition.

If the corpse has not gone lost[4], they should shave the hair, pare the nails, wash it and raise it on a pyre; here they

1. See note 1 on page 48.
2. Viz. Adherents of the Yajurveda.
3. This must mean: the rest of the sthâlipâka, of which has been sacrificed.
4. The translation of this corrupt passage is conjectural.

pile also his sacrificial utensils in the way described in the chapter of the brāhmaṇa which begins : "on it they place him ; on his nostrils he should put down the two sruva-ladles"[1]. Having previously taken four ladle-fuls of ghee, according to the prescripts of the chapter in the brāhmaṇa beginning : "He who knows thus, if he should fall ill"[2], (and then having made an oblation with this ghee in the fire) he puts, if possible, a piece of gold on the mouth of the corpse[3], propels the fires to the pyre and addresses it respectfully with the chaunts : with the one composed on the verse beginning : "The eagle flying in the vault"[4], according to the grāmageya ; when the smoke has risen upwards, with the one composed on the verse beginning : "Thy sparkling smoke arises"[5] and when the fire has risen, with one of the two composed on the verse beginning : "Agni, be gracious ; thou art great"[6]. The Sāmans should be chanted right off ("without returning" i. e. without repetition) : "without returning in yonder World" so says a brāhmaṇa.

II. 5.

If the wife of one who has consecrated his three sacred fires, comes to die before him, he should cremate her with a fire produced from the fire-drill or with a sāntapana-fire[7].

---

1. Jaim. bráhm. I. 48 (see journal of the American Oriental Society, vol. XIX, page 106).
2. Jaim. br. I. 46 (J. A. O. S. l. c. page 103) : the words ya evamvit syat precede immediately this passage.
3. I am far from certain to have rendered the meaning of the Sútrakára.
4. Jaim. S. I. 2. 3. 13; the chaunt is the yámam Sáma.
5. Jaim. S. I. 1. 9. 3. the chaunt is the Kaulmudam Sáma.
6. Jaim. S. I. 1. 3. 3: to this verse belong two Yama-samans.
7. Dry substances are put into an earthern pot and fire is laid around until the full in the pot takes fire.

Having selected as burial ground a spot, which by its nature is not saline, and whence the water flows down from right to left tortuously, or a spot, where herbs grow, and here having cremated the corpse, they go away without looking back in order to bring the libation of water to the deceased; this they do not perform in streaming water. The libation should be poured out so that always the youngest among them pours it out before the elder one; at the brink of the water; and if there is no brink, after having dug a well. With the nameless finger (i. e. the ringfinger) of the left hand he throws once some water forward, uttering the name of the deceased. If (the libation is made) in streaming water, they should first loosen the hair[1] on the head, they plunge into the water and having poured out the water-libation out of the hollow of the two open hands held together, they should tie up the hair and each of them should touch the fire of a firebrand with the formula: "O Agni śūkāhi (?), drive ye away my evil." He should touch a śamī-branch with the formula: "Thou art a śamī, remove (śamaya) my evil", a stone, with the formula: "A stone art thou; hard (steady) art thou; may I be steady"; then without any formula, a piece of bull's dung.

When he has poured out the libation of water he should sit down with his face directed toward the south, and those who have accompanied him should sit down near him. Another one addresses to them edifying words. At sunset they enter the village.

During this (day and the following) night they subsist on one single bean[2], or in complete indifference to all worldly enjoyments (i. e. eating nothing at all).

1. This seems here [cp. the following passage] to be the meaning of udgrathya.

2. Or: "solely on beans"? The commentator takes māsa as a measure: they subsist on so much food as has been bought for one māsa [a gold night].

On the next day he mixes milk and water (goes to the spot of cremation) and besprinkles the bones (with this mixture) by means of a goatshorn, a cow-horn or an earthen pail.

On the third day he should mix perfumes with herbs in water sprinkle the bones by means of a śamī or palāśa-branch and put them into an urn without making a noise (i. e. so that no grating sound is made by the bones touching one another). If the deceased was a woman, then in an earthen water-jar. Passing a crossway, a great arbour or a stream, he should bury (the urn) in the stair of a landing place of a stream.

On the third day after the decease they make them (i. e. the participants) bathe with apāmārga-plants, clay and cowding.

Having washed their clothes they remain idle during a period of ten days. From the fourth day on[1] they should subsist on food begged (from the neighbours). From this (begged food)[2] the offering into the fire has been demonstrated (and should in the well-known way take place during these ten days)[3], and with this begged food they should pass along together the time they expect[4].

After the lapse of the period of the ten days they should perform a śrāddha. Until they perform this śrāddha they should not give (alms). The restrictions for the nakṣatras are : (this śrāddha should take place) under (i. e. when the moon stands in conjunction with) the maghās, under nakṣatras consisting of one single star, under bharaṇī,

1. Reading caturthyâ [?].
2. Reading tasyāḥ.
3. Probably they must with this food perform the morning and evening offerings.
4. The meaning of this sentence is not clear to me.

and of the double nakṣatras under the former ; not under the fixed ones, viz. rohiṇī and under the later star of a double nakṣatra[1]. Having made (some) brahmins sit down who are worthy to partake of sacrificial substances, and having satiated these, he should give one single ball of boiled rice, (changing the plural of all the mantras with which it is offered) into the singular, and leaving out the addition : "and to those who accompany thee" (II. 2). He should satisfy all their (i. e. the brahmins') desires. Having accompanied them and having begged for the rest of the food, to do with it as he pleases (cp. II. 2, beg.), he should return. The rest he should not partake of ; only after having made the brahmins pronounce their blessing he may partake of it.

II. 6.

The rite of the house.

Now follows (the description) of the rite of the house. If he wishes that his house may flourish he should every month, every season or every year in the first half of the month under an auspicious nakṣatra undertake the rite for averting evil from his house. Having by means of indravallī-creepers tied together apāmārga, palāśa, śirīṣa, arka udumbara, sadabhadra and amṛtatṛṇa, and (with this kind o broom) having cleansed and swept his house, having be sprinkled it with water, having sprinkled it all over b means of a handful of darbha-grass with the five products of the cow, having strewn about white mustard seed, he should in the middle of the house perform the bali-offerings to the house and sacrifice oblations of ghee to Vāstoṣpati and then a thousand times sacrifice ghee with the verse addressed to Savitṛ. This same sacrifice then takes place in the south-

1. Fixed are called also by Varāhamihira [Bṛhatsaṃhitā] rohiṇ and uttaraphalgunī, uttarāṣāḍha, uttaraproṣṭhapada.

eastern, then in the south-western, then in the north-eastern and then in the north-western part of the house ; or in the middle (only). The sacrificial fee consists of a cow, a garment or a piece of gold. Then he should regale (some) brahmins with food and make them pronounce their benedictions.

Thus performing he enjoys endless and great prosperity, he gets many sons, who do not die young, the fire burns not his house, no biting animals will devour him, no thieves, rivals, demons or devils annoy him.

If his cows grow sick he should in the midst of his cows sacrifice a thousand ghee-offerings in the same way (*viz.* with the verse addressed to Savitṛ). The same holds good of the sickness of horses, camels, asses, goats and sheep, buffaloes, elephants and any of his bipeds or quadrupeds.

II. 7.

The allaying of prodigies.

Now we shall explain the allaying of prodigies. Now, when in his house the central pillar buds forth, when a dove enters into it, when a cow sucks another cow, when a draught-ox scrapes the sky (with his horns), when smoke or flames are seen while there is no fire, when honey is produced, when an ant-hill arises, when a frog croaks in the water-reservoir, when dogs roam about in the house—in case of these and other (prodigies and bad omens), he sacrifices ghee with the verses beginning : "What, O Indra, we fear"[1], "the prodigious master of the seat"[2], "adhyāyamutesumudasya"[3], "always, O Agni"[4], "when the lord of the

1. Jaim. S. I. 2. 2. 5. 2.
2. L. c. I. 2. 1. 6. 7.
3. This citation is corrupt.
4. Jaim. S. I. 1. 8. 8.

house is whetted"[1], "from all sides, O Agni"[2], "whom guard'[3] and with the verse addressed to Prajāpati[4]; at the beginning and end with "the great words"[5]. Then she should chant the sāmans composed on these same verses.

II. 8.

The recitation of the Veda during a fast.

Now we shall explain the rite of the recitation of the Veda during a fast. He should wear a clean garment or a dress made of bark; he should desire (i. e. partake of) food fit for sacrifice, water or fruit. But only a brahmin should bring it to him[6].

Having gone forth from the village in an eastern or northern direction; having smeared with cowdung, a sthaṇḍila,–a bull's hide in size; on a clean spot or in the neighbourhood of water, having sprinkled it; having drawn the lines on it; having besprinkled it with water; having heaped fuel on the fire (which he has carried to this spot); having sacrificed the two āghāras and the two ghee-portions, he offers burnt-oblations to Agni, to Soma, to Rudra, to Indra, to Brahman, to Prajāpati, to Bṛhaspati, to the All-gods, to the Seers, to the Ṛk-verses, to the Yajus-formulae, to the Sāman-chaunts, to Faith, to Knowledge, to Wisdom, to Sāvitrī, to the Lord of the seat, and to Anumati.

Having sacrificed he should, sitting on darbha-grass, the tufts of which are directed toward the east or the north, hold darbha-grass in his right hand. So sitting he should recite mentally four times "the great words" preceded by the syllable om, the verse addressed to Savitṛ and the

1. L. c. I. 1. 12. 8.
2. L. c. I. 1. 10. 6.
3. L. c. I. 2. 1. 8. 1.
4. See I. 4.
5. Bhûḥ, bhuvaḥ, svaḥ.
6. Translation doubtful.

chaunt composed on this verse, the chaunts composed on the verse beginning: "The king Soma"[1] and the two chaunts composed on the verse: "The Brahman born"[2]. Then he should begin with the beginning of the Veda and without interruption recite it silently, and he should not interrupt the recitation by stopping. Now were he to converse in between, or to stop, he should thrice hold his breath as long as he is able to, sip water, and begin just where he left off. If a passage does not occur to him, he should during the time the forgotten passage would have taken him, recite another passage either from the Ṛgveda, the Yajurveda or the Sāmaveda [thereby he reaches that forgotten part], or a Sāman that has the same brāhmaṇa, the same metre, and the same deity; or he may repeat (during the time which the forgotten passage would require) the Sāman belonging to the verse beginning: "The sea has roared"[3].—Standing, sitting, lying down or walking he should recite the Saṃhitā: thriving falls to his share. Or, according to Jaimini, he may recite the first triple section[4] a thousand times, or ending with the syallabe vāryam[5], or as much as he likes.

By reciting twelve times the Saṃhitā he removes from himself the faults committed by studying on forbidden days, by angering his teacher, and through improper acts. The Veda is by him sanctified and purified. If he recites the saṃhitā another twelve times, he gains thereby the world of Prajāpati. If he recites it another twelve times, he gains thereby the world of Uśanas. If, fasting, he re-

1. Jaim. S. I. 1. 10. 1.
2. L. c. I. 2. 3. 1. 9; to this verse belong the two ṛtusāmans.
3. Jaim. S. I. 3. 6. 5.
4. According to the comm. the three Sāmans on the first verse of the Saṃhitā are meant.
5. In this case the Sāmans belonging to Jaim. S. I. 1. 1. 11—I. 6. 8. 7. (1–61) are meant.

cites the saṃhitā one thousand times, he becomes one with Brahman and resplendent moving: unrestrained he gains the fulfilment of all his wishes. If he recites it during a year subsisting on begged food, he gains the (power of supernatural) vision; if during six months subsisting on barley-gruel, if during four months subsisting on water and barley-flour, if during two months subsisting on fruits, if during one month subsisting on water, or during twelve days eating nothing at all (he recites the saṃhitā), he obtains the power of suddenly disappearing, and sanctifies his kinsmen: seven kinsmen in the ascending, seven in the descending line and himself as fifteenth he rescues (from rebirth).

They call that the ladder of the gods. By means of that the gods reached their divine station and the seers the position of seers.

The beginning of this "session of Brahman" is threefold: at the morning pressing (of the Soma-sacrifice), at the midday pressing, or in the last part of the night: (the muhūrta) sacred to Brahman. Of this (session of Brahman) there are two intermissions of study (i. e. of reciting the Veda): if he himself is unclean, if the spot (where the recitation takes place) is unclean.

This rite was proclaimed by Prajāpati to the seven seers, by the seven seers to Mahājahnu, and by Mahājahnu to the Brahmins.

II. 9.

The appeasing of the Planets.

Now we shall explain the reception, the food-offering, and the victims for the grahas (i. e. the "Seizers", the Planets).

One who is devoid of faith, who is unclean, who does not mutter the sacred texts, who forsakes the auspicious ceremonies, that man the Seizers lead of a surety to the abode of Yama. I shall proclaim the hospitality to be offered to the Seizers of terrific action, who frequent the path of the stars. He should perform this (hospitality) for the sake of appeasing (them).

Red are the Sun and Mars, white are Venus and the Moon ; Mercury and Jupiter, these two are recorded to be yellow ; he should know Saturn as also Rāhu and Ketu to be black. The wise men should for this occasion get ready flowers which have the colour of the Seizers.

Having smeared with cowdung a sthaṇḍila, a bull's hide in size, having sprinkled it, having drawn the lines on it, having besprinkled it with water, having heaped fuel on the fire, having sacrificed the two āghāras and the two gheeportions, he calls to their places the Seizers : the Sun, to the middle ; to the south of this place, Mars ; to the south-east, the Moon ; to the north-east, Mercury[1]; to the north, Jupiter ; to the east, Venus ; to the west, Saturn ; to the south-west, Rāhu and to the north-west, Ketu. The place for the Sun is circular, for Mars triangular, quadrangular for the Moon, arrowshaped for Mercury, a traperium for Jupiter, a pentagon for Venus, a segment for Saturn, a half-circle for Rāhu, banner-shaped for Ketu.

He should know that the Sun represents the god Śiva, the Moon : Umā (i. e. the consort of Śiva), the planet Mars : the god of war Skanda; Mercury stands for Nārāyaṇa (i. e. Viṣṇu), Jupiter is Brahman itself and Venus is Indra. Saturn he should consider as Yama, Rāhu is the messenger of the God of Death, and Ketu is (his secretary) Citragupta. These are the deities of the Seizers.

Fire, Water, Earth, Viṣṇu, (Indra), Indrāṇī, Prajāpati, Sarpa (i. e. Śeṣa) and Brahman are in successive order their presiding deities.

1. Cp. the text of Baudh. gṛhya pariśeṣa I. 16. 12 (ed. of Mysore).

The Sun was produced in Kalinga-land, the Moon in the country of the Yamunā, the place of Mars is the Vindhya, that of Mercury is the "Midland", that of Jupiter the country of the Sindhu, that of Venus the Ghāts[1], Saturn belongs to Surāṣṭra, Rāhu to the eastern region and Ketu to the Parvata-mountain (i. e. the Himālaya ?). These are the regions where the Seizers are produced.

A piece of arka-wood, smeared with ghee, of the size of a span, he should put into the fire for the Sun[2], of khadira-wood for Mars, of palāśa-wood for the Moon, of the apāmārga-plant for Mercury, of aśvattha-wood for Jupiter, of udumbara-wood for Venus, of Śamī-wood for Saturn, of dūrvā-grass for Rāhu and a tuft of Kuśa-grass for Ketu.

He sacrifices twenty-eight oblations of ghee[3]. With these (i. e. the following verses ?) he sacrifices into his household-fire[4] to the Sun a simple mess of rice[5], to Mars sacrificial food, to the Moon a mess of rice boiled with ghee, to Jupiter a rice mess boiled with water, to Venus a rice mess boiled with milk, to Mercury a mess boiled with sour coagulated milk, to Saturn a mess of beans with sesamum-meal, to Rāhu a mess of meat, to Ketu a mess of rice boiled with turmeric. With the verse beginning: "With true light"[6] to the Sun; with the verse: "Agni is the head"[7] to Mars; with the verse: "Swell up, let be gathered"[6] to the Moon; with the verse: "The Brahman, born"[8] to Mercury; with the verse: "Bṛhaspati, what the enemies"[6]

---

1. This would point to Malabar, but it is uncertain; the Dictionaries do not record the word ghata in this sense; perhaps: "border" is meant.

2. Abbreviated, th. text being corrupt.

3. This is not clear.

4. Read: pakvágnau juhoti.

5. Read with Baudh. and Vaikh. s'uddhodanam.

6. These verses are not found in the texts of the Jaiminiyas. Most probably this chapter is taken from the Baudh. gṛhyasūtra.

7. Jaim. S. I. 1. 3. 7.

8. L. c. I. 2. 3. 1. 9.

to Jupiter; with the verse: "After his ancient splendour"[1] to Venus; with the verse: "To weal for us the divine ones"[2] to Saturn; with the verse: "With what aid the wondrous"[3] to Rāhu, with the verse: "Making a banner for the bannerless"[4] to Ketu.

As sacrificial fee he gives for (the offering to) the Sun a red milch cow, for (the offering to) Mars a red ox; for the (offering to the) Moon a conch; for (the offering to) Mercury a piece of gold; for (the offering to) Jupiter a garment; for (the offering to) Venus a horse; for (the offering to) Saturn a dark-blue cow; for (the offering to) Rāhu a piece of iron; for (the offering to) Ketu an elephant. Or for each a piece of gold or that by which his teacher is pleased.

As the arising of something terrible[5] is warded off by a mystical diagram, so is this evil-averting-rite a protection for those that are touched by a "Seizer"[6]. For him who abstains from hurting living beings, for him who practises self-control, for him who has gained possession of dharma, and for him who constantly checks himself, the "Seizers" are at all times favourable. The "Seizers" are the cows, they are the princes, and especially they are the brahmins; being revered, they revere, being disregarded, they torment.

---

1. l. c. III. 11. 1.
2. l. c. I. 1. 3. 13.
3. l. c. I. 2. 1. 6. 5.
4. l. c. III. 57. 10.
5. See the text of Baudh.
6. The following verse is omitted in this translation.

ओ३म्

अथातो ऽग्निं प्रणेष्यन्प्रागुदक्प्रवणमभ्युक्ष्य[१] स्थण्डिलं लक्षणं कुर्यान्मध्ये प्राचीं रेखामुल्लिख्योदीचीं च संहितां पश्चात्तिस्रो मध्ये प्राच्यो ऽभ्युक्ष्याग्निं प्रतिष्ठापयेद्भूर्भुवः स्वरिति लक्षणावृदेषा सर्वत्राथातः पाकयज्ञान्व्याख्यास्यामो हुतो ऽहुतः प्रहुतः प्राशित इति तेषामेकाग्नौ होमो नित्ये यज्ञोपवीतोदकाचमने दर्शपूर्णमासतन्त्राः स्वतन्त्रा वा दक्षिणतो ऽग्नेः पूर्णपात्रमुपनिदधाति स्रुवं चापां पूर्णमुत्तरतो ऽग्नेरिध्माबर्हिर्देवस्य त्वा सवितुः प्रसवे ऽश्विनोर्बाहुभ्यां पूष्णो हस्ताभ्यां प्रोक्षामीति[२] प्रोक्षितमुपक्लृप्तं भवति सकृद्यजुषा द्विस्तूष्णीं खादिरः पालाशो वेध्मस्तदलाभे विभीतकातिल्वकबाधकनिम्बराजवृक्षशल्मल्यरलुदधित्थकोविदारश्लेष्मातकवर्जं सर्ववनस्पतीनामिध्मः कुशालाभे शूकतृणशरशीर्यबल्बजमुतवनलशुण्ठवर्जं सर्वतृणानि शुक्लाः सुमनसस्तासामलाभे जपारूपकाकुत्थाभण्डीकुरण्डकवर्जं[३] गन्धवत्यो वा सर्ववर्णाश्चतस्र आज्यप्रकृतयो भवन्त्यूधन्यं[४] वा वाह्यं वा दधि वा[५] पयो वा पश्चादग्नेराचमनं त्रिराचामेद्द्विः[६] परिमृजेत्सकृदुपस्पृशेत्पादावभ्युक्ष्य शिरश्च शीर्षण्यान्प्राणानुपस्पृशेदप

---

१ प्रणेष्यन् M^1 ; प्रणष्यन् M^2; प्रणायिष्यन् B text and comm.

२ M^1 : देवस्य त्वेति सावित्रेण instead of देवस्य ... प्रोक्षामीति.

३ काकुत्थभ° M^1.　　४ ऊधन्यं B (comm.); उधन्यं B (t); उदन्यं M^1; ऊद्धन्य M^2 (t) ; उ(?)द्धन्यं M^2 (comm.).

५ om. all exc. M^1.

६ आचामे° B; आचमे° M^1, M^2.

उपस्पृश्य पश्चादग्नेरुपसमाहितस्योपविश्य दक्षिणेन पाणिना भूमिमारभ्य जपतीदं भूमेर्भजामह इदं भद्रं सुमङ्गलं परा सपत्नान्बाधस्वान्येषां विन्द ते धनमिति वस्वन्तं रात्रिश्चेदिमंस्तोम्येन तृचेनाग्निं परिसमूहेदाद्यया वा त्रिः प्रस्तरमुपसंगृह्य प्रातिदिशं परिस्तृणाति दक्षिणपुरस्तादुपक्रम्याग्रैर्मूलानि[2] छादयन्पश्चाद्वोपस्तीर्योलपराजिभ्यामुपहरेद्दक्षिणोत्तरः[3] सन्धिः ॥ १ ॥

प्रस्तरात्पवित्रे गृह्णाति प्रादेशमात्रे समे अप्रशीर्णाग्रे अनन्तर्गर्भे अङ्गुष्ठेनोपकनिष्ठिकया च धारयन्ननखेन छिनत्ति पवित्रे स्थो वैष्णव्याविति त्रिरूर्ध्वमद्भिरनुमार्जयेद्विष्णोर्मनसा पूते स्थ इति सकृद्यजुषा द्विस्तूष्णीं पात्रस्योपरिष्टात्पवित्रे धारयन्नाज्यमासिच्योत्तरेणाग्निमङ्गारान्निरूह्य तेष्वधिश्रित्यावद्योत्य दर्भतरुणाभ्यां प्रत्यस्य त्रिः पर्यग्नि[4] कृत्वोदगुद्वास्य प्रत्यूह्याङ्गारानुदगग्राभ्यां पवित्राभ्यां त्रिरुत्पुनात्याज्यं च हविश्च प्रणीताश्च स्रुवं च देवस्त्वा सवितोत्पुनात्वच्छिद्रेण पवित्रेण वसोः सूर्यस्य रश्मिभिरिति देवो व इति प्रणीताः पुनराहारमाज्यस्य सकृद्यजुषा द्विस्तूष्णीमुत्तरतोऽग्नेः प्रणीताः प्रणीय दर्भैः प्रच्छाद्य दक्षिणतोऽग्नेः प्रस्तरं निधाय प्रस्तरस्योपरिष्टात्पवित्रे निधाय विरूपाक्षं जपत्यों तपश्च तेजश्च सत्यं चात्मा च धृतिश्च धर्मश्च सत्त्वं[5] च त्यागश्च ब्रह्मा च ब्रह्म च तानि प्रपद्ये तानि मामवन्तु भूर्भुवः स्वरों महान्तमात्मानमध्यारोहामि विरूपाक्षोऽसि दन्ताञ्जिस्तस्य ते शय्या पर्णं गृहा अन्तरिक्षे[6] ते विमितं हिरण्मयं[7] तद्देवानां हृदयान्ययस्मये कुम्भे

१ आलभ्य B.

२ उपक्रम्य M², B (c); उपक्राम B (t); उपक्रमः M¹.

३ Thus M²; °श्चाद्वोपरिस्ती° B, M¹.

४ °ग्निं M¹.

५ सत्वं B. सत्यं M¹.

६ गृहान्तरि or ग्रहा° all.

७ हिरण्मयं B (text and comm.) M²; हिरण्ययं M¹.

अन्तः संनिहितानि तानि बलभृश्च बलधा च रक्ष णो[1] मा प्रमदः सत्यं ते द्वादश पुत्रास्ते त्वा संवत्सरेसंवत्सरे कामप्रेण यज्ञेन याजयित्वा पुनर्ब्रह्मचर्यमुपयन्ति त्वं देवानां ब्राह्मणो ऽस्यहं मनुष्याणां ब्राह्मणो वै ब्राह्मणमुपधावति तं त्वोपधावामि जपन्तं मा मा प्रतिजार्प्सीर्जुह्वन्तं मा मा प्रतिहौर्षीः कुर्वन्तं मा मा प्रतिकार्षीस्त्वां प्रपद्ये त्वया प्रसूत इदं कर्म करिष्यामि तन्मे समृध्यतां विरूपाक्षाय दन्ताञ्जये ब्रह्मणः पुत्राय ज्येष्ठाय श्रेष्ठायामोघाय कर्माधिपतये नम इति ॥ २ ॥

स्रुवं प्रणीतासु प्रणीय निष्टप्य दर्भैः संमृज्य संमार्गानभ्युक्ष्याग्नावाधाय दक्षिणं जान्वाच्यामेध्यं चेत्किंचिदाज्ये ऽवपद्येत घुणस्त्र्यम्बुका मक्षिका पिपीलिकेत्या पश्चभ्य उद्धृत्याभ्युक्ष्योत्पूय जुहुयात्परिधीन्परिदधाति मध्यमं स्थवीयसं पश्चाद्दीर्घं मध्यमं दक्षिणतः कनीयसमुत्तरतः संस्पृष्टान्दक्षिणतो ऽग्नेरपां कोशं निनयत्यादिते ऽनुमन्यस्वेत्यनुमते ऽनुमन्यस्वेति पश्चात्सरस्वते ऽनुमन्यस्वेत्युत्तरतो देव[2] सवितः[2] प्रसुवेति[2] त्रिः प्रदक्षिणमग्निं परिषिञ्चेद्देव सवितः प्रसुव यज्ञं प्रसुव यज्ञपतिं भगाय दिव्यो गन्धर्वः केतपूः केतं नः पुनातु वाचस्पतिर्वाचं नः स्वदत्विति सकृद्यजुषा द्विस्तूष्णीमथेध्ममादाय स्रुवेणाज्यं गृहीत्वाभिघार्याग्नावभ्यादधात्ययं त इध्म आत्मा जातवेदस्तेन वर्धस्व चेध्यस्व चेन्द्धि वर्धय चास्मान्प्रजया पशुभिर्ब्रह्मवर्चसेनान्नाद्येन समेधय स्वाहेति मनसाघारौ जुहोति संततमक्षणया प्रजापतये स्वाहेत्युत्तरं परिधिसन्धिमन्ववहृत्य स्रुवमिन्द्राय स्वाहेति दक्षिणं परिधिसन्धिमन्ववहृत्याघारौ[3] हुत्वाज्यभागौ[3]

---

१ रक्षणो B; लक्षणो M[1]; रक्षनो M[2]   २ only in M[1].

३ आघारैर्हुत्वा M[2]; not found in the other sources.

जुहोत्यग्नये स्वाहेत्युत्तरतः सोमाय स्वाहेति दक्षिणतस्तावन्तरेणाहुतिलोको भूः स्वाहा भुवः स्वाहा स्वः स्वाहा भूर्भुवः स्वः स्वाहेत्यग्नये ऽग्नीषोमाभ्यामिति पौर्णमास्यामग्नय इन्द्राग्निभ्यामित्यमावास्यायामुत्तरपूर्वामुत्तरपूर्वामाहुतिं जुहोत्यनभिजुह्वदाहुत्याहुतिं प्रत्यक् सौविष्टकृतस्थानान्नित्यो ऽग्निः पुरस्तात्स्विष्टकृदन्ते[1] ऽन्यत्र[1] वपाहोमाज्यहोमाभ्यां न स्विष्टकृतं प्रत्यभिघारयति स्रुवे सकृदाज्यमुपस्तृणाति द्विर्हविषो ऽवद्यति सकृदाज्येनाभिघार्य प्रत्यभिघारयत्यङ्गुष्ठेनाङ्गुलिभ्यां च मांससंहिताभ्यां द्विर्हविषो ऽवद्यति द्विराज्येनाभिघार्य[2] प्रत्यभिघारयति जामदग्न्यानां तद्धि पञ्चावत्तं भवत्यङ्गुल्या तृणकूर्चेन वा एषा होमावृत्सर्वत्र ॥ ३ ॥

सपवित्रं प्रस्तरमादत्ते तस्याग्राणि स्रुवे ऽनक्ति दिव्यङ्क्त्वेति मध्यमाज्ये ऽन्तरिक्षे ऽङ्क्त्वेति मूलानि हविषि पृथिव्यामङ्क्त्वेति प्रस्तरात्तृणं निरस्यत्यायुषे त्वेति प्रस्तरमग्नावनुप्रहरत्यग्नये ऽनुमतये स्वाहेति पश्चात्तृणमनुप्रहरति द्विषन्तं मे ऽभिधेहि तं चैव प्रदह स्वाहेति घृतेनाक्ताः[3] समिध आदधाति समृद्ध्यै स्वाहेति भूमिमारभ्य[4] शीर्षण्यान्प्राणानुपस्पृशेदप उपस्पृश्य द्वादश प्रायश्चित्ताहुतीर्जुहोत्याकूत्यै[5] स्वाहा ॥ कामाय स्वाहा ॥ समृद्ध्यै स्वाहा ॥ ऋचा स्तोमं समर्धय गायत्रेण रथंतरं बृहद्गायत्रवर्तनि स्वाहा ॥ उदु त्यं जातवेदसं देवं वहन्ति केतवः । दृशे विश्वाय सूर्यं स्वाहा ॥ चित्रं देवानामुदगादनीकं चक्षुर्मित्रस्य वरुणस्याग्नेः । आप्रा द्यावापृथिवी अन्तरिक्षं सूर्य आत्मा जगतस्तस्थुषश्च स्वाहा ॥ उद्वयं

१ स्विष्टकदन्तेनअन्यत्र M²; स्विष्टकृतंतेअन्यत्र M¹; स्विष्टकृतन्तेन्यत्र B.

२ अभिघार्य missing in B, M².

३ घृताक्ताः B.

४ आलभ्य M².

५ आकूत्यै M², B; आत्माले M¹.

तमसस्परि स्वः पश्यन्तो ज्योतिरुत्तरम् । देवं देवत्रा सूर्यमगन्म ज्योतिरुत्तमं स्वाहा ॥ प्रजापते न त्वदेतान्यन्यो विश्वा जातानि परि ता बभूव । यत्कामास्ते जुहुमस्तन्नो ऽस्तु वयं स्याम पतयो रयीणां स्वाहा ॥ भूः[१] स्वाहा ॥ भुवः स्वाहा ॥ स्वः स्वाहा ॥ भूर्भुवः स्वः[१] स्वाहेत्यथास्तीर्णान्दर्भानानीय[२] प्रणीतानां च स्रुवस्य चोपरिष्टात्कृत्वापस्रावयञ्ज्ञपति[३] सदसि सन्मे भूयाः सर्वमसि सर्वं मे भूयाः पूर्णमसि पूर्णं मे भूया अक्षितमसि मा मे क्षेष्ठा इति प्रतिदिशमप उत्सिञ्चति प्राच्यां दिशि देवा ऋत्विजो मार्जयन्तामिति[४] प्राचीनावीती दक्षिणस्यां[५] दिशि मासाः पितरो मार्जयन्तामिति[४] यज्ञोपवीती भूत्वाप उपस्पृश्य प्रतीच्यां दिशि गृहाः पशवो मार्जयन्तामित्युदीच्यां[४] दिश्याप ओषधयो वनस्पतयो मार्जयन्तामित्यूर्ध्वायां[४] दिशि यज्ञः संवत्सरो यज्ञपतिर्मार्जयन्तामिति समुद्रं वः प्रहिणोमीत्यपो निनीय[६] समुद्रं वः प्रहिणोम्यक्षिताः स्वां योनिमपि गच्छत । अरिष्टा अस्माकं वीराः सन्तु मा परासेचि नः स्वमिति यदप्सु ते सरस्वतीत्यङ्गुष्ठेनोपकानिष्ठिकया चाक्षिणी विमृजेद्यदप्सु[६] ते सरस्वति गोष्वश्वेषु यन्मधु । तेन मे वाजिनीवति मुखमङ्ग्धि सरस्वतीति दर्भान्परिधींश्चाग्नावाधाय वामदेव्येन शान्ति कृत्वा त्रिः पर्युक्षेत्सहविष्कं प्रदक्षिणमन्वमंस्थाः प्रासावी-

---

१ The Mss. om the visarga constantly before स्व°.

२ अथास्तीर्णान्दर्भान° B; यथास्तीर्णं दर्भान° M^1; विस्तीर्णान् दर्भान° M^2.

३ Read अवस्रावयन् ?

४ इति only in M^2.

५ दाक्षिणायां M^1, M^2.

६ Thus runs the text in M^1. In B M^2 the pratīka is not given at the first place, but the Mantra is found immediately Sakalapāṭhena and then, after इति, the act, if above p. 3. l. 15. Thus throughout further on.

रिति मन्त्रान्संनमयेत्पूर्णपात्रमुपनिहितं सा दक्षिणा यथाश्रद्धदक्षिणाः पाकयज्ञाः पूर्णपात्रं वा[1] ॥ ४ ॥

पुंसवनं तृतीये मास्यन्यत्र गृष्टेर्घृते चरुं श्रपयित्वा पृषदाज्यं वा स्थालीपाकवत्संस्कृत्य पुरुषसूक्तेन जुहुयान्माषौ च यवं च पुल्लिङ्गं कृत्वा दधिद्रप्सेनैनां प्राशयेत्प्रजापतिः पुरुषः परमेष्ठी स मे पुत्रं ददात्वायुष्मन्तं यशस्विनं सह पत्या जीवसूर्भूयासमिति न्यग्रोधशुङ्गं फलाभ्यामुपहितं शुक्लरक्ताभ्यां सूत्राभ्यां ग्रथित्वा कण्ठे[2] धारयेद्ध्रुवकुमारायेत्याचक्षते वासो दक्षिणा ॥ ५ ॥

अथातो नान्दीमुखेभ्यः पितृभ्यः पूर्वेद्युर्व्याख्यास्याम आपूर्यमाणपक्षे पुण्ये नक्षत्रे श्वः करिष्यामीति श्वो भूते वान्नं संस्कृत्य शुचीन् श्रोत्रियान्ब्राह्मणाननुमन्त्रयते शुचिः शुक्लमनार्द्रमाच्छाद्य यज्ञोपवीत्यप आचम्य चतुःशुक्लान्बलीन्हरती दधि तण्डुलाः सुरभि शुक्लाः सुमनस इत्यग्न्यायतने प्रागग्रान्दर्भान्संस्तीर्याग्नये सोमाय प्रजापतये विश्वेभ्यो देवेभ्य ऋषिभ्यो भूतेभ्यः पितृभ्यः सर्वाभ्यो देवताभ्यो नम इति हविष्यमन्नं ब्राह्मणेभ्यः प्रदाय दध्ना माषमत्स्यमांसभक्ष्याशनैरित्यपरमथ चतुष्टयमादाय व्रीहियवपुष्पसर्षपाणीति सह तैरेवोदकुम्भमादाय मनः समाधीयतां प्रसीदन्तु भवन्त इत्युक्त्वा सप्रणवं नान्दीमुखाः पितरः प्रीयन्तामित्येवं यथार्थमितरे प्रतिब्रूयुः[3] ॥ ६ ॥

सीमन्तोन्नयनं चतुर्थे मासि षष्ठे ऽष्टमे वा पूर्वपक्षे पुण्ये नक्षत्रे हस्तोत्तराभिर्वा कुर्यात्तिलमुद्गमिश्रं स्थालीपाकं श्रपयित्वान्वारब्धायां जुहुयान्महाव्याहृतिभिर्हुत्वा प्राजापत्यया[4] चाथैनां पश्चा-

---

१ Repetition of the last two words only in B.

२ Thus M²; कर्णे B.

३ B repeats the last three words.

४ प्राजापत्ययर्चा M².

दर्भैर्भद्रपीठ[1] उपवेश्यैरकायां वाहतोत्तरायां तस्यै त्रिः शुक्लया[2] शलल्या प्राणसंमितं सीमन्तं कुर्याच्छुक्लेना मूर्ध्नः प्राणाय त्वापानाय त्वा व्यानाय त्वेत्यथास्या दक्षिणं केशान्तं स्रग्भिरलंकृत्य तथोत्तरं हिरण्यवतीनामपां कांस्यं पूरयित्वा तत्रैनामवेक्षयन्पृच्छेद्धि भूर्भुवः[2] स्वः किं पश्यसीति परा प्रत्याह प्रजां पशून्सौभाग्यं मह्यं दीर्घमायुः पत्युरिति वासो दक्षिणा हिरण्यं वा ॥ ७ ॥

कुमारे जाते जातकर्म प्राक्स्तनप्राशनाद्व्रीहिं च यवं च जातरूपेणावघृष्येदमन्नमिति प्राशयेदिदमन्नमयं रस इदं प्राणेनामृतं सह पृथिवी ते माता द्यौः पिता जीवाहि शरदः शतं पश्याहि शरदः शतमित्यथैनमभिमन्त्रयते ऽङ्गादङ्गात्संभवसि हृदयादधि जायसे । आत्मा वै पुत्रनामासि स जीव शरदः शतं पश्याहि शरदः शतमित्यथैनं परिददात्यह्ने त्वा परिददाम्यहस्त्वा रात्र्यै परिददातु रात्रिस्त्वाहोरात्राभ्यां परिददात्वहोरात्रौ त्वार्धमासेभ्यः परिदत्तामर्धमासास्त्वा मासेभ्यः परिददतु मासास्त्वर्तुभ्यः परिददत्वृतवस्त्वा संवत्सराय परिददतु संवत्सरस्त्वा जरायै मृत्यवे परिददात्विति को ऽसि कतमो ऽसीत्याह सं मासं[3] प्रविशासावित्यथास्य गुह्यं नाम ददाति वेदो ऽसीत्यथास्य मूर्धानमुपजिघ्रत्यश्मा भव परशुर्भव हिरण्यमस्तृतं भव पशूनां त्वा हिंकारेणाभिजिघ्रामीत्येवमेव प्रवासादेत्य पुत्राणां मूर्धानमुपजिघ्रति फलीकरणमिश्रान्सर्षपान्दशरात्रमग्नौ जुहुयात् शण्डायेति द्वाभ्यां शण्डाय मर्कायोपवीराय शौण्डिकेर उलूखलो मलिम्लुचो द्रुणाशि[4] च्यवनो नश्यतादितः[5]

---

१ °पीठमुप° all; cp. Pār. Gṛhs. I. 15. 4. २ The Mss. om the visarga. ३ सम्मासं B. M¹; शर्मासं M² (cp. Mantr. br. I. 5. 14). ४ द्रुणांशि M². ५ Without visarga the Mss.

स्वाहा । आलिखन्विलिखन्ननिमिषन् किंवदन्त[1] उपश्रुतिरर्यम्णः कुम्भी शत्रुः पात्रपाणिर्निपुणहान्त्रीमुखः सर्षपारुणो नश्यतादितः[2] स्वाहेति दशरात्रं दम्पती सूतकौ भवतस्तस्यान्ते स्नात्वोत्थानम् ॥ ८ ॥

अथातो नामकर्म पूर्वपक्षे पुण्ये नक्षत्रे द्वादश्यां वा पिता नाम कुर्यादाचार्यो वा तमहतेन वाससा समनुपरिगृह्य पिताङ्केनासीत तस्य नामधेयं दद्याद् द्व्यक्षरं चतुरक्षरं वा घोषवदाद्यन्तरन्तस्थमनुनक्षत्रमनुदैवतमनुनामातद्धितमाकारान्तं स्त्रियै यथार्थं[3] वा[4] कुमारयज्ञेषु च नक्षत्रं नक्षत्रदैवतं तिथिमिति यजते ऽष्टावन्या जुष्टा देवता यजते ऽग्नि[5] धन्वन्तरि[5] प्रजापतिमिन्द्रं वसून्रुद्रानादित्यान्विश्वान्देवानित्येतासु[6] स्विष्टासु[6] सर्वा देवता अभीष्टा भवन्ति ॥ ९ ॥

अथातः प्राशनकर्म पूर्वपक्षे पुण्ये नक्षत्रे ब्राह्मणान्भोजयित्वा हविष्यमन्नं प्राशयेदन्नपते ऽन्नस्य नो देह्यनमीवस्य शुष्मिणः । प्र प्रदातारं तारिष ऊर्जं नो धेहि द्विपदे शं चतुष्पद इति ॥ १० ॥

तृतीये संवत्सरे जटाः कुर्वीत गर्भतृतीय इत्येक उदगयने पूर्वपक्षे पुण्ये नक्षत्रे ब्राह्मणान्स्वस्तिवाच्यापराह्णे ऽग्निं प्रणयित्वा दक्षिणतो ऽग्नेश्चत्वारि पूर्णपात्राणि निदध्याद्व्रीहियवानामभितो मध्ये तिलमाषाणामाचान्तोदके ऽन्वारब्धे जुहुयान्महाव्याहृतिभिर्हुत्वा

---

१ Thus B; किंवदन्तीम् M[1]; किंवदन्ती M[2]. For the two mantras cp. Pār. gṛhs. I. 16. 23.

२ Without visarga the Mss.

३ M[2] instead of यथार्थं : अभिधामसमर्थं.

४ In M[1] begins a new Khaṇḍa; consequently this recension has one Khaṇḍa more in the first praśna.

५ Thus B M[1]; अग्निं ध° M[2]; read अग्निंधन्वन्तरीं ?

६ Thus B; एतास्वष्टास् M[1]; एतास्वष्टा M[2].

त्रिरूपात्तेणात्र पञ्चमीं जुहोति सर्वौषधीभि स्फाण्टमुदकमानयन्ति[1] व्रीहियवास्तिलमाषा इत्येतत्सर्वौषधमायमगात्सविता क्षुरेणेति क्षुरमादत्त आयमगात्सविता क्षुरेण विश्वैर्देवैरनुमतो मरुद्भिः । स नः शिवो भवतु विश्वकर्मा यूयं पात स्वस्तिभिः सदा न इत्युष्णेन वाय[2] उदकेनेहीत्युदकमादत्त उष्णेन वाय[2] उदकेनेह्यदितिः केशान्वपत्वित्याप उन्दन्तु जीवस इति दक्षिणं केशान्तमभ्युन्द्यादाप उन्दन्तु जीवसे दीर्घायुष्ट्वाय वर्चस इति तस्मिंस्तिस्रो दर्भपिञ्जूलीरुपदधात्येकां वा धारयतु प्रजापतिरिति धारयेद्धारयतु प्रजापतिः [3]पुनः पुनः सुवप्तवा इत्यूर्ध्वं त्रिरादर्शेन स्पृष्ट्वा येन धातेति क्षुरेण छिन्द्याद्येन धाता बृहस्पतेरग्नेरिन्द्रस्य[4] चायुषेऽवपत् । तेन त आयुषे वपामि सुश्लोक्याय स्वस्तय इति येन तत्प्रजापतिर्मरुद्भ्यो[5] गृहमेधिभ्योऽवपत् । तेन त आयुषे वपामि सुश्लोक्याय स्वस्तय इति येन भूयश्चरात्ययं ज्योक् च पश्याति सूर्यम् । तेन त आयुषे वपामि सुश्लोक्याय स्वस्तय इत्येवं पश्चात्तथोत्तरतः[6] प्रतिमन्त्रं केशांश्च दर्भपिञ्जूलीशेषांश्चानडुहे गोमयेऽभूमिस्पृष्टे निदध्याद्ब्राह्मणस्य पुरस्तात्पश्चादितरयोर्वर्णयोर्यत्क्षुरेणेति नापिताय क्षुरं प्रयच्छेद्यत्क्षुरेण मम्ला[7] वप्त्रा वपसि नापिताङ्गानि शुद्धानि कुर्वायुर्वर्चो मा हिंसीर्नापितेति यथैषां गोत्रकल्पः कुलकल्पो वाप्लुते प्रायश्चित्तीर्जुहुयादावृतैव स्त्रियाः कुर्यादमन्त्रं समन्त्रं चेत्पश्चाज्जुहुयादथास्य

---

१ The MSS. have mostly स्फागड° (गड and ण्ट are often confounded in Grantha); is the text corrupted from °भिः फाण्टमु° or is स्फाण्ट equal to फाण्ट? Comm. मह क्वथितं.

२ Thus B, M[1]; वायवुद° M[2].

३ B M[2] om. पुनः पुनः

४ अग्नेर् alone in M[2].

५ Thus M[1] M[2]; instead of येन तत् B: यत.

६ Thus M[1], M[2]; पश्चादथो° B.

७ Thus B; क्षुरेणामम्ला M[1]; मन्मला M[2]

मूर्धानमारभ्य जपति त्रियायुषं[१] कश्यपस्य जमदग्नेस्त्रियायुषं[१] यद्देवानां त्रियायुषं[१] तत्ते अस्तु[२] त्रियायुषमिति धान्यपल्वले गोष्ठे वा केशान्निखनेत्कुशलीकर्ता पूर्णपात्राणि हरेद्गौर्दक्षिणा ॥ ११ ॥

सप्तमे ब्राह्मणमुपनयीत[३] पञ्चमे ब्रह्मवर्चसकामं नवमे त्वायुष्काममेकादशे क्षत्रियं द्वादशे वैश्यं नाति षोडशमुपनयीत[४] प्रसृष्टवृषणो[५] ह्येष वृषलीभूतो भवतीति तत एनं स्नातमलंकृतमाक्ताक्षं कृतनापितकृत्यमानयन्ति तमहतेन वाससा परिदधीत परीमं सोमेति यथावर्णं परीमं सोम ब्रह्मणा महे श्रोत्राय दध्मसि। यथेमं जरिमा ण[६] याज्ज्योक्[६] श्रोत्रे अधि जागराज्जीवाहि शरदः शतं पश्याहि शरदः शतमिति परीममिन्द्र ब्रह्मणा महे राष्ट्राय दध्मसि। यथेमं जरिमा ण[७] याज्ज्योग्राष्ट्रे[७] अधि जागराज्जीवाहि शरदः शतं पश्याहि शरदः शतमिति परीमं पोष ब्रह्मणा महे पोषाय दध्मसि। यथेमं जरिमा ण[८] याज्ज्योक्[८] पोषे अधि जागराज्जीवाहि शरदः शतं पश्याहि शरदः शतमित्यथैनं पश्चादग्नेः प्राङ्मुखमुपवेश्य यज्ञोपवीतिनमाचार्य आचामयत्याचान्तमुत्थाप्योत्तरतो ऽग्नेः प्राचो दर्भानास्तीर्य तेष्वक्षतमश्मानमत्याधाय तत्रैनं दक्षिणेन पादेनाश्मानमधिष्ठापयेदिममश्मानमारोहाश्मेव त्वं स्थिरो भव द्विषन्तमपबाधस्व[९] मा च त्वा द्विषतो वधीदित्यथैनं पश्चादग्नेः प्राङ्मुखमुपवेश्योत्तरत आचार्यो ऽन्वारब्धे जुहुयान्महाव्याहृतिभिर्हुत्वा वेदाहुतिभिश्च संपातमास्ये भूर्ऋचः[१०] स्वाहेति प्रतिमन्त्रं भूर्ऋचः[१०]

---

१ त्र्यायु° B. २ स्तु B. ३ उपनयते B; उपनयेत M². उपनीयत M¹

४ Thus B; उपनीयत M¹; उपनयेत M². ५ प्रस्रस्त° M¹, M².

६ णयाज्ज्यो° B, M¹, M². ७ णयनज्यो° B; णयाज्ज्यो° M¹; missing in M². ८ णयानज्यो° B; णयाज्ज्यो° M¹; missing in M².

९ अववाध° M¹ M². १० The Visarga not in the MSS.

स्वाहा भुवो यजूंषि स्वाहा स्वः सामानि स्वाहेति प्राशितमाचान्तमुत्थाप्य नमो वातायेत्येनं[१] प्रदक्षिणमग्निं परिणयेन्नमो वाताय नमो अस्त्वग्नये[२] नमः पृथिव्यै नम ओषधीभ्यो नमो वो ऽदृष्टाय बृहते करोमीत्यधिगन्तरधिगच्छ प्रदातः प्रयच्छामावमुष्मै वेदामित्यथैनं पश्चादग्नेः प्राङ्मुखमवस्थाप्य पुरस्तादाचार्यः प्रत्यङ्मुखस्तावञ्जली कुरुत उत्तरत आचार्यस्तमन्यो ऽद्भिः पूरयेन्निस्रावेणेतरस्य पूरणमथैनं संशास्ति ब्रह्मचर्यमगामुप मा नयस्वेति को नामासीत्यसाविति नामधेयं दद्यात्तत्राचार्यो जपति हिं भूर्भुवः स्वरागन्त्रा समगन्महि प्र सु मर्त्यं युयोतन। अरिष्टाः संचरेमहि स्वस्ति चरतादयमित्यथास्य दक्षिणेन हस्तेन दक्षिणं हस्तं गृह्णातीन्द्रस्ते हस्तमग्रभीद्धाता[४] हस्तमग्रभीत्पूषा हस्तमग्रभीत्सविता हस्तमग्रभीदर्यमा हस्तमग्रभीन्मित्रस्त्वमसि धर्मणाग्निराचार्यस्तवेति प्राणानां ग्रन्थिरसीति नाभिदेशमारभ्य[५] जपति प्राणानां ग्रन्थिरसि मा विस्रसामृत मृत्योरन्तरं कुर्विति दक्षिणमंसमन्ववमृश्य मयि व्रत इति हृदयदेशमारभ्य[५] जपति मयि व्रते हृदयं ते अस्तु मम चित्तमनु चित्तं ते अस्तु। मम वाचमेकव्रतो जुषस्व बृहस्पतिस्त्वा नियुनक्तु मयीत्यथैनं परिददात्यग्नये त्वा परिददामि वायवे त्वा परिददामि दवाय त्वा सवित्रे परिददाम्यद्भ्यस्त्वौषधीभ्यः परिददामि सर्वेभ्यस्त्वा देवेभ्यः परिददामि सर्वेभ्यस्त्वा भूतेभ्यः परिददाम्यरिष्ट्या इत्यथैनं संशास्ति ब्रह्मचार्यसि समिध आधेह्यपो ऽशान कर्म कुरु मा दिवा स्वाप्सीरित्यग्नये समिधमाहार्षमिति घृतेनाक्ताः समिध आदधात्यग्नये

१ Cp. page 5 note 6. २ स्वग्न॰ M¹, M².

३ आचार्यःनम॰ B ; आचार्यस्यनम॰ M² ; आचार्यस्थनम॰ M¹.

४ M¹ here and further on throughout अग्रहीत. ५ आलभ्य M², B.

समिधमाहार्षं[1] बृहते जातवेदसे । यथा त्वमग्ने समिधा समिध्यस एवमहमायुषा वर्चसा तेजसा सन्या मेधया प्रज्ञया[2] प्रजया पशुभिर्ब्रह्मवर्चसेनान्नाद्येन धनेन समेधिषीय स्वाहा ॥ अप्सरासु या मेधा गन्धर्वेषु च यन्मनः । दैवी मेधा मनुष्यजा सा मां मेधा सुरभिर्जुषतां स्वाहा ॥ भूः[3] स्वाहा भुवः[3] स्वाहा स्वः[3] स्वाहा भूर्भुवः[3] स्वः[3] स्वाहेतीयं दुरुक्तादिति मेखलामाबध्नीत इयं दुरुक्तात्परिबाधमाना वर्णं पवित्रं पुनती म आगात् । प्राणापानाभ्यां बलमाभरन्ती स्वसा देवी सुभगा मेखलेयम् ॥ ऋतस्य गोप्त्री तपसः परस्पी[4] घ्नती रक्षः सहमाना अरातीः । सा मा समन्तादभिपर्येहि भद्रे भर्तारस्ते मेखले मा रिषामेति मौञ्जीं ब्राह्मणस्य मौर्वीं राजन्यस्य मुञ्जमिश्रां तामलीं[5] वैश्यस्य मौञ्जीं वा सर्वेषामथ परिधानानि क्षौमं वा शाणं वान्तरं ब्राह्मणस्यैणेयमुत्तरं रौरवं राजन्यस्याजं वैश्यस्यैणेयं वा सर्वेषां स्वस्त्ययनोऽसीति दण्डं प्रयच्छेत्प्राणसंमितं पालाशं ब्राह्मणस्य बैल्वं ब्रह्मवर्चसकामस्य नैयग्रोधं राजन्यस्यौदुम्बरं वैश्यस्य पालाशं वा सर्वेषां मातरं प्रथमं भिक्षेताथान्याः[6] सुहृदो[7] भवत्पूर्वया ब्राह्मणो भिक्षेत भवति भिक्षां देहीति भवन्मध्यमया राजन्यो भिक्षां भवति देहीति भवदन्त्यया वैश्यो देहि भिक्षां भवतीति क्षां च हिं च न वर्धयेद्भवत्पूर्वया वा सर्वे प्रायश्चित्तं चेदुत्पद्येत जीवा स्थ जीवयत मेत्येनमप आचामयेज्जीवा स्थ जीवयत मापो नाम स्थामृता नाम स्थ स्वधा

---

१ आहारिषन B. २ प्रश्नया B. ३ All Mss. without visarga.

४ परस्नीः and परस्फा M² text and comm.; परिस्त्री B text and comm., M¹. ५ तामर्लां B ; तमर्लां M¹, M².

६ Thus only M² ; ॰न्यः B, M¹. ७ सुहृदः M¹, M²; सुहृदं B.

नाम स्थ तासां वो भुक्षिषीय[1] सुमतौ मा धत्त शिवा मे भवत नमो वो ऽस्तु मा मा हिंसिष्टेति भैक्षमुपन्याहृतमूर्ध्वं[2] त्रिरात्रात्सावित्रीं प्रब्रूयात्तदहर्वा पश्चादग्नेः पच्छो ऽर्धर्चशः सर्वामित्यनूच्य वेदमारभ्याग्ने व्रतपत इति घृतेनाक्ताः समिध आदधात्यग्ने व्रतपत व्रतं चरिष्यामि तच्छकेयं तन्मे राध्यतां स्वाहा। वायो व्रतपते व्रतं चरिष्यामि तच्छकेयं तन्मे राध्यतां स्वाहा। आदित्य व्रतपते व्रतं चरिष्यामि तच्छकेयं तन्मे राध्यतां स्वाहा। व्रतानां व्रतपते व्रतं चरिष्यामि तच्छकेयं तन्मे राध्यतां स्वाहेति तदेतद्व्रतादेशनं सर्वत्र व्रतसमाप्तावग्ने व्रतपते व्रतमचारिषं तदशकं तन्मे ऽराधि स्वाहेति मन्त्रान्संनमयेदथैनं संशास्ति ब्रह्मचार्याचार्याधीनः प्रशान्तो ऽधःशायी दण्डमेखलाजिनजटाधारी स्त्र्यनृतमधुमांसगन्धमाल्यवर्जी भवेति त्रिरात्रमक्षारालवणाश्यूर्ध्वं[3] त्रिरात्रात्प्राचीं वोदीचीं वा दिशमुपनिष्क्रम्य पलाशं[4] गत्वा व्याहृतिभिरभ्यज्य स्थालीपाकेनेष्ट्वा यज्ञोपवीतं[5] दण्डमित्युदस्य प्रत्येयाद्गोर्दक्षिणा ॥ १२ ॥

सायंप्रातरुदकान्ते पूतो भूत्वा सपवित्रो ऽद्भिर्मार्जयतापोहिष्ठीयाभिस्तिसृभिस्तरत्स मन्दी धावतीति चतसृभिर्वामदेव्यमन्ते शुचौ देशे दर्भेष्वासीनो दर्भान्धारयमाणः प्रत्यङ्मुखो वाग्यतः सन्ध्यां मनसा ध्यायेदा नक्षत्राणामुदयादुदितेषु नक्षत्रेषु त्रीन्प्राणायामान्धारयित्वा सावित्रीं सहस्रकृत्व आवर्तयेच्छतकृत्वो वा दशावरमथाग्निमुपतिष्ठते ऽग्ने त्वं नो अन्तम इत्यथ वरुणमुपतिष्ठते त्वं वरुण उत मित्र इत्येतयैवावृता प्रातः प्राङ्मुखस्तिष्ठन्नथादित्यमुपतिष्ठत उद्वयं तमस-

---

१ भुक्षीय B ; भिक्षिषीय M¹, M². २ उपव्याहृत° M².

३ Thus B; अक्षारलव° M² ; अक्षयरलव° M¹. ४ पालाशं the Mss.

५ Thus M² ; °पर्याप्तदण्ड° B, M¹.

स्परीत्यथ मित्रमुपतिष्ठते प्र मित्राय प्रार्यम्ण इति स यदि सूर्याभ्युदितः सूर्याभिनिम्रुक्तो वा तच्छेषं सावित्रीं मनसा ध्यायेत्सैव तत्र प्रायश्चित्तिः ॥ १३ ॥

श्रावण्यामुपाकरणं प्रौष्ठपद्यां वा हस्तेन त्रीन्प्राणायामानायम्याचम्य[1] सर्वे पुरस्ताज्जपं जपन्ति सह[2] नो[2] ऽस्तु सह नो भुनक्तु सह नो वीर्यवदस्तु मा विद्विषामहै सर्वेषां नो वीर्यवदस्त्विति तेभ्यः सावित्रीं प्रब्रूयाद्यथोपनयने मनसा सामसावित्रीं च सोमं राजानमित्यादितश्छन्दांस्यधीत्य यथार्थमक्षतधानानां दध्नश्च नवाहुतीर्जुहोत्यृषीन्देवांश्छन्दांस्यृचो यजूंषि सामान्यृचं साम यजामहे सदसस्पतिमद्भुतं मेधाकारमित्येतासामेव पूर्वाभिः षड्भिः पूर्वं तर्पयेदाचार्यमाचार्यांश्च[3] जैमिनिं तलवकारं सात्यमुग्रं राणायनिं[4] दुर्वाससं[5] च भागुरिं[6] गौरुण्डिं[7] गौर्गुलविं[8] भगवन्तमौपमन्यवं कारडिं[9] सावर्णिं गार्ग्यं वार्षगण्यं दैवन्त्यमित्येतांस्त्रयोदश[10] धानावन्तं दधिक्राव्ण[11] इत्येताभ्यामभिमन्त्र्य हविःशेषं प्राश्य प्राङ् प्रधीयत[12] आग्नेये समाप्ते ऽज ऐन्द्रे मेषो गौः पावमाने पर्वदक्षिणा सब्रह्मचारिणश्चोपसमेतान्भोजयेत्सावित्रमहः[13] काङ्क्षन्त उत्सर्गे च पक्षिणीं रात्रिं न मांसमश्नीयान्न श्राद्धं न लोमानि संहारयेन्न स्त्रियमुपेयादृतौ जायामुपेयाद्वर्षाशरदिकमेतद्व्रतमर्धमासमित्येके[14] ॥ १४ ॥

---

१ प्राणानायम्याथाचम्य M^1; प्राणायामानाचमाचम्य M^2; प्राणायामानाचम्य B.
२ शंनोऽस्तु M^2.
३ What follows, until the end of the khaṇḍa, is missing in M^2. आचार्य आचार्यं च M^1.
४ प्राणायनिं B; राणायिणीं M^1.
५ कुरुवाससं B; दर्वासस्र or दर्वासस्र M^1, cp. Simon, Beitr. zur Kenntnis der Vedischen Schulen, S. 28, note.
६ भागुरं M^1.
७ गौरारिण्डं B, गौरारिण्डं M^1.
८ गौद्गुलवं B; गौर्गलवं M^1
९ Thus B, but with Tamil-Malayalam *l*, instead of the *d*; गार्ग्य° M^1.
१० Thus B; दैवन्त्रम् M^1.
११ दाधिक्राव्णामित्ये° B.
१२ प्राधीयत M^1.
१३ सावित्रांम° the Mss.
१४ वर्षशर° M^1.

तेषामुत्सर्गो वेदेषु यथास्वं विश्रमन्तां छन्दांसि चतुरुत्तराणि शिवेन नो ध्यायन्त्वित्युत्सृज्याध्यायानध्यायौ व्रतानि चानुपालयन्तो यथास्वं वेदमधीयीरन्नत ऊर्ध्वमभ्रेषु नाधीयते ॥ १५ ॥

गौदानिकव्रातिकौपनिषदाः[१] संवत्सरास्तेषु सायंप्रातरुदकोपस्पर्शनं नानुपस्पृश्य भोजनं प्रातः सायमुपस्पृश्या समिदाधानादरण्यात्समिधमाहृत्यादध्यादादित्यव्रातिकः संवत्सर एकवासा न युक्तमारोहेदादित्यं नान्तर्दधीत छत्त्रेण महीमासनशयनाभ्यामुपानद्भ्यां च[२] नोर्ध्वं जान्वोरपः प्रस्नायादन्यत्राचार्यवचनाद्व्रातिके व्रतपर्वादित्यव्रातिके[३] शुक्रियारण्यौपनिषद उपनिषदं श्रावयेत् ॥ १६ ॥

द्वादश महानाम्निकाः[४] संवत्सरा नव षट् त्रय इति विकल्पाः संवत्सरमित्येके[५] पित्रा चेच्छ्रुता महानाम्न्यः[६] संवत्सरं ब्रह्मचर्यं चरेच्छुक्लैकवासा व्रतं तु भूयस्तिष्ठेद्दिवाथासीत नक्तं तस्य कृष्णे भोजनाच्छादने भवत इत्येके शुक्लं चैव[७] परिदध्याद्रागदोषान्न कृष्णं सर्वास्वप्सूपस्पृशेदबुक्नाः[८] शक्वर्य इति नावा न प्रस्नायात्प्राणसंशये तूपस्पृशेदुभयत[९] अपि वा गाः पाययेत्पशूक्नाः शक्वर्य इति वर्षं नान्तर्दधीत छत्त्रेण प्रति वर्षं निष्क्रामेदेवमस्य चरतः कामवर्षी पर्जन्यो भवति ब्रह्मचर्यान्त एकरात्रमुपोषित अरण्यं गत्वा शैवलमिश्राणामपां कांसं पूरयित्वा तमुपवेश्य समनुपरिगृह्य निमीलितं तिस्र स्तोत्रिया उपगायेत्सपुरीषा[१०] उपोत्थायाचार्यो ऽहतेन वाससा मुखमस्य परिणह्येत्प्रदक्षिणमुदपात्रं धारयंस्तिष्ठेदहःशेषं रात्रिमासीत

१ Thus B, M[2] ; गोदा° M[1]. २ उपनद्भ्यां च om. M[1].
३ व्रातिके B, M[2] ; व्रातिकस् M[1]. ४ °नाम्रीकाः B, M[2].
५ °वत्सर इत्येके B, M[2]. ६ °नाम्नयः the Mss.
७ चैव M[1] ; तैव (sic) B ; M[2] om. the words शुक्लं......दध्यात्.
८ Thus only B ; आपूक्ना M[1] ; अभुक्ना M[2]. ९ B ins. इति after °स्पृशेद्. १० Thus all (उपागायेत् M[1]); but as the comm. explains उपगायेत् by अध्यापयेत्, the correction उपगापयेत् is probable.

वाग्यतः श्वो भते ऽरण्यं गत्वाग्निमुपसमाधाय वत्समुपान्वानीय[१] वाम उद्वेष्टयेदुद्यम्य कांसमपोऽभिवीक्ष इति वीक्षेत्स्वरभिवीक्ष इत्यादित्यं ज्योतिरभिवीक्ष इत्यग्निं पशुमाभिवीक्ष इति वत्सं समन्या यन्तीत्यपः प्रसिच्य वासः कांसं वत्समित्यचार्यायोपहरेत्स्थालीपाकाद्विश्वामित्रेन्द्रौ महानाम्नीश्च यजत इत्याचार्यं सपरिषत्कं भोजयेद्गौर्दक्षिणा ॥ १७ ॥

द्वादश वर्षाणि वेदब्रह्मचर्यं[२] जननात्प्रभृतीत्येके यावदध्ययनं वा सदा सायं[३] समिदाधानं सायंप्रातर्भैक्षचरणं द्वे त्रिवृती वर्जयेत्त्रिवृतं च मणिं त्रिगुणे[४] चोपानहौ षोडशे गोदानकरणं तत्केशान्तकरणमित्याचक्षते चौडकरणेन मन्त्रा व्याख्याता[५] उपनयनेन व्रतादेशनं न त्विह नियुक्तमहतं वासः सर्वाणि लोमनखानि वापयेच्छिखावर्जमित्यौद्गाहमनिरुप्तकेशः स्नायाद्वनस्पतेरिति वनस्पतीनां स्नानीयेन त्वचमुन्मृद्नीते[६] वनस्पतेस्त्वगसि शोधनि शोधय मा तां त्वाभिहरे दीर्घायुष्ट्वाय वर्चस इति वनस्पतीनां गन्धो ऽसीति स्नात्वानुलेपनेन कुरुते वनस्पतीनां गन्धो ऽसि पुण्यगन्ध पुण्यं मे गन्धं कुरु देवमनुष्येषु तं त्वाभिहरे दीर्घायुष्ट्वाय वर्चस इति वनस्पतीनां पुष्पमसीति स्रजमाबध्नीते वनस्पतीनां पुष्पमसि पुण्यगन्ध पुण्यं मे गन्धं कुरु देवमनुष्येषु तं त्वाभिहरे दीर्घायुष्ट्वाय वर्चस इत्यादर्शो ऽसीत्यादर्श आत्मानं वीक्षेतादर्शो[७] ऽस्या मा दृश्यासन्देवमनुष्या उभये शोभो ऽसि शोभासमहं देवमनुष्येषु रोचो ऽसि

१ Thus B ; उपन्वर्नाय M[1] ; उपन्वार्नाय M[2]. २ चरेत् ins. M[1].
३ Thus B M[1]; सादामाये M[2]. ४ Thus B; त्रिगुण M[1]; त्रिगुणी M[2].
५ Thus M[1] ; °करणेनमन्त्रव्याख्यातं M[2] ; °करणेनव्याख्यातं B.
६ ऋन्मृदनीते B ; उन्मृध्नीते M[2] ; उन्मृर्भायने M[1].
७ Thus B M[2] ; अवेक्षेत M[1].

रोचासमहं देवमनुष्येष्वित्यपोद्धृत्य स्रजमादेशयेतोक्ता[1] धर्माः संवत्सरेषु गौर्दक्षिणा ॥ १८ ॥

वेदमधीत्य व्रतानि चरित्वा ब्राह्मणः स्नास्यन्संभारानुपकल्पयतेऽहतं वास एरकां स्नानमनुलेपनं सुमनस आञ्जनमादर्शमहते वाससी त्रिवृतं मणिं वैणवं दण्डं शुक्ले उपानहौ नापित उपक्लृप्त उत्तरत उपतिष्ठत्यैरकामास्तीर्याहतेन वाससोदग्दशेन प्रच्छाद्य तत्रैनं प्राङ्मुखमुपवेश्य दण्डमप्सु षादयेद्द्विषतां[2] वज्रोऽसीति मेखलां विस्रंसयेदुदुत्तममिति तां चैवाप्सु षादयेत्केशान्तकरणेन मन्त्रा व्याख्याताः परिवापनं च शिरोऽग्रे वपते[3] ततः श्मश्रूणि तत इतराण्यङ्गान्यनुपूर्वेण[4] केशश्मश्रुलोमनखान्यश्वत्थस्य मूले निखनेदुदुम्बरस्य[5] वापहतो मे पाप्मेति शीतोष्णाभिरद्भिर्हिरण्यान्तर्हिताभिरेनं स्नापयेच्छिवा नः शंतमा भव सुमृडीका सरस्वति मा ते व्योम संदृशीति रोहिण्यां स्नायात्प्रजापतेर्वा एतन्नक्षत्रं प्रजावान्भूयासमिति मृगशिरसि स्नायात्सोमस्य वा एतन्नक्षत्रं सोमेज्या मोपनमेदिति तिष्ये स्नायाद्बृहस्पतेर्वा एतन्नक्षत्रं ब्रह्म बृहस्पतिर्ब्रह्मवर्चसी भूयासमिति हस्ते स्नायात्सवितुर्वा एतन्नक्षत्रं सवितृप्रसूतो भूयासमित्यनूराधासु स्नायान्मित्रस्य वा एतन्नक्षत्रं मित्राणां प्रियो भूयासमिति श्रवणे स्नायाद्विष्णोर्वा एतन्नक्षत्रं यज्ञो वै विष्णुर्यज्ञो मोपनमेदिति तमहतेन वाससा परिदधीत परीमं सोमेति सव्यमग्रेऽभ्यञ्जीत यशसा मेत्यथ[6] दक्षिणं त्रिवृतं मणिं कण्ठे प्रतिमुञ्चते पालाशं स्वस्त्ययनकामः स्वस्त्ययनोऽसीति बैल्वं ब्रह्मवर्चसकामो ब्रह्मवर्चसी

१ आदेशयत B ; आदेशयेति M² (आदेशयेत comm.); आदेशयते M¹.

२ द्विषतो M¹. ३ वपेत M¹.

४ Thus B ; आनुपूर्व्येण M² ; आनुपूर्वेण M¹. ५ औदुम्बरस्य all.

६ यशसेमेतिअथ B ; यशसामेतिअथ M¹ ; यशसामेतिअथ M².

भूयासमित्यर्कमन्नाद्यकामो ऽर्कवानन्नादो भूयासमिति गन्धर्वो ऽसि विश्वावसुः स मा पाहि स मा गोपायेति वैणवं दण्डमुपादत्त उपानहावादधीत[1] नेत्रे स्थो नयतं मामिति दक्षिणमग्रे प्रतिमुञ्चते तस्य व्रतानि भवन्ति नाजातलोम्न्योपहासमिच्छेद्वर्षति न धावेन्नोपानहौ स्वयं हरेन्न फलानि स्वयं प्रचिन्वीत न प्रतिसायं ग्रामान्तरं व्रजेन्नैको न वृषलैः सह नोदपानमवेक्षेन्न वृक्षमारोहेन्न संक्रममारोहेन्नानन्तर्धायासीत नापरया द्वारा प्रपन्नमन्नमश्नीयान्न शुक्तं न द्विःपक्वं न पर्युषितमन्यत्र शाकमांसयवपिष्टान्नपृथुकफाणितदधिमधुघृतेभ्यो[2] नानर्मणि हसेन्न नग्नः स्नायाच्छुक्ला वाचो न भाषेत जनवादं कलहांश्च वर्जयेत्त्रयः स्नातका भवन्तीति ह[3] स्माहारुणिगौतमो[3] विद्यास्नातको व्रतस्नातको विद्याव्रतस्नातक इति तेषामुत्तमः श्रेष्ठस्तुल्यौ पूर्वौ स्नात्वाचार्यं [4]ब्रूयान्मधुपर्कं मे भवानानयत्वित्याचार्यकल्पो वा तस्मै प्राङ्मुखायासीनाय मधुपर्कमाहरेद्विष्टरपाद्यार्घ्याचमनीयान्येकैकमनुपूर्वेण[5] विष्टरमध्यास्ते पाद्येन पादौ प्रक्षालयते मयि श्रीः श्रयतामिति[6] सव्यं पादमग्रे शूद्रा चेन्मयि पद्या[7] विराडित्यथ[7] दक्षिणं मयि वर्च इत्यर्घ्यं प्रतिगृह्णीयादाचमनीयाभिराचामेत्[8] पात्रचमसं विष्टरोपहितमधस्ताद्विष्टरौ संहिताग्रौ भवत एकविष्टर उत्तरतस्तयोर्मध्ये दधि मधु संनिहिते भवतो दध्ना चेद्दधिमन्थो ऽद्भिश्चेदुदमन्थः पयसा चेत्पयस्यस्तं प्रतिगृह्णीयाद्देवस्य त्वेति तं प्रतिगृह्य[9] भूमौ प्रतिष्ठाप्यावघृष्याङ्गुष्ठेनोपकनिष्ठिकया च मह्यं

---

१ Thus M¹ M²; आददीत B. २ °फाणित° M²; °पाणित° B; °पाणि° M¹. ३ Thus B (only °रुणिगौत°); इति इह स्याहारुणीगौत° M¹; इति अस्नाहरुणिगौत° M². ४ प्रब्रूयात् B.

५ Thus M¹; आनुपूर्वेण B; आनुपूर्व्येण M². ६ Thus M²; श्रिय° M; श्रीय° B. ७ Thus B; विद्याविरा इति M¹; विपद्याविराडिति M².

८ Thus B; आचमेत् M²; °चामयेत् M¹.

९ Thus M¹; B M²: तं प्रतिगृह्य देवस्य त्वेति त्रिः प्रभूमौ।

त्वा यशसे श्रिये ऽन्नाद्याय ब्रह्मवर्चसायेति त्रिः प्राश्नीयाच्छेषमुत्तरतः प्रतिगृह्य[1] ब्राह्मणाय दद्यादभ्युक्ष्य वाब्राह्मणाय गर्ते वा निखनेत्परः स्वधितिपाणिर्गां दृष्ट्वाह गौर्गौरिति[2] तामभिमन्त्रयते गौर्धेनुरित्योमुत्सृजतेति ब्रूयात्कर्तव्या चेत्कुरुतेति ब्रूयाद्गौर्धेनुर्हव्या[3] माता रुद्राणां दुहिता वसूनां स्वसादित्यानाममृतस्य नाभिः । प्र नु वोचं चिकितुषे जनाय मा गामनागामदितिं वधिष्ट पिबतूदकं तृणान्यत्त्वित्यथ[4] षडर्घ्यार्हा भवन्त्यृत्विगाचार्यः स्नातको राजाभिषिक्तः प्रियः सखा श्रोत्रियश्चेति तेभ्य आतिथ्यं गां कुर्यात्तामतिथय इति प्रोक्षेत् ॥ १९ ॥

स्नात्वा मातापितरौ परिचरेत्तदधीनः स्यात्ताभ्यामनुज्ञातो जायां विन्देतानग्निकां समानजातीयामसगोत्रां मातुरसपिण्डां ज्यायसः कनीयसीं दूतमनुमन्त्रयते ऽनृक्षरा ऋजवः सन्तु पन्था एभिः[5] सखायो यन्ति नो वरेयम् । समर्यमा सं भगो नो ऽनुनीयात्सं[6] जास्पत्यं सुयममस्तु देवा इति पाणिग्रहणे ऽग्निमाह्रियमाणमनुमन्त्रयते[7] ऽग्निरैतु प्रथमो देवतानां सो ऽस्यै प्रजां मुञ्चतु मृत्युपाशात् । तदयं राजा वरुणो ऽनुमन्यतां यथेयं स्त्री पौत्रमघं न रोदादिति प्रज्वलितमुपतिष्ठत इमामग्निस्त्रायतां गार्हपत्यः प्रजामस्यै नयतु दीर्घमायुः । अशून्योपस्था जीवतामस्तु माता पौत्रमानन्दमभि प्रबुध्यतामियमिति पुरस्तादग्नेर्ब्राह्मणो वाग्यतः प्रत्यङ्मुख उदकुम्भं धारयंस्तिष्ठेद्दक्षिणतो ऽग्नेः शमीपलाशमिश्राँल्लाजाञ्छूर्पे माता धारयेन्मातुरभावे तन्मात्री प्रत्यगग्नेरेरकां तेजनीं वान्यद्वैवंजातीयं[9] संवेष्ट्य निदध्याद्यथा

---

१ परिगृह्य M². २ Thrice गौः M¹. ३ Thus B M¹ (cp. the comm.); भव्या M². ४ After इति (which is missing in B M²) M¹ has: ओमुत्सृजत तामुत्सृजेत. ५ Thus all (instead of येभिः), also the comm. ६ Thus all (instead of निनीयात्) also the comm.

७ °ह्रीयमाण° M¹ B; °हार्यमाणा° M². ८ Thus B; तेजनं M²; तेजनीयं M¹. ९ वा अन्यदेवजा° M¹.

प्रसार्यमाणं[१] पश्चार्धं बर्हिषः प्राप्नोत्यथास्यै[२] वाससी प्रोच्यानुमन्त्र्य ददाति[३] या अकृन्तन्नवयन्या अतन्वत याश्च देवीरन्तामभितो ऽददन्त। तास्त्वा देवीर्जरसा संव्ययन्त्वायुष्मतीदं परिधत्स्व वास इति तां ब्रूयादिमामेरकां दक्षिणेन पादेनाभिजहीति प्र मे पतियानः पन्थाः कल्पतामित्यजपत्यां[४] स्वयं जपेत्प्रास्या इति दक्षिणत एरकायां भार्यामुपवेश्योत्तरतः पतिरुभावन्वारभेयातां स्वयमुच्चैर्जुहुयाज्जाया-यामन्वारब्धायां महाव्याहृतिभिर्हुत्वा या तिरश्चीति सप्तभिर्जुहोति संपातं प्रथमया मूर्धन्यासिञ्चेद्या[५] तिरश्ची निपद्यसे ऽहं विधरणी इति। तां त्वा घृतस्य धारया संराधा राधयामसि संराधायै स्वाहा॥ मा ते गृहे निशि घोष उत्थादन्यत्र त्वद्रुदत्यः संविशन्तु। मा त्वं विकेश्युर आवधिष्ठा जीवपत्नी पतिलोके विराज प्रजां पश्यन्ती सुमनस्यमाना स्वाहा॥ अन्वद्य नो ऽनुमतिर्यज्ञं देवेषु मन्यताम्। अग्निश्च हव्यवाहनस्तत्करोतु समृध्यतां स्वाहा॥ द्यौस्ते पृष्ठं रक्षतु वायुरूरू अश्विनौ च स्तनं धयतस्ते पुत्रान्सविताभिरक्षतु। आ वाससः परिधानाद्बृहस्पतिर्विश्वे देवा अभिरक्षन्तु पश्चात्स्वाहा॥ अप्रजस्तां पौत्रमृत्युं[६] पाप्मानमुत वाघम्। शीर्ष्णः[७] स्रजमिवोन्मुच्य द्विषद्भ्य प्रतिमुञ्चामि पाशं स्वाहा॥ यानि कानि च पापानि सर्वाङ्गेषु तवाभवन्। पूर्णाहुतिभिराज्यस्य सर्वाणि तान्यशीशमं स्वाहा॥ प्रजापत इत्येका॥ २०॥

अथास्या दक्षिणेन पाणिना दक्षिणं पाणिं गृह्णाति प्रहस्तं पुंस

---

१ °माणः M[1]. २ Before अथ M[1] ins. इति. ३ दधाति M[1] M[2].

४ Thus D, कल्प्यतामित्य° M[2]; कल्प्यतामियामित्य° M[1].

५ Thus M[2]; मूर्ध्न्यासि° B; मूर्ध्नासि° M[1]. ६ Thus B M[2]; पौत्रं मृत्युं M[1]. ७ Without the visarga B M[2]; शीर्ष्णि M[1].

अङ्गुली स्त्रियः साङ्गुष्ठं मिथुनकामो[1] गृह्णामि[2] ते सौभगत्वाय हस्तं मया पत्या जरदष्टिर्यथासत् । भगो ऽर्यमा सविता पुरन्धिर्मह्यं त्वादुर्गार्हपत्याय देवाः ॥ सोमो ऽददद्गन्धर्वाय गन्धर्वो ऽददग्नये । रयिं च पुत्रांश्चादादग्निर्मह्यमथो इमाम् ॥ सोमः प्रथमो विविदे गन्धर्वो विविद उत्तरः । तृतीयो ऽग्निष्टे पतिस्तुरीयो[3] ऽहं मनुष्यजा इत्युपनयनावृताश्मानमधिष्ठापयेत्स्त्रीवत्[4] उत्तरपुरस्तादग्नेर्भार्यया संप्रेक्ष्यमाणो जपत्यघोरचक्षुरपतिघ्नी म[5] एधि शिवा पतिभ्यः[6] सुमनाः सुवर्चाः । जीवसूर्देवकामा स्योना शं नो भव द्विपदे शं चतुष्पदे ॥ आ नः प्रजां जनयतु प्रजापतिराजरसाय समनक्त्वर्यमा । अदुर्मङ्गलीः पतिलोकमाविश शं न[7] एधि[7] द्विपदे शं चतुष्पदे ॥ तां पूषञ्छिवतमामेरयस्व यस्यां बीजं मनुष्या वपन्ति । या न ऊरू उशती विस्रयातै यस्यामुशन्तः प्रहरेम शेफम् ॥ अमो ऽहमस्मि सा त्वं सामाहमस्म्यृक्त्वं मनो ऽहमस्मि वाक्त्वं द्यौरहं पृथिवी त्वं तावेहि संभवाव सह रेतो दधावहै पुंसे पुत्राय वेत्तवै मामनुव्रता भव सहशय्या मया भवासावित्यथास्या नाम गृहीत्वाग्निं परिक्रमेयातामीत्वमस्यूर्क्के माता नाम सा मामेहि सह प्रजया सह रायस्पोषेणेति तस्यां प्रत्याव्रजितायां भ्रातान्यो वा सुहृदभिघारितान्लाजाञ्छूर्पादञ्जलिनोपघातमञ्जलावावपेदुपस्तीर्णाभिघारितान्कृत्वा तानितराग्नौ जुहुयात्कन्यलेयं नार्यर्यम्णामिति कन्यला पितृभ्यः पतिलोकं यतीयमव दीक्षामयक्षत स्वाहा ॥ इयं नार्युपब्रूते ऽग्नौ

---

१ Here follow in M[1] the words (which are neither given by B M[2] nor explained in the comm.): मध्यमां परिवर्जयेत्

२ Thus B M[2] ; गर्भाणामि M[1]. ३ तुरियो B ; तुर्यो M[1] M[2].

४ M[1] inserts here the mantra इममश्मानम् with ūha.

५ Thus M[2] ; °घ्नामयेधि B ; °घ्नीमेति M[1]. ६ पशुभ्यः all Mss. of the text ; the comm., however, has पतिभ्यः

७ Thus B ; नयेति M[1] ; नो भव M[2].

लाजानावपन्ती । दीर्घायुरस्तु मे पतिरेधन्तां ज्ञातयो मम स्वाहा ॥ अर्यम्णं नु देवं कन्याग्निमयक्षत । स इमां देवो अर्यमा प्रेतो मुञ्चातु मामुतः स्वाहेति होमान्तेषु जपति चतुर्विंश्वा उत त्वया वयं धारा उदन्या इव । अतिगाहेमहि द्विष इति तूष्णीं धारिका कामाया-वपेच्चतुर्थं दक्षिणं शूर्पपुटं काम इत्याचक्षत उत्तरपुरस्तादग्नेः सप्त पदान्यभ्युत्क्रमयेदेकमिष इति प्रतिमन्त्रमेकमिषे विष्णुस्त्वान्वेतु । द्वे ऊर्जे विष्णुस्त्वान्वेतु । त्रीणि रायस्पोषाय विष्णुस्त्वान्वेतु । चत्वारि मयोभवाय विष्णुस्त्वान्वेतु । पञ्च प्रजाभ्यो विष्णुस्त्वान्वेतु । षडृतुभ्यो विष्णुस्त्वान्वेतु । सखा सप्तपदी भवेति सप्तमे प्राचीमवस्थाप्योदकुम्भेन मार्जयेरन्नापोहिष्ठीयाभिस्तिसृभिः प्रेक्षकाननुमन्त्रयते सुमङ्गलीरियं वधूरिमां समेत पश्यत । सौभाग्यमस्यै दत्त्वायाथास्तं विपरेतनेति प्रेक्षयेद्ध्रुवमरुन्धतीं सप्त ऋषीन्पश्यानीति प्रतिजानानां ध्रुवो ऽसीति ध्रुवमुपतिष्ठते ध्रुवो ऽसि ध्रुवाहं पतिकुले भूयासममुष्येति पतिनाम गृह्णीयादसावित्यात्मनो ऽरुन्धतीमरुन्धत्यरुद्धाहं[1] पत्या भूयासममु-नेति पतिनाम गृह्णीयादसावित्यात्मनः ॥ २१ ॥

पूषा त्वेत इति प्रस्थितामनुमन्त्रयते पूषा त्वेतो नयतु हस्तगृह्या-श्विनौ त्वा प्रवहतां रथेन । गृहान्गच्छ गृहपत्नी यथासो वशिनी त्वं विदथमावदासीति स्वं कुलं प्राप्तां कल्याणशीलाः कल्याणप्रजाः समवजीर्णाः प्रत्यवरोपयन्तीह प्रियं प्रजया ते समृध्यतामस्मिन्गृहे गार्हपत्याय जागृहि । एना पत्या तन्वं संसृजस्वाथाजीव्री विदथमा-वदासीति प्रत्यवरोप्यानडुहे चर्मण्युत्तरलोमन्युपवेशयेदिह[2] गावो निषीदन्त्विहाश्वा इह पुरुषाः । इहो सहस्रदक्षिणो ऽभि[3] पूषा

---

१ After अरुन्धतीं B ins. : दृष्ट्वा उपतिष्ठते अरुन्धतीति. २ Thus M^1 M^2; °लोम्न्युप° B. ३ Thus B; °दक्षिणा अभि M^1; °दक्षिणोपि M^2.

निषीदत्विति कुमारमुपस्थ आधाय शकलोटानावपेत्फलानि वोत्थाप्य कुमारमन्वारब्धायां जुहुयादिह धृतिरित्यष्टाभिः[१] स्वाहाकारान्तैरिह धृतिरिह स्वधृतिरिह रन्तिरिह रमस्व । मयि धृतिर्मयि स्वधृतिर्मयि रमो मयि रमस्वेति[२] त्रिरात्रमक्षारालवणाशिनौ[३] ब्रह्मचारिणावधः संवेशिनावसंवर्तमानौ[४] सह शयातामूर्ध्वं त्रिरात्रात्संभवो[५] निशायां जायापतिकर्मण्यं प्रायश्चित्तीर्जुहुयादग्ने प्रायश्चित्ते त्वं देवानां प्रायश्चित्तिरसि ब्राह्मणस्त्वा नाथकाम उपधावामि यास्यै प्रजाघ्नी तनूस्तामस्या अपजहि स्वाहा । वायो प्रायश्चित्ते त्वं देवानां प्रायश्चित्तिरसि ब्राह्मणस्त्वा नाथकाम उपधावामि यास्यै पशुघ्नी तनूस्तामस्या अपजहि स्वाहा । सूर्य प्रायश्चित्ते त्वं देवानां प्रायश्चित्तिरसि ब्राह्मणस्त्वा नाथकाम उपधावामि यास्यै पतिघ्नी तनूस्तामस्या अपजहि स्वाहा । चन्द्र प्रायश्चित्ते त्वं देवानां प्रायश्चित्तिरसि ब्राह्मणस्त्वा नाथकाम उपधावामि यास्यै गृहघ्नी तनूस्तामस्या अपजहि स्वाहा । अग्ने वायो सूर्य चन्द्र प्रायश्चित्तयो यूयं देवानां प्रायश्चित्तय स्थ ब्राह्मणो वो नाथकाम उपधावामि यास्यै यशोघ्नी तनूस्तामस्या अपहत स्वाहेति स्थालीपाकादाग्नेयं प्रजापतिं चेष्ट्वा संपातांश्चमस आनीय स्नातास्याङ्क्ष्वेत्येनां[६] ब्रूयान्नाभिं प्रथमं ततो यान्यूर्ध्वं ततो यान्यर्वाञ्च्यूर्ध्वमधरात्रात्संवेशनं विष्णुर्योनिं कल्पयत्वित्येतेन[७] तृचेन[७] विष्णुर्योनिं कल्पयतु त्वष्टा रूपाणि पिंशतु । आसिञ्चतु प्रजापतिर्धाता गर्भं दधातु ते ॥ गर्भं धेहि सिनीवालि गर्भं धेहि सरस्वति । गर्भं ते अश्विनौ देवावाधत्तां पुष्करस्रजौ ॥ हिरण्ययी अरणी यं निर्मन्थतामाश्विनौ । तं ते गर्भं दधाम्यहं दशमे

---

१ Thus M¹ M²; इत्येताभि B. २ Before इति M ins. स्वाहा.
३ Thus B; अक्षारलवना° M¹ M². ४ Thus B; अधस्संवर्त° M¹; M² defective. ५ संभवतः B. ६ अङ्क्ष्वेति B ७ विष्णु°...तृचेन om. M¹.

मासि सूतवा[१] इत्यृतावृतावेवमेव संवेशने[२] हुत्वाचार्याय गां दद्याददर्शने[३] ब्राह्मणेभ्यो गां दद्यात् ॥ २२ ॥

सायंप्रातर्होमे ऽग्नय इति प्रथमामाहुतिं जुहोति प्रजापतय इत्युत्तरामेवं प्रातरग्निस्थाने सूर्यः सायंप्रातरशनस्य बली वर्धयित्वा पूर्वस्मादग्नौ जुहोत्यग्नये स्वाहा सोमाय स्वाहा धन्वन्तरये[४] स्वाहा द्यावापृथिवीभ्यां स्वाहा विश्वेभ्यो देवेभ्यः स्वाहा सर्वाभ्यो देवताभ्यः स्वाहा प्रजापतये स्वाहेति मनसोत्तरां तत एवोत्तरतो ऽग्नेर्बलिं[५] हरति[५] ये हर्षणा वेपना स्फातिमाहरा वातस्य ध्राजमनुसंचरन्ति । तेभ्यो बलिमन्नकामो हराम्यन्नं पयस्वद्बहुलं मे अस्त्वित्येवमशनायत्यायस्थाने[६] मृत्योरधिष्ठानाय स्वाहेति शेषस्य बलिहरणं प्रदक्षिणं गृह्याभ्यो देवताभ्यो बलिं नयामि तन्मे जुषन्तां ता मा पान्तु ता मा गोपायन्तु ता मा रक्षन्तु ताभ्यो नमस्ताभ्यः स्वाहेत्युदधाने मध्ये ऽगारस्योत्तरपूर्वार्धे शयने देहल्यां[७] संवरणे ब्रह्मायतन[८] एतेष्वायतनेषु[८] शेषं धन्वन्तरये निनयेत्सदा गृहेषु स्वस्तिवाचनं सा महाशान्तिरित्याचक्षते ॥ २३ ॥

नवेन यक्ष्यमाणः पुराणेनाग्नि यजेताग्निधन्वन्तरी प्रजापतिमिन्द्रं तिस्रश्च नवाहुतीर्नवेन यजेत शरदि व्रीहीणां वसन्ते यवानां वर्षासु श्यामाकानामैन्द्राग्नो वैश्वदेवो द्यावापृथिव्यश्चरव एकचरुर्वोक्ते एवोपस्तरणाभिघारणे द्विर्हविषो ऽवद्यत्यथ प्राश्नीयाद्भद्रान्नः श्रेयः समनैष्ट देवास्त्वयावसेन समशीमहि त्वा । स नो मयोभूः पितो

---

१ Thus M^2; सूतवै (इति) B ; सूतवाह (इति) M^1. २ Thus B M^1; °शनं M^2. ३ Thus B ; आदर्शने M^1 M^2. ४ °न्तरे the MSS.
५ Thus M^2 only ; बलीमाहरति B ; बलीन् हरति M^1. ६ Thus M^1 M^2 ; आयु° B. ७ देहिन्यां B ; देहिल्यां M^1 ; देवड्यां M^2.
[८] ब्रह्मायनेषु एतेष्व° M^1 ; ब्रह्मायतनेषु तेष्व° M^2 ; ब्राह्मणायतने एतेष्व° B.

आविशस्व शं तोकाय तनुवे स्योन इत्येतमु त्यं मधुना संयुतं यवं सरस्वत्या अधि मनावचर्कृषुः[१] । इन्द्र आसीत्सीरपतिः शतक्रतुः कीनाशा आसन्मरुतः सुदानव इति यवस्य प्राश्नीयादग्निः प्रथमः प्राश्नातु स हि वेद यथा हविः । शिवा अस्मभ्यमोषधीः कृणोतु विश्वचर्षणीरिति श्यामाकस्य प्राश्नीयात्प्राश्नीयात्[२] ॥ २४ ॥

॥ इति जैमिनिसूत्रं पूर्वम् ॥

श्राद्धं करिष्यन्तः स्नाताः शुचिवाससस्तिलैर्वास्त्ववकीर्य[३] सव्यमाचरन्तो ऽन्नमुपसाधयेरन्हविष्यैरुपसिच्यैवं दद्याद्यद्दद्यात्तत्तद्धविष्यैरुपसिच्यैव हविष्या इति तिलानामाख्या दन्तधावनं स्नानीयानि पाद्यमानीय प्रथमोद्धृतं ब्राह्मणांस्त्र्यवदातानुपवेशयत्या मे गच्छन्तु पितरो भागधेयं विराजाहूताः[४] सलिलात्समुद्रियात्[५] । अक्षीयमाणमुपजीवतैनन्मया प्रत्तं स्वधया मदध्वमित्युपमूललूनान्दर्भान्विष्टरान्प्रसव्यान्कृत्वा ब्राह्मणेभ्यः प्रदद्यादेतत्ते पितरासनमसौ ये च त्वात्रानु तेभ्यश्चासनमित्येवं पितामहायैवं प्रपितामहाय हविष्योदकं तिरः पवित्रं गन्धान्सुमनसश्च दद्यादन्नमवत्त्वा घृतेनाभिघार्य दर्भान्परिस्तरणीयानीति[६] तदादायाग्नौ करिष्यामीति ब्राह्मणाननुज्ञाप्य प्राग्दक्षिणामुखो ऽग्निं प्रणयित्वा त्रिर्धून्वन्प्रदक्षिणमग्निं[७] परिस्तृणाति प्राचीनावीती त्रिः प्रसव्यं त्रिः पर्युक्षेत्प्रदक्षिणं प्राचीनावीती त्रिः प्रसव्यमौदुम्बर इध्मः परिधयो भवन्ति मेक्षणं च पवित्रं संस्कृत्या-

---

१ °वर्चाकिषुः M^2; °विचाकिषुः B; M^1 defective. २ The repetition acc. to the comm.; the MSS. do not repeat.

३ Thus M^2; अर्कार्य B M^1. ४ °हुताः MSS. ५ Thus M^2 and the comm.; समृद्यान् M^1; समुद्रात् B. ६ Thus M^1; B M^2: °स्तरणीयानीति ७ धुन्वन् B (comm.: धून्वन्).

अमुत्पूयाग्नौ पवित्रं प्रास्य मेक्षणेन जुहोत्यग्नये कव्यवाहनाय स्वधा नमः स्वाहा सोमाय पितृमते स्वधा नम स्वाहेति यज्ञोपवीती भूत्वाप उपस्पृश्य यमायाङ्गिरस्वते स्वाहेति मेक्षणमग्नावनुप्रहरति नमस्कारान्कृत्वा यथादैवतं त्रिः पर्युक्षेत्प्रदक्षिणं प्राचीनावीती त्रिः प्रसव्यं सव्यञ्जनमन्नं पात्रेषु वर्धयित्वामासु पक्कमिति क्षीरं घृतं वा सिञ्चत्यामासु पक्कममृतं निविष्टं मया प्रत्तं स्वधया मदध्वमिति वर्धितान्यादिशत्येतद्वः[1] पितरो भागधेयं पात्रेषु दत्तममृतं स्वधावत् । अक्षीयमाणमुपजीवतैनन्मया प्रत्तं स्वधया मदध्वम् ॥ अमृता वागमृता वाचो अग्रे वाचो ऽमृत[2] त्वं त्रिवृत्तैकधामा[3] । एभिर्मन्त्रप्रत्तैः स्वधया मदध्वमिहास्मभ्यं वसीयो ऽस्तु देवाः ॥ अयं यज्ञः परमो यः[4] पितृणां पात्रदेयं पितृदेवत्यमग्ने । वाक्च मनश्च पितरो नः प्रजानीमाश्विभ्यां प्रत्तं स्वधया मदध्वम् ॥ य इह पितरः पार्थिवासो य अन्तरिक्ष[5] उत ये समुद्रियाः[6] । ये वाचमाप्त्वा अमृता बभूवुस्ते[7] ऽस्मिन्मखे[8] हविषि मादयन्ताम् ॥ एषा व ऊर्गेषा वः स्वधा चामत्त च पिबत च मा च वः क्षेष्ट । स्वधां वहध्वममृतस्य योनिं यात्र स्वधा पितरस्तां भजध्वम् ॥ येह पितर ऊर्ग्देवता च तस्यै जीवेम शरदः शतं वयम् । ज्योतिष्मद्भ्राजरं म आयुरित्यथैतानि ब्राह्मणेभ्य उपनिक्षिप्य स्वाङ्गुष्ठेनानुदिशत्यमुष्मै[9] स्वधामुष्मै स्वधेति यन्मे ऽप्रकामा इति भुञ्जतो ऽनुमन्त्रयते यन्मे ऽप्रकामा उत वा प्रकामा समृद्धे[10] ब्राह्मणे ऽब्राह्मणे वा । य स्कन्दति निर्ऋतिं वात उग्रां येन नः प्रीयन्ते

---

१ In B M² first are given all the mantras, then follow the words : व° आदि°. २ मृतत्वं B ; अमृतत्वं M¹ (M² defective). ३ त्रिविधैक° M ; त्रिवृदेक° B (M² defective). ४ यं the MSS. ५ Thus B ; आन्तरिक्षा M¹; अन्तरिक्षां M². ६ समुद्रा : M² ; समृद्धया M¹ ; समुद्राः B. ७ Thus M² ; ते अस्मि° M¹ ; तेस्मि° B. ८ माचवक्षेष्ट M² ; मावचेष्ट B ; माधवक्षेषु M¹. ९ ब्राह्मणस्यांगुष्ठेन M¹. १० Thus B ; समृद्धे M² ; समृध्ये M¹.

पितरो देवताश्च । वायुष्टत्पवं शुन्धतु तेन शुद्धेन देवता मादयन्तां तस्मिञ्छुद्धे पितरो मादयन्तामित्यक्रान्समुद्र इत्याश्वं गीत्वा संपन्नं पृष्ट्वाथाचामयेद्यज्ञोपवीती[1] भूत्वाभिरमन्तां[2] भवन्त इत्युक्त्वा प्रदक्षिणं कृत्वा यन्मे रामेति गच्छतोऽनुमन्त्रयते यन्मे रामा शकुनिः श्वापदश्च यन्मेऽशुचिर्मन्त्रकृतस्य प्राशत् । वैश्वानरः सविता तत्पुनातु तेन पूतेन देवता मादयन्तां तस्मिन्पूते पितरो मादयन्तामिति ॥१॥

शेषमनुज्ञाप्य प्रत्येत्य प्राग्दक्षिणायतं चतुरश्रं गोमयेनोपलिप्यापहता असुरा रक्षांसि पिशाचाः पितृषद इति मध्ये रेखां काष्ठेनोल्लिख्य ये रूपाणि प्रतिमुञ्चमाना असुराः सन्तः स्वधया चरन्ति परापुरो निपुरो ये भरन्त्यग्निष्टांल्लोकात्प्रणुनोत्त्वस्मादित्युल्मुकं[3] दक्षिणतो निदधात्यनुलेखं दर्भानास्तीर्योदपात्रेणाचामयत्याचाम पितरसौ ये च त्वात्रानु ते चाचामन्त्वित्येवं पितामहायैवं प्रपितामहाय तेषु पिण्डान्निदधात्यनुनामापहस्तेनैतत्ते पितरसौ ये च त्वात्रानु तेभ्यश्च स्वधा नम इत्येवं पितामहायैवं प्रपितामहाय नामान्यजानतः पितरेतत्ते पितामहैतत्ते प्रपितामहैतत्त इति बन्धवजानत इदं पितृभ्यः पृथिवीषद्भ्य इदं पितामहेभ्योऽन्तरिक्षसद्भ्य इदं प्रपितामहेभ्यो दिविषद्भ्य इत्यत्र पितरो मादयध्वं यथाभागमावृषायध्वमित्युदगावृत्त्या तमितोरासीतामीमदन्त पितरो यथाभागमावृषायिषतेति जपित्वा पूर्ववदाचामय्य[4] नीवीं[5] विस्रंस्य[6] नमस्कारान्कृत्वा यथादैवतमेतद्वः पितर इति वस्त्राण्यादिशत्यूर्णास्तुकां दशाम्बरं वा एतद्वः पितरो वासो गृहान्नः पितरो दत्ताधत्त पितरो गर्भं कुमारं पुष्करस्रजं यथेह

---

१ Thus B; आचामेत् M^2; आचामइति M^1. २ M^1 has after भूत्वा the words: अप उपस्पृश्य. ३ प्रणुनोत्व॰ the MSS. ४ आचम्य the MSS. ५ Thus all (निवीं B). ६ Thus M^2; विस्रस्य B; विमृश्य M^1.

पुरुषो ऽसदित्यञ्जनाभ्यञ्जने ददात्याङ्क्ष्वासावित्यभ्यङ्क्ष्वासाविति गन्धान्सुमनसश्च दद्यान्नमो वः पितर इति षड्भिर्नमस्कारैरुपतिष्ठते नमो वः पितरो रसाय[1] नमो वः पितरः शुष्माय[1] नमो वः पितरो जीवाय[1] नमो वः पितरो घोराय[1] नमो वः पितरो बलाय[1] नमो वः पितरो मन्यवे स्वधायै च पितरो नमो व इत्यूर्जं[1] वहन्तीरमृतं घृतं पयः कीलालं परिस्रुतं[2] स्वधा स्थ तर्पयत मे पितॄनित्यपः प्रसिच्य[3] मा मे क्षेष्टेत्यभिमन्त्र्य[4] मा मे क्षेष्ट बहु मे पूर्तमस्तु ब्रह्माणो मे जुषन्तामन्नमन्नम् । सहस्रधारममृतोदकं मे पूर्तमस्त्वेतत्परमे व्योमन् ॥ देवाश्च पितरश्चैतत्पूर्तं मे अत्रोपजीवन्ताम् । अक्षीयमाणमुपजीवतैतन्मया प्रत्तं स्वधया मदध्वमिति ये समानाः सुमनस[5] इति प्रदक्षिणं कृत्वा ये समानाः सुमनसो[6] जीवा जीवेषु मामकाः । तेषां श्रीर्मयि कल्पतामस्मिँल्लोके शतं समा इत्यामयावी पिण्डान्प्राश्नीयादन्नाद्यकामो वाग्नौ वा संक्षपयेदप्सु[7] वाभ्यवहरेयुरजं गां ब्राह्मणं वा प्राशयेयुः[8] शेषस्य[9] प्राश्नीयान्न चान्नतृप्तिं गच्छेत् ॥२॥

ऊर्ध्वमाग्रहायण्यास्त्रयो ऽपरपक्षास्तेषामेकैकस्मिन्नेकैकाष्टका भवति शाकाष्टका मांसाष्टकापूपाष्टकेति तत्र शाकमांसापूपानि हवींष्योदनं च तेषां हविषां स्थालीपाकावृताग्नौ जुहुयादष्टकायै स्वाहा एकाष्टकायै स्वाहा अष्टकायै[10] सुराधसे स्वाहा संवत्सराय परिव-

---

१ In the following passage the recension of M^1 is received after each dative we find in B M^2 partly abbreviated, partly corrupt, the words : स्वधायै च पितरो नमो वः ; M^1 has this addition only after the six namaskāramantras and ins. after इति the word: पर्यान्तेषु. Did the text run originally: नमस्कारैरुपतिष्ठते नमो वः...स्वधायै च पितरो नमो व इत्यन्ततः ? २ परिस्रुतं the MSS. ३ अपः प्रसिच्य om. M^1. ४ क्षेष्टेत्यामन्त्र्य M^1. ५ Thus M^1. ६ Here M^1 : समनसो : सुम° B M^2 (also the comm.). ७ सक्षापयेत् M^1. ८ Thus M^1 : °शयेत् B M^2. ९ न ins. M^1. १० Thus M^1: °काय B M^2.

त्सरायेदावत्सरायेद्वत्सरायावत्सराय[१] कृणुता नमोभिः । त्वया वयं सुमतौ यज्ञियानां ज्योगजीता अहताः स्याम स्वाहेति हुत्वोपतिष्ठत एहि भगेहि भगेहि भगेति[२] मध्यमायां गां कारयेत्तामष्टकायै प्रोक्षेत्तस्यास्त्रीणि सक्थ्यान्युपोद्धरति पार्श्वमपघनीं[३] श्रोणीमिति[४] श्वो भूते श्राद्धमन्वष्टक्यं वदहर्वा ब्राह्मणान्हविरर्हानुपवेश्य तांस्तर्पयित्वा तस्मादग्नेर्दक्षिणतः षडग्नीन्प्रणीय तेषामेकैकस्मिन्नेकैकां कर्षूं खानयेदायामेन प्रादेशमात्रीं पार्थवेन त्र्यङ्गुलामवाग्वैकाङ्गुलामिति तासु पिण्डान्निदधात्यनुनामापहस्तेन मन्त्राः पितृभ्य उपकर्षति[५] पार्श्वानि स्त्रीणां तत्राध्वर्यवः केचिदधीयते मध्यमं पिण्डं पत्नी प्राश्नीयात्प्रजाकामस्य तथा श्राद्धस्य स्थालीपाकं वा श्राद्धस्य स्थालीपाकं वा[६] ॥३॥

आहिताग्नेः शरीरनाशे त्रीणि षष्टिशतानि पलाशत्सरूणामाहृत्य तैः प्रतिकृतिं कुर्यात्कृष्णाजिने ऽशीन्यर्धं शिरसि दध्याद्ग्रीवायां तु दशैव तु बाह्वोश्चैव शतं दध्यादङ्गुलीषु पुनर्दश उरसि त्रिंशतं दध्याज्जठरे विंशतिं तथोर्वोश्चैव शतं दध्यात् मेढ्रे[७] चापि दशैव तु जानुजंघयोस्त्रिंशतं दध्यात् दश पादाङ्गुलीष्वपि[८] इत्येतावन्तीह[९] पुरुषस्य शरीराणि भवन्तीति विज्ञायते मध्ये शरीरं सतीशरीरमुप्तकेशं[१०] निकृत्तनखं प्रक्षालितं चितामारोपयन्त्यत्र पात्राण्यपि[१२]

---

१ Uncertain ; before इद्वत्सराय B inserts: इदुवत्सराय : moreover B has: इद्वत्सरायायवत्सराय : after इद्वत्सराय M^2 has: वत्सरायायवत्सराय, M^1 : वत्सवत्सराय. Five are required acc. to the comm. २ Thus B ; M^2 only twice एहि भग. M^1 twice and at the end : भगेत्रिः ३ Thus B : अपघ्नीं M^2 : अपगनिं M^1. ४ Thus B M^2 ; श्रौणिमिति M^1. ५ Thus B ; कर्षन्ति M^2 ; पितृभ्योवकर्षति M^1. ६ The repetition of the closing words alone in M^1. ७ मेध्रे B (in the comm., this passage is missing in the text); मेद्र M^1. ८ अपि not in M^1. ९ Thus all MSS. The correct reading is no doubt : एतावन्ति ह. १० सति B M^1 ; सती comm. ; instead of my restitution : उप्तकेश°, the MSS. have लुप्त°. The text probably is corrupt. Are we to read : सति शरीर उप्त° ? ११ Not in B. १२ अपं B instead of अपि.

चिनोति तस्यामेनमादधाति[1] तस्य नासिकयोः स्रुवौ निदध्यादित्येतेनानुवाकेन य एवंवित्स्यात्स यदोपतापी स्यादिति[2] पूर्वमेव चतुर्गृहीतं गृहीत्वान्यं[3] यथासंभवमास्ये हिरण्यशकलमाधायाग्नीनुपोह्य[4] सामभिरुपतिष्ठते नाके सुपर्णमिति ग्राम्यं गेयमुदिते धूमे त्वेषस्ते धूम ऋण्वतीत्यग्नौ समारूढे ऽग्ने मृड महं[5] असीत्येतयोरन्यतरेण पराक्[6] पराग्वा[7] असौ लोक इति ब्राह्मणम् ॥४॥

आहिताग्नेश्चेत्पूर्वं जाया म्रियेत तां निर्मन्थ्येन दहेत्सांतपनेन वा श्मशानकृतं स्वकृतमनिरिणमपसलवक्रोदकं[8] कृत्वा यत्र वौषधयो जायन्ते तत्र शरीरं दग्ध्वोदककरणाय यान्त्यनवेक्षमाणा न वाहिनीषु कुर्वन्ति तेषां योयः पश्चाज्जातः ससो[9] ऽग्रं कुर्यादुपकूलमकूले कूपं खात्वा सव्यहस्तस्यानामिकया सकृदुदकं प्रोहति प्रेतस्य नामकरणेन वाहिनीषु चेदुद्ग्रथ्य[10] केशान्निमज्यैकाञ्जलिं दत्त्वोपसंगृह्य केशानुल्मुकस्याग्निमारभेताग्ने शूकाहे[11] पापं मे ऽपहतेति शमीमारभेत शम्यसि शमय मे पापमित्यश्मानमारभेताश्मासि स्थिरो ऽस्यहं स्थिरो भूयासमिति तूष्णीं गोमयं कृतोदकं दक्षिणामुखमासीनं तमनुगन्तार उपविशन्ति तानितरः कल्याणीभिर्वाग्भिः प्रत्याहोपास्तमनवेलायां ग्रामं[12] प्रविशन्ति तां रात्रिमेकमाषेण वसन्ति शान्त्या वा श्वो भूते क्षीरोदके संसृज्य शरीराण्यवसिञ्चत्यजशृङ्गेण गोशृङ्गेण[13] मृण्मयेन कोशेन वा[14] तृतीयायां गन्धौषधीभिः संसृज्य शमीशाखया पलाशशाखया वासंह्लादयन्कुम्भ्यामवदध्यात्स्त्री

१ °दधाति B. २ इति only in B. ३ अन्यं only in B. ४ आदाय the MSS; उपोष्य M[1], प्रोह्य B. ५ Thus (rightly!) the MSS. ६ परात् M[1]; B om. ७ After वा both MSS. insert इति. ८ स्वकृतं not in B. ९ B omits the first demonstr. pronoun; °जातामसो M[1]. १० MSS. corrupt; M[1]: चेन्दुकूले; B: दुतग्रत्थ्य (here only the syllable चे seems to fail). ११ Thus B (and the comm.); शोकाहे M[1]. १२ Not in M[1].

चेद्घट एव[१] दध्याच्चतुष्पथमतीत्य महावृक्षं नदीं वा तीर्थेषु निखनेत् प्रेतस्य तृतीयायां स्नापयन्त्यपामार्गेण मृदा गोमयेन च[२] वासांसि प्रक्षाल्य दशरात्रमासते[३] चतुर्थ्यां भिक्षामावर्तयेरन्तस्य सिद्धमग्नौकरणं[४] कालं च यावदाकांक्षेयुर्भिक्षयानुसंतरेयुरूर्ध्वं[५] दशरात्राच्छ्राद्धं दद्युर्न दद्युरा श्राद्धस्य प्रदानान्नक्षत्रेषु[६] नियमो मघास्वेकतारेषु भरणीषु च पूर्वसमयेषु[७] न रोहिण्यामुत्तरेषु ध्रुवेषु ब्राह्मणान्हविरर्हानुपवेश्य तांस्तर्पयित्वैकवत्पिण्डं दद्यान्न चान्विति[८] ब्रूयात्सर्वैः कामैस्तर्पयेदनुगमनं कृत्वा शेषमनुज्ञाप्य प्रत्येत्य शेषं[९] न प्राश्नीयाद्ब्राह्मणान्स्वस्ति वाच्य प्राश्नीयात् ॥५॥

अथातो गृहकर्मणो गृहवृद्धिमिच्छन्मासिमास्यृतावृतौ संवत्सरेसंवत्सरे वा[१०] पूर्वपक्षे पुण्ये नक्षत्रे गृहशान्तिमारभेतापामार्गपलाशशिरीषार्कौदुम्बरसदाभद्रामृततृणमिन्द्रवल्लीभिर्बद्ध्वा गृहान्परिमार्ज्य परिसमूह्यापो ऽभ्युक्ष्य पञ्चगव्यैर्दर्भमुष्टिना संप्रोक्ष्य सिद्धार्थकान्संप्रकीर्य[११] वास्तुबलिं कृत्वा वास्तोर्मध्ये वास्तोष्पतिं हुत्वा सावित्र्या सहस्रं जुहुयात्ततो दक्षिणपुरस्तात्ततो दक्षिणपश्चात्तत उत्तरपुरस्तात्तत उत्तरपश्चान्मध्ये वा गौर्वासो हिरण्यं दक्षिणा ब्राह्मणानन्नेन परिविष्य पुण्याहं स्वस्त्यृद्धिमिति वाचयित्वैवं प्रयुञ्जानो ऽनन्तं महान्तं पोषं पुष्यति बहवः पुत्रा भवन्ति न च बालाः प्रमीयन्ते नाग्निर्दहति न दंष्ट्रिणः खादयेयुर्न तस्कराः सपत्ना रक्षांसि पिशाचा अपि

---

१ Not in M^1. २ चा M^1; missing in B: the comm., however has च. ३ Thus B: दशरात्रशेषं M^1. ४ Not in B: the comm., however, seems to indicate, that these words, which run thus in M: तस्यासिद्धंकर्मौकरणं, belong to the text. ५ अनु not in B: M^1 has: कालश्चकांक्षयुः भिक्षयानुसंतर्नायुः ६ Before नक्षत्रेषु M^1 has the following, to me unintelligible words: पशुछेदेकपम्यत्रो ७ M^1 ins. वा ८ च not in B. ९ om. B: शेष्य M^1. १० Not in M^1. ११ °सं° only in M^1.

बाधन्ते यदि गावः प्रतप्येरन्गवां मध्य आहुतिसहस्रं जुहुयादित्येतेनैव कल्पेनाश्वोष्ट्रखराजाविकमहिषहस्तिकुलमन्यतरद्द्विपदां चतुष्पदां च[१] व्याख्यातम् ॥६॥

अथातोऽद्भुतशान्तिं व्याख्यास्यामोऽथ यद्यगारे स्थूणा विरोहेत्[२] कपोतो वागारं गच्छेद्गौर्वा गां धयेदनड्वान्वा[३] दिवमुल्लिखेदनग्नौ[४] वा धूमो जायेतानग्नौ वा दीप्येत मधु[५] वा[५] जायेत वल्मीकं वोपजायेत मण्डूको वाम्भृणे[६] वाश्येच्छ्वानो[६] वा गृहे पर्यटेयुरित्येतानन्यांश्च यत इन्द्र भयामहे । सदसस्पतिमद्भुतम् । अधायामुतेसुमुदस्य[७] । सनादग्ने । यद्वा उ विश्पतिः शितः । प्रत्यग्ने । यं रक्षन्ति । प्राजापत्ययर्चा[८] पुरस्ताच्चोपरिष्टाच्च[९] महाव्याहृतिभिर्जुहोति[१०] एतान्यृक्सामानि गायेत् ॥७॥

अथातोऽनक्षत्रसंहितायाः कल्पं व्याख्यास्यामः शुचिवासाः स्याच्चीरवासा वा हविष्यमन्नमशनमिच्छेदपः फलानि वा ब्राह्मणस्त्वेव[११] प्रत्याहरेत्प्राङ् वोदङ् वा ग्रामान्निष्क्रम्य शुचौ देश उदकान्ते वा गोमयेन गोचर्ममात्रं स्थण्डिलमुपलिप्य प्रोक्ष्य लक्षणमुल्लिख्याद्भिरभ्युक्ष्याग्निमुपसमाधायाघारावाज्यभागौ हुत्वाज्याहुतीर्जुहोत्यग्नये सोमाय रुद्रायेन्द्राय ब्रह्मणे प्रजापतये बृहस्पतये विश्वेभ्यो देवेभ्य ऋषिभ्य ऋग्भ्यो यजुर्भ्यः सामभ्यः श्रद्धायै प्रज्ञायै मेधायै सावित्र्यै सदसस्पतयेऽनुमतये च हुत्वा दर्भेष्वासीनः प्राक्तूलेषूदक्तूलेषु वा दक्षिणेन पाणिना दर्भान्धारयन्नोंपूर्वा व्याहृतीः सावित्रीं च चतुरनुद्रुत्य मनसा सामसावित्रीं च सोमं राजानं ब्रह्मजज्ञानीये चोभे

१ Not in B. २ वरोहेन ३ गन्धयेयु अनड्वा ४ °खेन अग्नौ ५ मधुना ६ वाभ्रमणोवाशयेच्छ्वानो ७ Citation corrupt. ८ प्राजापत्यायाच ९ °पुरस्तात् वोपरि° १० °व्याहृतीर्जु° ११ °स्त्वेवा B ; °स्त्वेवं M^2 ; °स्त्वैव M^1.

वेदादिमारभेत संततमधीयीत मौनी न चान्तरा विरमेत्[1] अथान्तरा व्याहरेदथान्तरा विरमेत्[2] त्रीन्प्राणानायम्यातम्याचम्य[3] वृतान्तादेवारभेताप्रतिभायां यावता कालेन वेदमधीयीत तावत्कालमधीयीत यज्ञानीयादृक्तो यजुष्टः सामतस्तदवाप्नुयात्तद्ब्राह्मणं तच्छान्दसं तद्दैवतं साम वा अक्रानित्येतदेव वाभ्यस्येत्तिष्ठन्नासीनः शयानश्चङ्क्रम्यमाणो[4] वा संहितां प्रयुञ्ज्यात्समृद्धिरेवास्य भवत्याद्यं त्रिवर्गं वा सहस्रकृत्व इति जैमिनिश्च वार्यमन्तं[5] वा यथाकामी वा द्वादश संहिता अधीत्य यदनेनानध्यायेष्वधीतं यद्गुरवः कोपिता यान्यकार्याणि कृतानि ताभिः पवते शुद्धमस्य पूतं ब्रह्म भवत्यथापरा द्वादश संहिता अधीत्य ताभिः प्रजापतेर्लोकमवाप्नोत्यथापरा द्वादश संहिता अधीत्य ताभिरुशनसो लोकमवाप्नोत्यनश्चत्संहितासहस्रमधीत्य ब्रह्मभूतो विरजो भवति कामचारी सर्वान्कामानवाप्नोति संवत्सरं भैक्षभक्षः प्रयुञ्जानश्चक्षुर्लभते षण्मासान्यावकभक्षश्चतुरो मासानुदकसक्तुभक्षो द्वौ मासौ फलभक्षो मासमब्भक्षो द्वादशरात्रं वानश्नन्[6] क्षिप्रमन्तर्धीयते ज्ञातीन्पुनाति सप्तातीतान्सप्तानागतानात्मानं च पञ्चदशं तारयते तामेतां देवनिश्रेणीत्याचक्षत एतया वै देवा देवत्वमगच्छन्नृषय ऋषित्वं तस्य ह वा एतस्य ब्रह्मसत्त्रस्य त्रिविध एवारम्भो भवति प्रातःसवने माध्यंदिने सवने ब्राह्मे वापररात्रे तस्य ह वा एतस्य द्वावेवानध्यायौ यदात्माशुचिर्यद्देशस्तद्वा एतत्प्रजापतिः सप्तऋषिभ्यः प्रोवाच सप्तऋषयो महाजह्नवे महाजह्नुर्ब्राह्मणेभ्यो ब्राह्मणेभ्यः ॥ ८ ॥

---

१ Thus B M^2; व्याहरेत् M^1. २ Thus M^2; B om. अन्तरा before विरमेत्; M^1 om. अथान्तरा व्याहरेत्. ३ आतम्य only in B, instead of it M^2: आचम्य; M^1 om. ४ शयानः only in M^1; °चक्रम्य° both MSS. ५ Thus emended; °चावार्यन्तं B; चवाप्यन्तं M^1. ६ वानश्नान् B; वाप्राश्नात M^1.

अथ ग्रहाणामातिथ्यं बलिकर्मोपरुतं[१] व्याख्यास्यामः अश्रद्धानमशुचिकरणमजाप्यं[२] त्यक्तमङ्गलं । सुव्यक्तं ग्रहा नयन्ति[३] पुरुषं यमसादनम्[४] । ग्रहाणां दीप्रचेष्टानां नक्षत्रपथचारिणाम् । ग्रहातिथ्यं[५] प्रवक्ष्यामि शान्तिकर्मणि कारयेत् । भास्कराङ्गारकौ[६] रक्तौ श्वेतौ शुक्रनिशाकरौ । सोमपुत्रो[७] गुरुश्चैव तावुभौ पीतकौ स्मृतौ । कृष्णं शनैश्चरं विद्याद्राहुं केतुं तथैव च । ग्रहवर्णानि पुष्पाणि प्राज्ञस्तत्रोपकल्पयेत् । गोमयेन गोचर्ममात्रं स्थण्डिलमुपलिप्य प्रोक्ष्य लक्षणमुल्लिख्याद्भिरभ्युक्ष्याग्निमुपसमाधायाघारावाज्यभागौ हुत्वा ग्रहानावाहयन्त्यादित्यं मध्ये लोहितं[८] पूर्वदक्षिणतः सोमम् । पूर्वोत्तरतो बुधमुत्तरेण[९] गुरुं पूर्वेण भार्गवम् । पश्चिमे शनैश्चरं विद्याद्राहुं दक्षिणपश्चिमे[१०] पश्चिमोत्तरतः केतुं[११] वृत्तमादित्याय त्रिकोणमङ्गारकस्य चतुरश्रं[१२] सोमाय बाणं बुधाय दीर्घचतुरश्रं बृहस्पतये पञ्चकोणं शुक्राय धनुः शनैश्चराय राहोः शूर्पं केतोर्ध्वजमिति[१३] ईश्वरं भास्करं विद्यात[१४] उमां सोमं तथैव च । स्कन्दमङ्गारकं चैव बुधो[१५] नारायणः स्थितः । बृहस्पतिः[१६] स्वयं ब्रह्म शुक्रः शक्रस्तथैव[१७] च । यमं शनैश्चरं विद्याद्राहोः कालदूतिनः[१८] केतोश्चित्रगुप्तश्चेत्येते ग्रहदेवताः अग्निरापो भूमिर्विष्णुरिन्द्राणी प्रजापतिः सर्पो ब्रह्मेत्येते प्रत्यधिदेवताः जातमर्क[१९] कलिङ्गेषु यामुनेषु च चन्द्रमाः । विन्ध्य अङ्गारकदेशो[२०] मध्यदेशो[२१] बुधः स्मृतः । बृहस्पतिः सिन्धुदेशः शक्रदेशो[२२] घटेषु च । शनैश्चरस्तु सौराष्ट्रो राहुस्तु पूर्वदे-

---

१ Sic ! are we to read: °कर्मोपहूतं ? २ Sic ! °करण° must probably be cancelled. ३ नावाहयन्ति ४ °दने ५ ग्रहातीर्थं ६ °ङ्कारकौ ७ सोपुत्रो ८ After लोह्तिं the word दक्षिणतः is inserted. ९ नुधंउत्त° १० दक्षिणतः प° ११ केतु १२ °श्रां १३ ध्वजग्रमिति १४ चैव instead of विद्यात् १५ बुधं १६ °पातिं १७ शुक्र शक्र १८ Sic ! १९ Sic ! जातो ऽर्कः to be restored ? २० विन्ध्यामङ्गारको देशो २१ मघादेशो २२ शक्रोदशो

शिकः केतुः पर्वत इत्येते देशानां ग्रहजात[1] इति अर्कसमिधमादित्याय प्रादेशमात्राभिघारितानाम्यादिभिर्जुहुयात्[2] खादिरमङ्गारकाय पालाशं सोमायापामार्गं बुधायाश्वत्थं बृहस्पतय औदुम्बरं शुक्राय शमीं शनैश्चराय राहोर्दूर्वाः केतोः कुशाग्रमित्यष्टाविंशतिमाज्याहुतीर्जुहोत्येताभिः पक्काग्नेर्जुहोत्यादित्याय इलोदनं[3] हविष्यमन्नमङ्गारकाय[4] सोमाय घृतपायसं पयोदनं बृहस्पतये क्षीरोदनं[5] शुक्राय दध्योदनं बुधाय[6] तिलपिष्टमाषोदनं शनैश्चराय राहोर्मांसोदनं केतोश्चित्रोदनमिति आ सत्येनेत्यादित्याय[7] अग्निर्मूर्धा दिव इत्यङ्गारकाय आप्यायस्व समेतु इति सोमाय ब्रह्म जज्ञानमिति बुधाय बृहस्पते अति यदर्य इति बृहस्पतये अस्य प्रत्नामनु द्युतमिति शुक्राय शं नो देवीरभिष्टय इति शनैश्चराय कया नश्चित्र आभुवदिति राहोः केतुं कृण्वन्नकेतव इति केतोः रक्तां[8] धेनुमादित्याय रक्तमनड्वाहमङ्गारकाय सोमाय शङ्खं बुधाय काञ्चनं बृहस्पतये वासः शुक्राय हयं नीलां गां शनैश्चराय राहोः कृष्णायसं केतोः कुञ्जरमिति सर्वेषामपि हिरण्यं वा येन वा तुष्यत्याचार्यस्तद्ददाति यथा समुत्थितं यन्त्रं[9] यन्त्रेण प्रतिहन्यते । तथा ग्रहोपसृष्टानां शान्तिर्भवति दारुणम्[10] ॥ नादिशेत्तपसा युक्तं नादिशेद्दिवमाश्रितम् । न च वेदान्तकं विप्रं वृत्तान्तां नारीं परिवृताम्[11] ॥ अहिंसकस्य दान्तस्य धर्मजितधनस्य च । नित्यं च नियमस्थस्य[12] सदानुग्रहा ग्रहाः ॥ ग्रहा गावो नरेन्द्राश्च ब्राह्मणाश्च विशेषतः । पूजिताः पूजयन्त्येते निर्दहन्त्यवमानिताः ॥९॥

॥ इति जैमिनिसूत्रं समाप्तम् ॥

---

१ Sic ! must we restore इत्येतेषु देशेषु ग्रहा जाता इति २ Sic ! ३ Sic ! ४ हविष्य° ५ वीतोदनं ६ This word added by me. ७ सासत्यनेत्य° ८ रक्तु ९ °त्थितय°; यन्त्रं must be corrupt ; Baudh. has घोरं १० Sic ! ११ A corrupt Sloka ! १२ तिश्चनीयसस्थस्य

FXTRACTS

FROM THE

COMMENTARY.

श्रीनिवासाध्वरिविरचिता जैमिनिसूत्रव्याख्या सुबोधिनी ॥

जैमिनिसूत्रं पूर्वम् ।

प्रथमः खण्डः ॥

पादैर्हस्तैः शिरोभिश्च भूर्भुवःस्वरधिष्ठितम् ।
ज्योतिष्पूर दुरालोकं ज्वलज्जाम्बूनदप्रभम् ॥
संप्रवृत्तिनिवृत्तिभ्यां संविदः सलिलस्य च ।
विराजमानं विश्वेषां हृदि सूर्ये च संततम् ॥
अनाद्यन्तमनोज्ञं तमन्तराध्यायपूरुषम् ।
प्राकारिकाश्च वृत्तीश्च मन्वादेर्वचनान्यपि ॥
न्यायांश्च शिष्टाचारांश्च समालोच्य पुनः पुनः ।
संचिताखिलसारापि स्वल्पग्रन्था सुबोधिनी ॥
व्याख्यया व्यक्तयोपेता मन्त्राणां च यथामति ।
टीका जैमिनिसूत्रस्य श्रीनिवासेन तन्यते ॥
नात्र प्रमाणेन विना कश्चिदप्यर्थ उच्यते ।
नानूद्यते प्रमाणं तु ग्रन्थविस्तरशङ्कया ॥

ad p. 1, l. 1—2. अथेति मङ्गलार्थमत इत्यारम्भार्थम् । अग्निं प्रणेष्यन्प्रदेशान्तरे स्थापयितुमिच्छन्विहितकर्मण इति शेषः । प्रागुत्तरप्रदेशावनतं स्थण्डिलं कृत्वाभ्युक्ष्य तस्य मध्ये वक्ष्यमाणपञ्चरेखात्मकलक्षणं दर्भादिना लिखेत् । गोमयेनोपलिप्य त्रिरुद्धृत्यावोक्षितायां भुवि पञ्चप्रस्थमिताभिः सिकताभिर्मृद्भिर्वा कृतमरत्निचतुरश्रं धिष्ण्यं स्थण्डिलमिति पूर्वाचार्यसंज्ञा ॥

ad p. 1, l. 2—3. स्थण्डिलमध्यात्प्राङ्मुखीं रेखामुल्लिख्य तस्याः पश्चात्तया संहितां संयुक्तामुदङ्मुखीमरत्न्यायतां रेखामुल्लिख्य तस्याः पश्चात्तस्या मध्ये समासन्ये तिस्रः प्राङ्मुख्यो रेखाः प्रादेशायामा उल्लिखेरन् । तथा च प्रत्यङ्मुखशलाकृतिलक्षणं भवति ॥

ad p. 1, l. 4. यस्मिन्होममात्रं प्रधानं स हुतः औपासनादिः । यस्मिन्न विद्यते होमः स अहुतः सन्ध्यावन्दनादिः । यस्मिन्होमो ऽन्यच्च प्रधानं स प्रहुतः पुंसुवनादिः । पुंसुवने हि पुरुषसूक्तहोमः पुल्लिङ्गप्रश्नश्च प्रधानं । प्राशितं श्राद्धकर्म । एवं चतुर्धा पाकयज्ञान्व्याख्यास्यामः । यस्मादेते दर्शपूर्णमासादिभ्यो ऽल्पे भवन्ति तस्मादेषु पाकयज्ञाख्या । पाकशब्दो ह्यत्राल्पार्थकः ॥

ad p. 1, l. 5. तेषां पाकयज्ञानां होम एकाग्नौ कर्तव्यः। न तु कर्मणिकर्मणि पृथगग्निरुपादेयः। सर्वकर्मार्थमेको ऽग्निर्धार्यः। स चार्थादौपासनाग्निरिति प्रसिद्धं। ब्रह्मचर्याद्यर्थसमिदाधानादिस्तु तेषामौपासनाग्न्यसंभवाल्लौकिके इति सिद्धम्॥

ad p. 1, l. 5. एते कर्मादौ स्तः विकल्पानुक्तेरेव नित्यत्वे सिद्धे नित्यशब्दग्रहणं स्त्रिया अपि यज्ञोपवीताकारेण उत्तरीयं कर्माङ्गं भवति। श्रोतस्पर्शाद्यनुकल्पव्यावृत्त्यर्थमुदकग्रहणम्॥

ad p. 1, l. 5. एते पाकयज्ञा दर्शपूर्णमासतन्त्रसदृशतन्त्रा भवन्ति। एतेन यद्येतेष्वनुक्तमाकाङ्क्षितं तद्दर्शपूर्णमासाभ्यामानेतव्यं। यथा खादिरः पालाशो वेध्म इत्युक्ते एकविंशतिरिध्मदारूणीति॥

ad p. 1, l. 6. वाशब्दश्चार्थः। एते स्वतन्त्राश्च भवन्ति न सर्वत्रैषां दर्शपूर्णमासतन्त्रमानेतव्यमित्यर्थः। तेनात्र न ऋत्विग्वरणादि। तथा च सूत्रद्वयार्थं आचाराद्व्यवस्थापनीयः॥

ad p. 1, l. 6. पूर्णपात्रस्य दक्षिणात्वं वक्ष्यति (p. 6, l. 1)। तद्योग्ययथाशक्ति व्रीह्यादिपूर्णं पात्रमित्यर्थः॥

ad p. 1, l. 6. पूर्णपात्रस्य पुरस्तात्खादिरादिमयं जलपूर्णं स्रुवं चोपनिदधाति॥

ad p. 1, l. 7. इध्मश्च बर्हिश्चेध्माबर्हिः। उपलक्षणमेतत्। अनिर्दिष्टस्थानं सर्वमुत्तरत उपनिदधाति। प्रोक्षणीनामग्नेः पश्चादुपनिधानमाचारात्॥

ad p. 1, l. 12—13. शुक्लानां सुमनसामलाभे जपापुष्पादीनि पञ्च वर्जयित्वा। गन्धवत्यश्चेतसर्ववर्णाः कृष्णरक्तादिवर्णाः सुमनसो ग्राह्याः। वाशब्दश्चार्थः॥

ad p. 1, l. 13—14. ऊधन्यं नवनीतं वा। वाह्यं वा घनीभूतं। दधि वा पयो वा। एताश्चतस्र आज्यप्रकृतय आज्यहेतव आज्यकार्ये भवन्ति यद्याज्यं न लभ्यते॥

ad p. 1, l. 14. प्राग्विहितस्याचमनस्य प्रदेशानियमो ऽयम्॥

ad p. 1, l. 14—15. प्रसङ्गात्सार्वत्रिकस्याचमनस्यायमनुष्ठानक्रम उच्यते॥

ad p. 1, l. 15. शीर्षण्यान्प्राणान् चक्षुषी नासिके श्रोत्रे चेत्यर्थः॥

ad p. 2, l. 3. रात्रिश्चेन्मन्त्रजपकालः धनमिति पदमपोह्य तत्स्थाने वस्विति ब्रूयात्॥

ad p. 2, l. 4. परिसमूहनं नाम आर्द्रेण पाणिना अग्निं परितः संमार्जनं तच्च प्रत्यृचमन्ते सकृत्सकृद्भवति॥

ad p. 2, l. 4—5. प्रस्तरमुपसंगृह्य सप्रस्तरेण पाणिना प्रतिदिशं प्राङ्दक्षिणादिक्रमेण दक्षिणपुरस्तादुपक्रम्य प्राचीनानां मूलानि दक्षिणोत्तराग्रैस्तन्मूलानि च प्रतीचीनाग्रैश्छादयन्सर्वत्र प्रागग्रैर्दर्भैः पूर्वपश्चिमयोः प्रादेशमात्रैरितरेतरयोररत्निमात्रैः परिस्तृणाति ॥

ad p. 2, l. 5. पश्चिमतो वा प्रथमं परिस्तीर्यानन्तरं द्वाभ्यामुलपराजिभ्यां दर्भमुष्टिभ्यामरत्निमात्राभ्यां पश्चिमपरिस्तरणदक्षिणोत्तरयोः संसक्तमूलाभ्यां पूर्वस्यां मध्ये संहिताग्राभ्यामुपहरेत्परिस्तृणीयात् ॥

ad p. 2, l. 6. पूर्वस्यामुक्तः परिस्तरणसन्धिस्तु दक्षिणोत्तरो भवति। दक्षिणपरिस्तरणमुत्तरमुपरिगतं यस्मिन्तादृशो भवतीत्यर्थः। पक्षद्वये प्रथमश्चतुरश्रः द्वितीयस्त्रिकोण इति वेदितव्यम् ॥

द्वितीयः खण्डः ॥

ad p. 2, l. 7. पूर्वगृहीतात्प्रस्तरात्पवित्रसंज्ञे भाविनी तृणे अप्रशीर्णाग्रे अच्छिन्नाग्रे अनन्तर्गर्भे अन्तस्तृणान्तररहिते प्रादेशमात्रे ते गृह्णाति ॥

ad p. 2, l. 10—14. ते पवित्रे कस्यचित्पात्रस्योपरिष्टाद्वामकरेण धारयन्तस्मिन्पात्रे पवित्रे प्लावयन्नाज्यमासिच्य अग्नेरुत्तरतः परिस्तरणस्यान्तरेव कतिचिदङ्गारान्पृथक्कृत्य तेषु तदाज्यमारोप्य दर्भज्वालया प्रदीप्य दर्भाग्राभ्यां क्षिप्त्वा त्रिर्दर्भज्वालया प्रदक्षिणीकृत्य परिस्तरणादुत्तरत आज्यमवरोप्याङ्गारानग्नौ संयोज्य उदगग्राभ्यां पवित्राभ्यामाज्यं च हविश्च प्रणीताश्च स्रुवं चानेन यजुषा त्रिरुत्पुनाति प्रागपवर्गं मन्त्रोक्तिः सकृत्सकृदिति वक्ष्यति (p. 2. l. 15)। देवः सविता त्वा त्वां। उत्पवनीयं वस्तु पुनातु पवित्रीकरोतु। अच्छिद्रेण पवित्रेणादित्येनासौ वा आदित्यो ऽच्छिद्रं पवित्रमिति ब्राह्मणं। वसोस्तेजस्विनः सूर्यस्य रश्मिभिश्चोत्पुनात्विति मन्त्रार्थः ॥

ad p. 2, l. 15. आज्यस्य विहितमुत्पवनं। पश्चिमतः पवित्रे पुनराहृत्य आहृत्य कर्तव्यं। तथा च पवित्रे प्रागानीय पश्चान्नीत्वा प्रागानेतव्ये इति सिद्धम् ॥

ad p. 2, l. 15—p. 3, l. 8. प्रणीतार्थमुत्पूता अपः परिस्तरणाद्बहिरुत्तरतो ऽग्नेः प्रतिष्ठाप्य दर्भैः प्रच्छाद्य तथा दक्षिणतो ऽग्नेः पूर्णपात्रस्रुवयोरुत्तरतः प्रस्तरं निधाय तदुपरिष्टात्पवित्रे निधाय विरूपाक्षदैवतमिमं मन्त्रं जपति। परिस्तरणादौ प्रस्तरोपसंग्रहणस्य प्रणीताप्रणयनानन्तरं प्रस्तरनिधानस्य च विधानात्तदन्तर्विहितानि कर्माणि प्रस्तरपाणिना कर्तव्यानीति गम्यते। तप इत्यादि दश पदार्थाधिदैवतानि विरूपाक्षविभूतिभूतानि पूर्वं प्रपद्ये। तानि मामवन्तु महादेवभजनशक्तं कुर्वन्तु। अनन्तरं भूर्भुवःस्वः त्रैलोक्यात्मतया वर्तमानमोमिति प्रणवान्तवेद्यशुद्धचैतन्यरूपं। महान्तमपरि-

च्छिन्नमात्मानं परमात्मानं त्वामध्यारोहामि शरणीकरोमि। त्वं भक्तेषु प्रकटितरौद्रवेषतया विरूपाक्षो ऽसि भयंकरनेत्रो ऽसि। दन्ताभ्यां दंष्ट्राभ्याम-नाक्ति व्यक्तीभवति प्रकाशते इति दन्ताञ्जिरसि। तादृशस्य ते शय्या निवासः पर्णे पर्णपटलाच्छन्नतया दुर्गमेकान्तरे भवति। नमः पर्ण्याय च पर्णशद्याय चेति श्रूयते (cp. T. S. IV. 5. 9. m)। परमार्थस्वरूपस्य ते तव तु गृहा गृहं निवासस्थानमन्तरिक्षे विशुद्धहृदयदहराकाशे तच्च विमितं विगतमान-मपरिच्छिन्नं। हिरण्मयं हितं च रमणीयं चादित्यवर्णमिति वा। यस्मादेवं तस्माद्देवानां सर्वेषां तानि हृदयानि सारांशा अयस्मये कुम्भे इवाच्छिद्रदुरस्व-भावे त्वयि अन्तः तदन्तर्भागे संनिहितानि संगृहीतानि। नमो वः किरिके-भ्यो देवानां हृदयेभ्य इति श्रूयते (cp. T. S. l. c. p)। सर्वदेवतात्मासीति यावत्। बलभूर्बलाकरश्च त्वं बलधा च भजतां बलपोषकश्च। रक्ष णो अस्मान् णत्वमार्षं। मा प्रमदः प्रमादादन्तरा मा त्याक्षीः। सत्यं खलु ते तव स्वरूपमेव कथमन्तरात्यागो भवेदिति भावः। द्वादश ते तव कालरूपस्य पुत्राश्चैत्रादिमासरूपा यदङ्गेषु वसन्तादिषु सर्वो ऽपि यज्ञस्त्वां संवत्सरे संवत्सरे कामं प्राति पूरयतीति कामप्रः कामपूरकः। तादृशेन दर्शपूर्णमासा-दिना यज्ञेन सर्वेण याजयित्वा पुनःपुनर्ब्रह्मचर्यं दीक्षां यष्टुमेवोपयन्ति पुनः पुनः परिवर्तमानैश्चैत्रादिभिर्यजनादेवमुच्यते त्वमेव खलु सर्वकामात्मा सर्व-यज्ञानामाधारभूतो यजनीयश्चेति यावत्। लौकिकदृष्ट्या साजात्येनापि विशे-षरक्षणीयतामाह। त्वं देवानामित्यादि। उपधावति शरणीकरोति। जपन्त-मित्यादि कृतस्य प्रतिकरणं प्रतिहननं तन्मा कार्षीरिति भावः। त्वामित्यादि प्रसूतो ऽनुज्ञातः। शिष्टं स्पष्टम्॥

तृतीयः खण्डः॥

ad p. 3, l. 9—11. स्रवगता अपः प्रणीतास्वासिच्य। स्रुवं निष्टप्य दर्भैः संमृज्य संमार्गान्संमार्जनसाधनभूतान्दर्भानभ्युदयाग्नौ क्षिप्त्वा जानु दक्षिणमाच्य अवनम्य। घृतं निरीक्ष्य। तस्मिन्नाज्ये घुणस्त्री अम्बुका (sic) पिपीलिका इत्यादिजन्तुजातममेध्यं पवित्रं किंचिदा पश्चभ्यः पञ्चानधिकम-वपद्येत संभाव्येत चेत्तदुद्धृत्य देवस्य त्वेत्यभ्युदयैताभ्यामेव पवित्राभ्यां प्राग्वदुत्पूय होतव्यं जुहुयात्। अधिकाशुद्धावन्यदाज्यमुपादाय यथाविधि संस्कार्यमिति भावः॥

ad p. 3, l. 11—13. स्थवीयसं स्थवीयांसं स्थूलतमं मध्यममायामेन न्यूनमग्नेः पश्चाद्भागे। दीर्घं मध्यमं स्थौल्येन न्यूनमग्नेर्दक्षिणतः। कनीयसं कनीयांसमायामेन स्थौल्येन कनीयांसमग्नेरुत्तरतः। एवं त्रीन्परिधीन्प-रस्परसंस्पृष्टान्परिदधाति। विहितशुक्लसुमनोभिरन्यायतनमलंकुर्यात्॥

ad p. 3, l. 13 कोशं धारां निनयति सिञ्चति॥

ad p. 3, l. 18—20. हे जातवेदः अयमिध्मः ते आत्मा शरीरं। तेन इध्मेन वर्धस्व च इध्यस्व च दीप्यस्व चास्मानिन्द्धि दीपय वर्धय च प्रजया पशुभिर्ब्रह्मवर्चसेनान्नाद्येन समेधय संपन्नान्कुरुष्व च ॥

ad p. 3, l. 20—22. अग्नावेव। उत्तरं परिधिसन्धिमनुगताद्देशात् वायुकोणादारभ्येत्यर्थः। अदणया विदिङ्मुखतया यावदाग्नेयकोणमित्यर्थः। सततं निरन्तरमाज्यमासिञ्चन्प्रजापतये स्वाहेति मनसोच्चरन्स्रुवमवहृत्य नीत्वा। अथ दक्षिणं परिधिसन्धिमनुगताद्देशादिन्द्राय स्वाहेति मनसा मन्त्रमुच्चरन्प्राग्वद्यावदीशानकोणं स्रुवं नीत्वा। एवमाघारौ नाम द्वे आहुती जुहोति ॥

ad p. 4, l. 1—3. तावाज्यभागदेशावन्तरेण तयोर्मध्य इत्यर्थः। आहुतीनामासां चतसृणां वक्ष्यमाणानां च लोकः स्थानं भवतीति। एताव दग्निमुखं नाम सर्वाग्निकर्मणां पूर्वाङ्गम् ॥

ad p. 4, l. 4—5. इदमादीनि परिभाषासूत्राण्या खण्डसमाप्तेः। स्विष्टकृत्संबन्धिनः स्थानात्प्रत्यगाहुत्या आहुतिमनभिजुह्वदसंयोजयन्। हुतस्यहुतस्य उत्तरपूर्वामुत्तरपूर्वामाहुतिं जुहोति ॥

ad p. 4, l. 5—6. लाजान्वपतीति विधानात् वपनरूपहोमो लाजहोमः। लाजहोमाज्यहोमाभ्यामन्यत्र सर्वाहुतीनामन्ते सर्वाहुतीनामुत्तरपूर्वभागे स्विष्टकृदग्निर्नित्यः। अग्नये स्विष्टकृते स्वाहेति तदीयाहुतिर्नित्या सार्वत्रिकेत्यर्थः ॥

ad p. 4, l. 6—7. अवदानानन्तरं स्थालीस्थे हविषि यत्प्रत्यभिघारणं विधास्यते तत्स्विष्टकृतमवदाय न कुर्यात् शेषस्य स्विष्टकृत्प्रकारस्यानभिधानात्। उपस्तीर्य सकृदवदाय द्विरभिघारणमिति दर्शपूर्णमासत आनीयते द्विरवदानमपि पञ्चावत्तिनामिति च ॥

ad p. 4, l. 7—8. प्रत्यभिघारयति स्थालीस्थं हविरिति शेषः। अङ्गुष्ठेन संनिधानात्तर्जनीमध्यमाभ्यां चाङ्गुलिभ्याम् ॥

ad p. 4, l. 9—10. जामदग्न्यानां भार्गवाणां। तद्धि पञ्चावत्तं भवतीति पूर्वाचार्यमतानुवादः। प्रत्यभिघारणं विना स्रुवोपस्तरणेन सह पञ्च संख्या ॥

ad p. 4, l. 10. विहितमुपस्तरणमभिघारणं चाङ्गुल्या तर्जन्या दर्भकूर्चेन वा कर्तव्यमित्यर्थः ॥

चतुर्थः खण्डः ॥

ad p. 4, l. 13. निरस्यति निष्कर्षति ॥

ad p. 4, l. 14—15. अनुप्रहरति जुहोति। द्विषन्तं मे अभिधेहि जानीहि तं प्रतिदह चेति ॥

ad p. 5, l. 5—7. दर्भान्परिस्तरणानि। सदसि शुभकर्मसीति। प्रणीताचमसं प्रति ॥

ad p. 6, l. 8—12. ऋत्विजो देवाः पृथिव्यादयः पृथिवी होतेत्येवमादि श्रूयते। मासास्तद्देवता। गृहा गेहाधिष्ठात्र्यः ॥

ad p. 6, l. 1—2. यथाश्रद्धदाक्षिणा येषां ते यथाश्रद्धदक्षिणा इमे सर्वे पाकयज्ञा भवन्ति। विहितहिरण्यादौ ब्राह्मणविहितेतरदानं च यथाश्रद्धं भवेदित्यर्थः ॥

ad p. 6, l. 2. विहितहिरण्यादिदानाशक्तौ सर्वपाकयज्ञेषु पूर्णपात्रमात्रं वा दक्षिणा भवति। दक्षिणा चाध्यापकाय तदभावे श्रोत्रियायेति वक्ष्यति। आवृत्तिः प्रश्नसमाप्तिद्योतनार्थः ॥

पञ्चमः खण्डः ॥

ad p. 6, l. 3. गृष्टेः प्रथमगर्भाया नार्याः पुंसुवनं। अन्यत्र चतुर्थे मासि स्यात् ॥

ad p. 6, l. 3—4. पृषदाज्यं दधियुक्तमाज्यं। स्थालीपाकवत्संस्कृत्य हविरिवोत्पूयेत्यर्थः। प्रसङ्गादस्माकं पुरुषसूक्तं सप्तर्चमत्र व्याख्यायते ॥

ad p. 6, l. 4—6. माषौ च वृषणवत् यवं च शिश्नवत् संनिवेश्य रेतोबिन्दुवदग्रेगेन दधिबिन्दुना सहानेन मन्त्रेण प्राशयेत् ॥

ad p. 6, l. 7—8. फलाभ्यामुपहितं मूलतः संसक्तं न्यग्रोधशुङ्गं वटसमिदग्रं। तथा च वृषणोपहितशिश्नसदृशमिति यावत् ॥

ad p. 6, l. 8. एवं कृतमिदं कर्म निश्चयेन कुमारोत्पत्तये स्यादिति पूर्वाचार्या आचक्षते ॥

षष्ठः खण्डः ॥

ad p. 6, l. 10—11. श्व इत्यादि नान्दीमुखदिनात्पूर्वेद्युर्वा। नान्दीमुखदिने एवान्नं संस्कृत्य तदनन्तरं वा इत्यर्थः ॥

ad p. 6, l. 12—15. दध्यादिभिश्चतुर्भिः शुक्लद्रव्यैरष्टाभ्यो देवताभ्यः प्रतिद्रव्यमेकैका पंक्तिरिति चतुर्धा हरति। नमःशब्दस्य पृथक्पृथग्योगः। अग्न्यायतने यत्राग्निः प्रणीयते तत्रेत्यर्थः ॥

ad p. 6, l. 16. माषाशनेन मत्स्याशनेन मांसाशनेन भक्ष्याशनेन वा मिश्रयेदित्यपरं मतमित्यर्थः ॥

सप्तमः खण्डः ॥

ad p. 7, l. 2—3. आ मूर्ध्नः मूर्धपर्यन्तं। प्राणसंमितं नासमभिकृत्य। सीमन्तं केशविभागं प्रत्यङ्मुखस्तिष्ठन्कुर्यात्। मन्त्रे विभजामीति शेषः। प्रतिमन्त्रं सकृत्सकृदिति आहः ॥

ad p. 7, l. 5. परा अन्या भार्येत्यर्थः ॥

अष्टमः खण्डः ॥

ad p. 7, l. 7—10. जातरूपेण समांशसुवर्णेन शिलादौ संघोष्य बालं प्राशयेत्। इदं व्रीहियवमन्नमयं सुवर्णशकलो रसः इदं सुवर्णं प्राणेनान्नस्य प्राणत्वात्तेन सह सहितममृतं पिबेति शेषः। पृथिवीत्यादि द्यौरादित्यस्तदन्तर्वर्ती पुरुषः पिता तद्वीर्यत्वाद्वर्षस्य तस्य धात्री पृथिवी माता। तस्याः खल्वोषधीशरीरेणास्य पूर्वं जननं। ततो ऽन्नरूपेण। ततः शुक्ररूपेण। ततः क्रमाच्छरीरत्वेन। ततो ऽस्य पितुरेव स्तनौ व्रीहियवौ। तौ हैतौ प्रजापतेः स्तनौ यद्व्रीहियवश्चेति श्रुतिः। हिरण्यं च प्राजापत्यो रस इति। शतं शरदः शतं संवत्सरान् जीवाहि जीव। पश्याहि पश्य ॥

ad p. 7, l. 16. वाक्यद्वयमेतत्। पुत्रं प्रत्याह पूर्वं कतमो ऽसि त्वमस्मिन् जन्मनि। सं समस्तगुणैर्मा मां संप्रविशानुकुरु। असावित्यस्य स्थाने अश्विनेत्यादि नाक्षत्रं नामास्य संबुद्ध्या निर्दिशेत् ॥

ad p. 7, l. 18. पशूनां हिंकारः सामात्मकतया शुद्ध इति ॥

ad p. 7, l. 19—p. 8, l. 3. तण्डुलावयवाः फलीकरणाः। लौकिकाग्नावौपासनवद्धोमः। शण्डादयो ऽष्टौ बालघातिग्रहाः। चतुर्थीत्रयं प्रथमार्थे। तथा लिखन्विलिखन्नित्यादि दश। अर्यम्णः शत्रुः कुम्भीत्येकः। निपुणहा अन्त्रीमुख इति पदच्छेदः। एते सर्वे इतःप्रदेशान्नश्यन्त्विति ॥

ad p. 8, l. 3. सूतकौ सूतकवन्तौ ॥

ad p. 8, l. 3--4. उत्थानमशुचित्वान्मोक्षः ॥

नवमः खण्डः ॥

ad p. 8, l. 5. द्वादश्यं जन्मदिनाद्द्वादशे दिवस इत्यर्थः ॥

ad p. 8, l. 8. (अनुनक्षत्रं) यथा कथंचिदस्य जन्मनक्षत्रसंबन्धसहितं वा। यथा सुकृत्तिकः अग्निमित्रः मेष इति ॥

ad p. 8, l. 8. (अनुदैवतं) देवतासंबन्धसहितं वा। यथा केशवः शंकर इत्यादि ॥

ad p. 8, l. 8. (अनुनाम) पित्रादेर्नामानुगतं वा। यथा विश्वामित्रः पराशर इत्यादि ॥

ad p. 8, l. 8. (अतद्धितं) सर्वत्र तद्धितान्तवर्जम् ॥

ad p. 8, l. 8. (आकारान्तं स्त्रियै) विहितं नामैव स्त्रियै चेदाकारान्तं कुर्यात् स्त्रीप्रत्ययोपलक्षणमेतत्। यथा जया शंकरीत्यादि ॥

ad p. 8, l. 8--9. (यथार्थं वा) उक्तसर्वविशेषानपेक्षया यथार्थमर्थानुरूपं ज्योतिर्दशाभाविकर्मनिर्णये यो ऽर्थो ऽभिलषितो ऽभिधातुं तदभिधानसमर्थं वा नाम कुर्यात्। यथा सुयज्ञः पुण्यकीर्तिः महामतिरिति ॥

ad p. 8, l. 9. (कुमारयज्ञेषु च) नामकर्मार्थं वक्ष्यमाणदशाहुतयो होतव्या इत्यर्थः ॥

ad p. 8, l. 9. नामाधानानन्तरं कुमारस्य जन्मनक्षत्रं तद्दैवतं जन्मतिथिं च यजते । तेभ्यः स्वनामभिर्जुहुयात् ॥

ad p. 8, l. 10—11. जुष्टाः सेविताः सर्वैरित्यर्थः । अग्निधन्वन्तरिभ्यां स्वाहा प्रजापतये स्वाहेत्यादि सप्ताहुतयः ॥

एकादशः खण्डः ॥

ad p. 8, l. 16. जटा इति शिखाशब्दवाच्याः केशाः ॥

ad p. 9, l. 1. स्फाण्डं (sic) सह कथितम् ॥

ad p. 9, l. 7. दर्भपिञ्जूलीति दर्भद्वयमूलप्रदेशः ॥

ad p. 9, l. 8—9. कोतच्चित्क्लिन्नान् केशान् सदर्भपिञ्जूलीकान्सव्यहस्तेनानेन मन्त्रेण धारयेत् । सुवप्तवै सुखेन वपनं कर्तुमित्यर्थः ॥

ad p. 9, l. 13—14. तथेति चार्थे । एताभ्यां मन्त्राभ्यां क्रमात्पश्चादुत्तरतश्च एवमेव छिन्द्यात् क्षुरादानं विना सर्वमावर्ततेत्यर्थः । तादिति पूरणः । अयं कुमारस्त्वं येन क्षुरेण कृतवपनः भूयः दीर्घकालं चराति अस्मिन्लोके चरिष्यसि ज्योक् चिरकालं च सूर्यं पश्याति द्रक्ष्यसि च ॥

ad p. 9, l. 18. एकार्षेयाणामेका चूडा त्र्यार्षेयाणां तिस्र इत्यादि गोत्रकल्पः । कुलकल्पस्तु पित्रादिभिराश्रितः प्रकारः । तथा नापितं बोधयेदिति शेषः ॥

ad p. 9, l. 19. पश्चाद्वपनस्नानानन्तरं प्रधानाहुतयः ॥

ad p. 10, l. 2—3. धान्यपल्वले धान्यक्षेत्रे । निखनेत् निगूहेत्कर्मकरः ॥

द्वादशः खण्डः ॥

ad p. 10, l. 5—6. अतिक्रान्तषोडशवयस्कं ब्राह्मणं नोपनयीत । अनियतेन्द्रियतया ह्येष शूद्रप्रायो भवतीति ॥

ad p. 10, l. 8—14. हे सोम ब्रह्मणा मन्त्रेण महे महते श्रोत्राय श्रोत्रियत्वाय परिदध्मसि परिधानवन्तं करोमि । इमं यथा जरिमा जरा अशक्तिः न यात् न प्राप्नुयात् यथा च ज्योक् सदा श्रोत्रे श्रोत्रियत्वे अधिजागरादधिकं जागरूको भवेत् तथा त्वमनुगृहाणेति शेषः । ण यादिति सांहितं णत्वं । अथ कुमारं प्रति जीवाहीत्यादि व्याख्यातं । राष्ट्राय राज्यरक्षायै । हे पोषेति पोष्याधिष्ठात्रीं देवतां प्रति । पोषाय पुष्ट्यै समृद्ध्यै ॥

ad p. 10, l. 18. द्विपन्त (sic) इत्यकारान्तं प्रथमैकवचनं द्विपन्नित्यर्थः (!) ॥

ad p. 11, l. 1—4. वः तुभ्यं । अदृष्टाय बृहते परमात्मने नमः करोमीत्यन्वयः । लिङ्गात्कुमारेण वक्तव्यो मन्त्रः ॥

ad p. 11, l. 4. (अधिगन्तरधिगच्छ) अधिगन्तव्यमिति शेषः । एवमाचार्यः कुमारं ब्रूयात् ॥

ad p. 11, l. 4—5. इत्थमाचार्यं कुमारो ब्रूयात् । असावित्यत्राचार्यनाम संबुद्ध्या अमुष्मै इत्यत्रात्मानं चतुर्थ्या च निर्दिशेत् ॥

ad p. 11, l. 6—7. आचार्याञ्जलिगतानामपां नीचैःस्रावेण इतरस्य शिष्याञ्जलेः पूरणं स्यात् । इदमुदकप्रदानरूपेण गुरोर्वेदप्रदानप्रतिज्ञानम् ॥

ad p. 11, l. 7. एनमाचार्यं कुमारः संशास्ति प्रार्थयति ॥

ad p. 11, l. 9—10. सु मर्त्यं प्रयुयोतन प्रमिश्रय भगवन्वयं तु आगन्त्रा अस्मानागच्छता सह समगन्महि संगच्छेमहि ॥

ad p. 11, l. 12—14. स त्वं मा विस्रसः मा विश्लथितो भव । हे अमृत । रुलापः सवर्णदीर्घश्च छान्दसः । मृत्योरन्तरं प्रवेशरन्ध्रं च मा कुरु॥

ad p. 11, l. 14—17. हृदयदेशमालभ्य जपति नाभेरविच्छेदेन दक्षिणमंसमन्ववमृश्य ततो हृदयदेशमालभ्य कुमारस्य इमं मन्त्रं जपति आचार्यत्वेन व्रते मयि मम वाचं वेदमयीमेकव्रतः अचञ्चलब्रह्मचर्यं त्वां मयि नियुनक्तु नियोजयतु मद्वश्यं करोत्वित्यर्थः ॥

ad p. 12, l. 8—10. (ऋतस्य etc.) ऋतस्य आश्रमधर्मस्य गोप्त्री तपसश्च परस्पी पालयित्री अरातीश्च शत्रून्सहमाना प्रसह्य वर्तमाना मा रिषाम मा नश्येम भर्तारो धर्तारः । शिष्टं स्पष्टम् ॥

ad p. 12, l. 12. कौपीनं कटिवस्त्रं चान्तरं तत्क्षौमं वा शणसंबन्धि वास्यात्सर्वेषामित्यर्थः ॥

ad p. 12, l. 18. भिक्षावाक्ये क्षा इति च हि इति चाक्षरे न वर्धयेन्नोच्चैर्ब्रूयात् । नीचैस्तरामितरवर्णेभ्यो ब्रूयादित्यर्थः ॥

ad p. 13, l. 3—4. (अनूच्य etc.) एवमुक्तां वटुः सावित्रीमनूच्य वेदमादितः किंचिदेकसामावरमृक्पूर्वमाचार्यादधीत्य पठिष्यमाणैश्चतुर्भिर्मन्त्रैश्चतस्रो घृतेनाक्ताः समिधोऽग्नावादध्यात् । उपनयनप्रभृत्यासमावर्तनपर्यन्तं यद्ब्रह्मचर्यं तद्व्रतमात्र एभिर्मन्त्रैरादिश्यते । तदिदं षोडशे गोदानकरणे विसृज्य पुनरपि तत्रापोद्धृत्य स्रजमादेशयेतेति विधास्यति (cf. p. 17, l. 1)। समावर्तने त्वस्यात्यन्तविसर्गः । इदं विसृज्यैव गौदानिकाद्यन्तरालव्रतादेशः॥

ad p. 13, l. 8. तदेतन्मन्त्रचतुष्टयेन समिदाधानं वस्त्रादेरप्युपलक्षणं सर्वत्र गौदानिकादिव्रतोपक्रमेऽपि कर्तव्यम् ॥

ad p. 13, l. 9--10. व्रतसमाप्तावत्रादिष्टस्य महतो व्रतस्य समाप्त्यर्थं समावर्तनाङ्गदण्डसादनात्पूर्वकाले गौदानिकादिसमाप्तौ च एभिर्मन्त्रैः समिध आधेयाः तदानीं च मन्त्रानेवमूहेदित्यर्थः ॥

ad p. 13, l. 12. (त्रिरात्रम् etc.) अक्षारमलवणं च भैक्षमाचार्यानुज्ञयाश्नीत ॥

ad p. 13, l. 13--14. अभ्यज्य आज्येनासिच्य । स्थालीपाकेन चरुणा व्याहृतिभिरिष्ट्वा तन्मूले हुत्वेत्यर्थः । यज्ञोपवीतं दण्डं च ब्रह्मचारिणस्तस्मिन्नेव पलाशे उत्क्षिप्य प्रत्येयात् प्रत्यागच्छेत् । ततश्च यज्ञोपवीतं दण्डं चान्यदाददीत ॥

त्रयोदशः खण्डः ॥

ad p. 13, l. 15—16. मार्जयेत आत्मानं प्रोक्षयेत् । तन्मध्ये सूर्यश्चाग्निश्चेति सायंप्रातर्मन्त्राचमनं स्मृतिसिद्धम् ॥

ad p. 13, l. 16. (वामदेव्यमन्ते) अन्ते वामदेव्यं प्रोक्षणमन्त्रः स्यात् । अन्तग्रहणमिदमन्यैरपि स्मृत्यन्तरसिद्धैः प्रोक्षणं तरत्समन्दीयादूर्ध्वं ज्ञापयति ॥

ad p. 13, l. 16—18. नक्षत्रोदयोपलक्षितकालादधि सन्ध्यां परमात्मानमादित्यान्तर्वर्तिनं ध्यायेदित्यर्थः । स्मृतिसिद्धार्घ्यदानानन्तरकृत्यमेतत् । प्रातर्विशेषो वक्ष्यते (p. 13, l. 21) । सायमपेक्षो ऽयं विधिः ॥

ad p. 13, l. 18—19. प्राणायामप्रकारस्तु सव्याहृतिकमित्यादि मनूक्तः (cp. Mānavadharmaśāstra VI. 70; II. 78) । स्मृत्यन्तरसिद्धतर्पणानन्तरकृत्यमेतत् । आवर्तयेत् पठेत् ॥

ad p. 13, l. 19. (शतकृत्वो वा दशावरम्) दशावृतस्त्ववरं मतमित्यर्थ. (B: दशावृत्तयस्त्ववरम्मत°) ॥

ad p. 14, l. 1—2. यस्मिन्सुप्ते ऽनुत्थिते सूर्य उदेति स सूर्याभ्युदितः । यस्मिन्सुप्ते ऽनुत्थिते सूर्यो निम्रोचति अस्तमेति स सूर्याभिनिम्रुक्तः । तच्छेषं तस्मात्सुप्तिकालादहःशेषं रात्रिशेषं वा ॥

चतुर्दशः खण्डः ॥

ad p. 14, l. 4. श्रवणसमवस्थितचन्द्रयुक्तपौर्णमासी श्रावणी । तथा प्रौष्ठपदी । वर्षापौर्णमास्योरन्यतरः स्यादित्यर्थः ॥

ad p. 14, l. 4. (हस्तेन) तन्नक्षत्रयोगिपूर्णिमाभावे संनिधानाद्वार्षिकेण हस्तेन उपाकुर्यादित्यर्थः ॥

ad p. 14, l. 4--6. सर्वे आचार्यः शिष्याश्च । पुरस्ताज्जप इत्युक्त्वा भूम्यालम्भजपात्प्रागेव कार्यः । अध्येष्यमाणो वेदः नः सहास्तु सर्वे-

षामधीनोऽस्तु । तथा भुनक्तु परिपालयतु । तथा शेषमपि ज्ञातव्यं । मा विद्विषामहै वयं परस्परम् ॥

ad p. 14, l. 8--9. छन्दांस्याग्नेयैन्द्रपवमानानि । आदितः ऋक्पूर्वं । अधीत्य अध्याप्य । यथार्थं यथाशक्ति एकर्चावरमित्यर्थः ॥

ad p. 14, l. 9--10. ऋषिभ्यः स्वाहेत्यादिप्रकारेण । ऋष्यादीन् षडिष्ट्वा ऋचं सामेत्यादि ऋग्भिश्च तिसृभिस्तिस्र आहुतीर्जुहुयादित्यर्थः । ऋषय ऋक्सामद्रष्टारः । देवा ऋकसामवाच्याः । छन्दांसि ऋक्सामयोर्यानि गायत्र्यादीनि । यजूंषि यानि सूत्रब्राह्मणमन्त्राणि ॥

ad p. 14, l. 10. एताभिरेव धानाभिः पूर्वाभिः षड्भिः षडाहुतिमन्त्रैरित्यर्थः । तानेव ऋष्यादींस्तृप्तिभाजः कुर्यात् । तानावाहनादिभिः संपूज्य हुतशेषा धानास्तेभ्यो निवेद्याचार्य्यः शिष्याश्च तानद्भिस्तर्पयेयुः ॥

ad p. 14, l. 10—13. (आचार्यमाचार्यांश्च) आचार्यं जैमिनिमाचार्यांस्तलवकारादीनेतांस्त्रयोदश ऋष्यादीनिव तृप्तिभाजः कुर्यादित्यर्थः ॥

ad p. 14, l. 16. (सावित्रमहः काङ्क्षन्ते) सावित्रमहः हस्तनक्षत्रं । तदेव पर्वदक्षिणा कर्मणि च काङ्क्षन्ते केचिदाचार्याः ॥

ad p. 14, l. 16. (उत्सर्गे च) सावित्रमहः अन्यच्च कर्मजातमुपाकृतिवदेव स्यात् ॥

ad p. 14, l. 16—17. (पक्षिणीं... अश्नीयात्) पक्षिणीं पक्षतुल्यागामिवर्तमानाहर्युक्तां रात्रिमुत्सर्गे इति शेषः । आचार्यस्यैवैतानि वर्णानि (sic) स्युः ॥

पञ्चदशः खण्डः ॥

ad p. 15, l. 1--2. यथास्वं स्वस्थानेषु । छन्दांसि गायत्र्यादीनि । चतुरुत्तराणीत्युपलक्षणमन्येषामपि शिनेन सहेति शेषः । नो अस्मानिति । इत्थमर्थाभि (?) सन्धिपुरःसरमुक्त्वा उत्स्रष्टव्यमित्यर्थः । ततश्च स्विष्टकृदादि हविःशेषप्राशनान्तमुपाकर्मवत् ॥

ad p. 15, l. 2--3. (उत्सृज्या°...अधीयीरन्) अध्यायदिने ऽध्ययनमनध्यायदिने तदभावश्च । उभयोरनुपालनं । यथास्वं स्वायत्तं (B: स्वायुक्तं) पठितमेव वेदावयवमित्यर्थः ॥

ad p. 15, l. 3. अतस्तैष्याः पूर्णिमाया ऊर्ध्वमभ्रेषु सत्सु मेघछन्ने ऽह्नीत्यर्थः । नाधीयते नाध्येतव्यम् ॥

षोडशः खण्डः ॥

ad p. 15, l. 4. गोदानसमाप्तिकं पवमानपर्यन्ताध्ययनमत्र गोदानशब्देनोच्यते । व्रतानीति आरण्यपर्वादौ । दशाध्यायी उपनिषदिति ।

तंवशाव्यव्याहृतिसामगायत्राणि यदुपनयनादि षट् द्वादश वा वर्षान्[1] यावदध्ययनकालं वा ब्रह्मचर्यमिति वक्ष्यमाणकालमध्ये गोदानसमावृतसामोपनिषत् साम्नामध्ययनार्थास्त्रयः संवत्सरा भवन्ति। औपनिषदस्तु समानव्रतत्वादत्रोपात्तः वक्ष्यमाणादादित्यव्रातिकात् (p. 15, l. 6) परो विज्ञातव्यः। इदं च सूत्रं तत्तत्संवत्सरानुष्ठेयव्रतविधानार्थम् ॥

ad p. 15, l. 4-5. तेषु त्रिषु संवत्सरेषु उदकोपस्पर्शनं स्नानम् ॥

ad p. 15, l. 5. अनुपस्पृश्य अस्नात्वा प्रातर्भोजनं न कुर्यात्। भैक्षचरणादि त्वस्नातेनापि कार्यमिति भावः। दिनचतुर्भागे ऽत्र प्रातःशब्दः ॥

ad p. 15, l. 5. (साय°...आधानात्) न भुञ्ज्यादिति शेष। भैक्षचरणं तु स्नानात्प्राक् समिदाधानादनन्तरमन्तरा वा स्नानसमिदाधानयोर्भवति। प्रदोषान्ते दिवसचतुर्भागे ऽत्र सायंशब्दः ॥

ad p. 15, l. 5—6. (अरण्यात्... दध्यात्) सदा सायं समिदाधानमिति वक्ष्यमाणस्य (p. 16, l. 8) अयमेतद्व्रतविषयो गुणविधिः। इदं व्रतं गौदानिकनिमित्तत्वेन त्रित्वं गौदानिकं व्रातिकमौपनिषदमिति तत्तत्संज्ञां च लभते। तथा च संवत्सरत्रयस्यादौ त्रिरादेशनमन्ते त्रिः समाप्तिश्च तदेतद्व्रतादेशनं सर्वत्रेत्यादि विधिः। तत्र व्रतादावग्ने व्रतपत इत्यादिमन्त्रेषु गौदानिकं व्रतं चरिष्यामि अन्ते अचारिषमित्यादि तत्तन्नामनिर्देशः। उपनयनादिष्टं सामान्यव्रतं तु सर्वेष्वेष्वनुसरति। एवमुत्तरत्र ग्राह्यं। अत्र औपासनवत्पूर्वोत्तरमन्त्रमध्ये व्रतसमिदाधानं व्रतादौ तु पूर्वपरिषेकात्प्रागुपनयनवत्। वस्त्रोपवीतमेखलाजिनदण्डधारणं च प्रायः कुर्वन्ति। उपाकृतेः प्रागेव गौदानिकादेशः ॥

ad p. 15, l. 6. (आदित्यव्रातिकः संवत्सरः) आदित्यव्रतानि शुक्रियसामानि। उक्तकालमध्ये तदध्ययनार्थः संवत्सरो भवति। इदं तद्व्रतविधानार्थम् ॥

ad p. 15, l. 6. (एकवासाः) एकसहायं वासो यावद्ध्वंसं वसीत ॥

ad p. 15, l. 6—7. (न युक्तमारोहेत्) युक्तमनोरथप्रभृति ॥

ad p. 15, l. 8. (नोर्ध्वं...प्रस्नायात्) अपः प्रस्नायात् प्रस्यन्दयेत्। अशुचित्वनिमित्तं तु स्नानं भवति ॥

ad p. 15, l. 8—9. तस्मिंस्तस्मिन्संवत्सरे व्रते समाप्ते सति श्रावयेदध्यापयेदित्यर्थः। इति गौदानिकादीनि चत्वारि समाप्तानि ॥

---

१ These difficult and doubtless corrupt words are handed down thus in M²: वश्शव्यव्याहृतिसामगायत्री...(lacuna)...दिषुयद्वा दश वर्षान्

सप्तदशः खण्डः ॥

ad p. 15, l. 10. महानाम्न्य इति विदा मघवन्निति शक्करीत्रयं ससाम (वसामि M)। तदध्ययनार्थाः द्वादश संवत्सराः नव षड्वा । त्रयो वा संवत्सरा इति विविधास्तत्र कल्पा भवन्ति ॥

ad p. 15, l. 11. श्रुता अध्यापिता भविष्यन्ति चेदित्यर्थः ॥

ad p. 15, l. 11—12. शुक्लत्वमत्र शुचित्वं । विहिते काले संवत्सरमात्रमेव चरेत् ॥

ad p. 15, l. 12. (व्रतं...दिवा) व्रतं समग्रं चरन्दिवा भूयः बहुशस्तिष्ठेत् ॥

ad p. 15, l. 12. (अथासीत नक्तं) भूय इति शेषः ॥

ad p. 15, l. 12—13. (तस्य...परिदध्यात्) अन्नं तु तदुक्तवद्वा भवत्विति भावः ॥

ad p. 15, l. 13. (रागदोषान्न कृष्णं) रागदोषाद्धेतोः कृष्णं न परिदध्यात् ॥

ad p. 15, l. 14. उपस्पृशेत् स्नायात् । प्रत्यहमनेन (प्रत्यग्गमनेन M) या स्नानयोग्या यवृच्छया (°पृच्छया M)[1] संगम्यन्ते (संगम्यते M) तासु सर्वास्वित्यर्थः । अप इत्युक्ता अबुक्ता (thus emended; चयुक्ता B, अभुक्ता M) इति हेतोः । अस्ति हि श्रुतिः आपो वै शक्वर्य इति ॥

ad p. 15, l. 14. (नावा न प्रस्नायात्) नावा अपो न प्रविशेत् । अवतीर्यैव नद्यादिकं लङ्घयेदित्यर्थः ॥

ad p. 15, l. 14—15. (प्राण°...उभयतः) प्राणसंशये तु नावैव लङ्घयन्नुभयतस्तीरयोरुपस्पृशेत् स्नायात् ॥

ad p. 15, l. 15. उभयत इति शेषः । पशूक्ता इति । अस्ति हि श्रुतिः पशवो वै महानाम्न्य इति ॥

ad p. 15, l. 15—16. प्रतिवृष्टि गृहान्निर्गतः किंचित्क्लिन्नो गृहं प्रविशेदित्यर्थः ॥

ad p. 15, l. 16—17. (एवमस्य...उपोषितः) ब्रह्मचर्यान्ते महानाम्नीब्रह्मचर्यान्ते इत्यर्थः । एकरात्रं एकमहोरात्रमुपोषितः स्यादिति शेषः ॥

ad p. 15, l. 17—19. (अरण्यं...सपुरीषा:) तस्मिन्नुपोषणदिने । आचार्यकृत्यमेतत् । अपामद्भिरित्यर्थः । तं ब्रह्मचारिणमुपवसन्तं । समनुपरिगृह्यालिङ्ग्य । निमीलितं मीलिताक्षं कृत्वा । स्तोत्रियाः स्तोत्रियसामसहिता महानाम्नीः । उपगायेत् अध्यापयेत् । एवा ह्येवेत्यादि पञ्च पुरीषपदानि ॥

ad p. 15, l. 19—20. शिष्यो ग्रामं प्रत्येत्येति शेषः ॥

---

[1] Read: यदृच्छया ।

ad p. 15, l. 20—p. 16, l. 1. (रात्रिम°...वाग्यतः) उदपात्रं धारयन्निति शेषः ॥

ad p. 16, l. 1—2. (श्वो°...वेष्टयेत्) आचार्यकृत्यं । श्वो भूते प्रभाते । वासः मुखवेष्टनवस्त्रम् ॥

ad p. 16, l. 2. (उद्यम्य...वीक्षेत्) ता एवापः । ब्रह्मचारिकृत्यम् ॥

ad p. 16, l. 2—4. (स्वर°...°पहरेत्) अपः कांस्यगताः । प्रकृतमेव वासःप्रभृति । उपहरेत् दद्यादाचार्याय गृहं गताय ॥

ad p. 16, l. 4—5. स्थालीपाकात् हविषेत्यर्थः (sic) । पुरस्तन्त्रान्ते इदमिति व्रतसमाप्तिद्योतकः । तस्मादत्रैव व्रतान्तसमिध आधाय स्विष्टकृदाद्युत्तरतन्त्रम् ॥

ad p. 16, l. 6—7. (गौर्दक्षिणा) दत्तस्य वत्सस्य माता गौरेव दीयते । महानाम्नीकव्रतं समाप्तम् ॥

अष्टादशः खण्डः ॥

ad p. 16, l. 7. वेदार्थं ब्रह्मचर्यं यदुपनयन आदिष्टं तद्द्वादश वर्षाणि चरितव्यम् ॥

ad p. 16, l. 7. (जननात्...एके)तथा चोपनीय (तथा चोपरि M) षड्वर्षाणीत्यर्थः । सप्तमे ह्युपनीयते ॥

ad p. 16, l. 7—8. (यावदध्ययनं) ब्रह्मचर्यचरणमिति शेषः ॥

ad p. 16, l. 8. (सदा...आधानं) औपासनवत्तन्त्रं । अग्नये समिधमित्याद्युपनयनवदाहुतिः ॥

ad p. 16, l. 8—9. द्वे त्रिवृती त्रिप्रकारे वस्तुनी केते इति चात्रिवृतं मणिं त्रिगुणे उपानहौ च वर्जयेत् ॥

ad p. 16, l. 9. (षोडशे गोदानकरणं) गोदानमिति केशान्तकरणं तत्संस्कारः । तदस्मिन्पाकयज्ञे इति । तद्गोदानकरणमिदमपि वृणोति ॥

ad p. 16, l. 9—10. (तम्...आचक्षते) अत एवोपनयनाद्येतावत्कालं केशा धार्या इति ज्ञायते । ब्रह्मचर्यान्ते एतत्कर्म । पञ्चमे चोपनयनं तदादि द्वादश वर्षाणि ब्रह्मचर्यं तन्मध्ये चानुकल्पाश्रयेण महानाम्न्यासमाप्तामेधाविना च अध्येतव्यजातस्य सर्वस्याप्यध्ययने चार्थादिदं षोडशे भविष्यतीति मुख्याभिप्रायेणेदं (मुख्यान्तप्रा° M) षोडश इत्युक्तं पक्षान्तरेण तदाग्वापरं (sic B; तदन्याग्वापरं M) वा यथाकथंचित् ब्रह्मचर्यावसान एवेदं कुर्यात् ॥

ad p. 16, l. 11. अविकृतं विरूपाक्षहोमान्तं कर्तव्यं । स्नानीयादि(भि)श्च प्रोदय इति विशेषः ॥

ad p. 16, l. 10—11. (उपनयनेन व्रतादेशनं) वक्ष्यमाणमपोद्धृत्य स्रजमादेशयेतेति (p. 17, l. 1) आदेशनमुपनयनेन व्याख्यातमिति शेषः। तदेतद्व्रतादेशनं सर्वत्रेति सिद्धे इदमुपनयनादिष्टस्य महतो व्रतस्येह निवृत्तिं ज्ञापयति। अतो विरूपाक्षाहुत्यनन्तरं व्रतान्तसमिध आधेयाः। पुनरादेशकालं तु वक्ष्यत्यपोद्धृत्य स्रजमादेशयेतेति ॥

ad p. 16, l. 11. (न त्विह...वासः) इह व्रतादेशे ऽहतं वासः न नियुक्तं न नियतं। अस्तु वा मा वेत्यर्थः। अत एव सर्वत्र व्रतादेशेषूपनयनवन्नूतनवस्त्रायस्तीति ज्ञायते ॥

ad p. 16, l. 11—12. (सर्वाणि...औद्वाहमनिः) समिदाधानादनन्तरमुदकदानाद्या (sic M; °मुदगादानाद्याः B) वपने त्वयं विशेषः। औद्वाहमनिराचार्यः। आचार्यग्रहणं पूजार्थम् ॥

ad p. 16, l. 12. (उप्तकेशः स्नायात्) उप्तकेशः धान्यपल्वले गोष्ठे वा निखातकेशः ॥

ad p. 16, l. 12—14. वनस्पतीनां चर्मणा संपिष्टेन स्नानीयेन। वनस्पतेस्त्वगसि त्वं हे शोधनि मा शोधय। तां त्वाभिहरे धारयामि ॥

ad p. 16, l. 15. (स्नात्वा°...कुरुते) कुरुते आत्मानमलंकुरुते। देवेषु मनुष्येषु च मध्ये मे पुण्यं गन्धं कुरु। शिष्टं स्पष्टम् ॥

ad p. 16, l. 19—p. 17, l. 1. आदर्शो ऽसि त्वं देवमनुष्या उभये मामादृश्यासन्नादरेण दृश्यासुः। शोभो ऽसि शोभयितासि त्वं देवेषु मनुष्येषु च मध्ये अहं शोभासं शोभिषीय। रोचो ऽसि रोचयितासि त्वं देवमनुष्येषु अहं रोचासं रोचिषीय ॥

ad p. 17, l. 1. (अपोद्धृत्य...°देशयेत) अपोद्धृत्य अपनीय स्रजमस्याचार्य आदेशयेत व्रतसमिध आधापयेत्। एतत्कर्मादौ निवर्तितस्य व्रतस्य पुनरत्राधानं। कुतः ॥

ad p. 17, l. 1—2. (उक्ता...संवत्सरेषु) प्राक्संवत्सरेषूक्ता एवात्रापि नियमा न नूतनमिति भावः। तत उत्तरतन्त्रं प्रायश्चित्तान्तं कृत्वा मूर्धारम्भजपः ॥

एकोनविंशः खण्डः ॥

ad p. 17, l. 3—5. स्नास्यन्यथाशक्ति दक्षिणां दत्त्वा गुरुणानुमतः समावर्तनं करिष्यमाण इत्यर्थः। स्नानं स्नानीयं। शुक्ले अनुपभुक्ते उपानहौ ॥

ad p. 17, l. 5. उपक्लृप्तः संनद्धः ॥

ad p. 17, l. 6—7. पूर्वतन्त्रान्ते व्रतान्तसमिध आधायानन्तरकृत्यमेतत्। आस्तीर्य पश्चादग्नेरिति शेषः। अप्सु तत्रैव पात्रावस्थितास्वप्सु ॥

ad p. 17, l. 8. (तां...षादयेत्) आचार्य एव ॥

ad p. 17, l. 8. (केशान्त°...व्याख्याताः) वक्ष्यमाणस्नानीयानुलेपनसुमनआदर्शान्वनस्पतेस्त्वगसीत्यादिमन्त्रैर्विनियुञ्जीतेत्यर्थः ॥

ad p. 17, l. 9. (परिवापनं च) वक्ष्यमाणवपने प्रकारश्च मेखलां सादयित्वा महाव्याहृतिभिर्विरूपाक्षेण च हुत्वा सर्वौषधीभिरित्यादिकृत्यं। तत्रायं विशेषः ॥

ad p. 17, l. 9—11. शिष्यकृत्यमेतत् ॥

ad p. 17, l. 11—12. आचार्यकृत्यमेतत् । हे सरस्वति नः शिवा शंतमा शोभनतमा भव । सुमृडीका सुखकरतमा भव । ते तव व्योम व्यापकं परं धाम मा संदृशि मां प्रति संदर्शनाय भवतु ॥

ad p. 17, l. 18—19. स्नानीयगन्धस्रजां गोदानकरणवद्विनियोगादनन्तरकृत्यमेतत् । अन्तरीयमात्रस्य परिधानमत्र ॥

ad p. 17, l. 19—20. (सव्य°...दक्षिणं) तयैव ऋचा। मा मा द्यावापृथिवी यशसा संयोजयतां। इन्द्रबृहस्पती भगेन भाग्येन संयोजयतां। भगस्य यद्यशस्तन्मां विन्दतु । यशः मा मां प्रतिमुच्यतां न विमुञ्चन्तु। यशस्वी अहं अस्याः संसदः प्रवदिता प्रकर्षेण वाग्मी स्यां भवेयं। अस्याः संसदः अहमुत्तमश्च भूयासमित्यर्थः ॥

ad p. 17, l. 20. (त्रिवृतं...°मुञ्चते) आदर्शमादर्शो ऽसीत्यादिमन्त्रेणावेक्ष्य धृतोत्तरीयस्येदमुच्यते । प्रतिमुञ्चते सूत्रप्रोतमासञ्जयति ॥

ad p. 17, l. 20—21. पालाशं त्रिवृतं मणिं। स्वस्त्ययनकामः सुष्ठुजीवनकामः ॥

ad p. 17, l. 21—p. 18, l. 2. अर्कवानश्ववान् । पालाशमेवैषां मुख्यम् ॥

ad p. 18, l. 3. (उपानहाव°...मामिति) करेण युगपदावधीत (sic) ॥

ad p. 18, l. 3. अथ सव्यमिति शेषः । नेत्रे नेत्रिणी इत्यर्थः । अथोत्तरतन्त्रः समूर्धारम्भजपः सगोदक्षिणः समाप्यते ॥

ad p. 18, l. 3. [तस्य...भवन्ति] यावज्जीवमिति शेषः ॥

ad p. 18, l. 4. [नाजात°...इच्छेत्] स्वभावाद्बाल्याद्वा नाभेरधो यस्या न लोमानि तया उपहास्यतीति [उपहास्यन्तीति M] उपहासं मैथुनं नेच्छेत् न तादृशीं परिणेतुं कामयेतेत्यर्थः ॥

ad p. 18, l. 5. [न फलानि...°चिन्वीत] वृक्षादिभ्य इति शेषः ॥

ad p. 18, l. 6. [नैकः] ग्रामान्तरं व्रजेत् ॥

ad p. 18, l. 6. (न वृषलैः सह) ग्रामान्तरं व्रजेत् ॥

ad p. 18, l. 6—7. [न संक्रममारोहेत्] संक्रमश्चक्रमं पिण्डशिला वा (sic; the Comm. on this sūtra is missing in M)॥

ad p. 18, l. 7. [नान्तर्धायासीत] आसनादिभिर्भूमिमनन्तर्धायानाछाद्य॥

ad p. 18, l. 7. [नापरया...अश्नीयात्] अपरया द्वारा गृहस्याप्रधानद्वारेण प्रपन्नमानीतम्॥

ad p. 18, l. 7. (न शुक्तं) शुक्तं गतरसम्॥

ad p. 18, l. 8. (न द्विःपक्वं) गतोष्णस्योष्णतावाप्तये॥

ad p. 18, l. 8—9. (न पर्युषितम°...°घृतेभ्यः) पर्युषितं पुरातनं शाकादिभ्यो ऽन्यत्र तानि विनेत्यर्थः। यवान्नपिष्टान्नादीत्यन्वयः। फाणितं शर्करा॥

ad p. 18, l. 9. [शुक्ता...भाषेत] शुक्ताः परेषां प्रीतिकरीः॥

ad p. 18, l. 10—11. अशक्त्या अव्रतो ऽधीतवेदस्नातो विद्यास्नातकः। अबुद्धया अवेदो ऽनुष्ठितव्रतस्नातो व्रतस्नातकः। अधीतवेदो ऽनुष्ठितव्रतस्नातश्च विद्याव्रतस्नातक॥

ad p. 18, l. 11—12. [तेषा°...श्रेष्ठः] उत्तमस्तृतीयः विद्याव्रतस्नातकः॥

ad p. 18, l. 12—13. (स्नात्वा°...°नयत्विति) स्नात्वा एवं स्नानाख्यं पाकयज्ञं निर्वर्त्य॥

ad p. 18, l. 13. (आचार्यकल्पो वा) आचार्यस्य पुत्रादिर्वा तथा वाच्य इत्यर्थः॥

ad p. 18, l. 13. (तस्मै...आहरेत्) आचार्यस्तत्कल्पो वेति शेषः॥

ad p. 18, l. 13—14. विष्टरमासनकूर्चं दद्यादिति शेषः॥

ad p. 18, l. 15. शूद्रा चेदस्य पादं प्रक्षालयेत॥

ad p. 18, l. 16. (मयि वर्च...°ह्रीयात्) परमेष्ठी प्रजापतिः मयि वर्चश्च गन्धश्च। अथो अथ। यज्ञस्य यत्पयः यो रसः तत्सर्वं दिवि आकाशे द्यां सूर्यमिव दृंहतु दृढीकरोतु॥

ad p. 18, l. 16—17. (आचमनीयाभि°...अधस्तात्) यस्मिन्नद्यते तच्चमसं। पात्रचमसं चमसपात्रं भक्षणपात्रमित्यर्थः। अधस्ताद्विष्टरेण तृणकूर्चेण उपहितं संसक्तं भवति॥

ad p. 18, l. 17. (विष्टरौ...भवतः) प्रागेव तौ द्वौ विष्टरौ संहिताग्रौ संबद्धाग्रौ भवतः यश्चमसस्याधस्तान्निहितो यश्चोपरि निधास्यते॥

ad p. 18, l. 18. (एक°...उत्तरतः) उत्तरतश्चमसस्योपरि निधातव्यः॥

ad p. 18, l. 18. (तयो°...भवतः) दधि च मधु च तयोर्विष्टरयोर्मध्ये यथा भवेतां तथा तौ विष्टरौ कृत्वा संनिहिते अन्तश्चमसासिक्ते भवतः। इदमितरयोर्मधुपर्कयोरुपलक्षणम् ॥

ad p. 18, l. 18—19. (दध्ना...°मन्थः) दध्ना चेन्मधुसंनिहितं स दधिमन्थनामा मधुपर्कः ॥

ad p. 19, l. 3. (परः...गौरिति) परः अन्यः। स्वाधीतपाणिः खड्गपाणिर्भूत्वा। गां तस्मै स्नातकाय दृष्ट्वा दर्शयित्वाह ॥

ad p. 19, l. 3—4. (ताम°...धेनुरिति) गौर्धेनुरित्यादिमन्त्रेण तामभिमन्त्र्य ॥

ad p. 19, l. 4. (कर्तव्या...ब्रूयात्) कर्तव्या भोजनार्थं संस्कर्तव्या चेत्। कुरुतेति संस्कुरुतेति ब्रूयात्। न त्वभिमन्त्रयेत ॥

ad p. 19, l. 4—8. इति मन्त्रः। गौः धेनुः पातव्याक्षीरा। हव्या हविर्योग्या ॥

ad p. 19, l. 7—8. विष्टरादिगवान्तमिहार्घ्यशब्देनोच्यते ॥

ad p. 19, l. 8. (तेभ्य...कुर्यात्) आतिथ्यमतिथिभोजनभूतां गामर्घ्यादेरप्युपलक्षणं कुर्यात् संस्कुर्यात् अनुत्सर्गे सति ॥

ad p. 19, l. 8—9. तां संस्करिष्यमाणां गामतिथये त्वा जुष्टं प्रोक्षामीत्यन्तेन सावित्रेण प्रोक्षेत् ॥ इति समावर्तनम् ॥

विंशः खण्डः ॥

ad p. 19, l. 10—11. अनग्निकां यस्मिन्वयसि स्वयमेव लज्जया वासः परिदधाति तद्वयस्कां। समानजातीयामसवर्णां मातुरसपिण्डां मातुरर्धशरीरत्वात्पितुरप्युपलक्षणं। संगतः पिण्डे शरीरो यस्याः सा सपिण्डा। वरस्य मात्रा पित्रा च रक्तधातुसंबन्धरहितामित्यर्थः। तच्च सापिण्ड्यं सप्तपुरुषमितिवत् सप्तमे शरीरे निवर्तते। तथा च मातुलदुहितुर्दुहिता पितृष्वसृदुहितुर्दुहिता इत्येवमादयः अपरिग्राह्याः मातुः स्वपित्रा तस्य स्वपुत्रेण तस्य स्वदुहित्रा तस्याश्च स्वदुहित्रा धातुसंबन्धो ऽस्तीति मातुलदुहितृदुहिता मातुः पञ्चमीति त्याज्या। एवमन्यत्राप्यूह्यम् ॥

ad p. 19, l. 11—12. (ज्यायसः कनीयसीं) ज्यायसः वयसा ज्येष्ठतमस्य वरस्य। कनीयसीं वयसा यवीयसीं जायां कुर्यात् ॥

ad p. 19, l. 12—14. दूतं दुहितृगतिगमननिर्णयाय प्रस्थापयमानं गणपतिसंकल्पस्य सत्यं कुरु। नान्दीप्रतिसरानन्तरकृत्यमेतत् ॥ अनृक्षराः अशर्कराः। ऋजवः पन्थाः पन्थानः सन्तु। एभिः पथिभिः नः सखायः

वरेयं कन्यागृहं यन्ति प्राप्नुवन्ति । अर्यमा च नः समनुनीयात् भगश्च नः समनुनीयात् । हे देवाः जास्पत्यं जायापत्यं सं सम्यक् सुयममस्तु सुकरमस्तु ॥

ad p. 19, l. 14—16. दूत्यकृत्यानुष्ठानस्वस्तिवाचनकन्यावेश्मगमनमधुपर्कग्रहणसंभारकल्पनानन्तरकृत्यमेतदनुमन्त्रणम् ॥

ad p. 19, l. 19. पूर्णपात्रनिधानानन्तरकृत्यमेतत् प्रोक्षणाद्या कर्मसमाप्तेः ॥

ad p. 19, l. 20. [मातु°...मात्री] मातुरभावे अशक्तौ तन्मात्री तत्सदृशा धारयेत् । मातुः स्वसा मातामही वा ॥

ad p. 19, l. 21—p. 20, l. 1. एवंजातीयं एवंप्रकारमन्यद्वा आस्तरणं कशिपु कम्बलादि । यथा संवेशनकाले प्रसार्यमाणं परिस्तरणबार्हिषः पश्चार्धं प्राप्नोति स्पृशति ॥

ad p. 20, l. 1—3. अथ समुपनिहितं देवस्य त्वेति प्रोक्ष्यानन्तरमेवास्यै वाससी ददाति । प्रतिवासो मन्त्रावृत्तिः । याः देवीः देव्यः इदं वास अवयन् तन्तुसंतानं कृतवत्यः । या अतन्वत विस्तारितवत्यः । या अकृन्तन् खण्डितवत्यः । या अभितः अन्तान् (thus also the text is to be emended) दशाः अददन्त कृतवत्यः । तास्त्वा देवीर्देव्यः जरसा सह संव्ययन्तु संयोजयन्तु । आयुष्मतीत्यादि स्पष्टम् ॥

ad p. 20, l. 3—4. परिहितोपसंवीतवस्त्रद्वयां आचान्तोपसन्नां वधूमग्न्यात्मनोर्मध्येन नीत्वा उपवेश्य श्रीसूक्तेन मङ्गल्यसूत्रं बद्ध्वा भूषणान्यलंकृत्य प्रत्यङ्मुखः श्वशुरेण संकल्प्य यथाशक्ति दत्त्वा गोत्रनामपुरःसरं दत्तामनामुपवेश्य । भूम्यालम्भादिपुरस्तन्त्रः आज्यानन्तरं लाजानां वा इत्युत्पवनं । तन्त्रान्ते एरकां प्रसार्यानन्तरमिदं । अभिजहि आरोहेत्यर्थः ॥

ad p. 20, l. 4—5. (प्र मे...कल्पतामिति) वधूरेरकां प्राङ्मुखी आरोहति ॥

ad p. 20, l. 5. (अजपत्यां...प्रास्या इति) प्र मे इत्यादि तस्यामजपत्यां वरः स्वयं प्रास्याः पतियानः पन्थाः कल्पतामिति जपेत् ॥

ad p. 20, l. 5—6. (दक्षिणतः...पतिः) उपविशेदित्यर्थः ॥

ad p. 20, l. 6. (उभावन्वारभेयातां) उभौ दम्पती तामेरकामन्वारभेयातां सहैवारोहेताम् ॥

ad p. 20, l. 8—19. संराधा नाम देवता सा च पृथिव्यात्मका सात्रेज्यते । संराधा हे संराधे । या त्वमहं विधरणी इति सर्वस्य प्रपञ्चस्य धारयित्री इति संकल्प्य तिरश्ची निपद्यसे तिर्यक् भूता शेषे पृथिवीरूपेण त्वा त्वां घृतस्य धारया राधयामसि तर्पयामः । अत्र ऋगर्थे न सिद्धे ऋचः परं चतुर्थ्यन्त आददात् ॥

एकविंशः खण्डः ॥

ad p. 20, l. 20. संपातसेकानन्तरमिदम् ॥

ad p. 20, l. 20. (प्रहस्तं पुंसः) पुंसः प्रजाः कामयमानः प्रहस्तं मणिबन्धनप्रदेशं गृह्णाति ॥

ad p. 21, l. 15--17. हे जानकि त्वं ईरसि ईर्नाम (इद् नाम B) देवता श्रियो ऽधिष्ठात्री इषे त्वेत्यादि प्रसिद्धा सासि । दीर्घरेफौ (°रेभौ MSS) प्रमादपठितावार्षौ वा । ते माता ऊर्क् ऊर्क् नाम देवता प्रजानामन्नानां चाधिष्ठात्री । सा ते माता । यस्मात्त्वमूर्जः पुत्री ईर् (इद् B) चेति नाम सिद्धं तस्मात्सा तादृशी त्वं प्रजया सह रायस्पोषेण सह मामेहि प्राप्नुहि ॥

ad p. 21, l. 17—18. तस्यां प्रत्यागतायां भ्राता वा अस्या अन्यो वा बन्धुः लाजानभिघारितान् कृत्वा कारयित्वा वा शूर्पादञ्जलिनोपहत्योपहत्यास्या अञ्जलौ द्विर्द्विरावपेत् ॥

ad p. 21, l. 18--19. तान् लाजान् । इतरा पत्नी । कृत्वा भर्त्रा कारयित्वेत्यर्थः । प्रत्याहुति अग्निं परिक्रम्यपरिक्रम्य तिष्ठन्ती जुहुयात् । कन्यलेत्यादिमन्त्रांस्तु लिङ्गात्पतिरेव वदेत् ॥

ad p. 21, l. 19--p. 22, l. 3. इयं कन्यला कन्या पितृभ्यः पतिलोकं यती पितृगृहात्पतिगृहं प्राप्नुवती दीक्षां सहधर्मचारिणीनियममवयक्षत अवाप्नोति स्मेत्यर्थः । इयं नारी मम भार्या उपब्रूते मन्मुखेन ब्रूते । कथमिति चेत् । दीर्घायुरित्यादि । इयं कन्या मम भार्या अर्यमणं नु देवमिममग्निं भावयित्वा अयक्षत अयजत । स देवो अर्यमा इमां मां च इतः प्रदेशात् प्रमुञ्चतु मद्गृहं प्राप्तुमनुजानातु ॥

ad p. 22, l. 3—4. होमत्रयस्यास्य वक्ष्यमाणधारिकावपनस्य चान्ते चतुःकृत्व इमं मन्त्रं जपेत् ।

ad p. 22, l. 4—5. (तूष्णीं...चतुर्थं) चतुर्थमग्नावावपेत् लाजधारिका कामाय वध्वा इष्टप्राप्त्यर्थम् ॥

ad p. 22, l. 5. (दक्षिणं... °चक्षते) अतस्तेनावपेदिति भावः । कामसाधनत्वात्तस्मिन् कामशब्दः ॥

ad p. 22, l. 9—10. सप्तमे पदे एनां निवर्त्य प्राङ्मुखीमवस्थाप्य उदकुम्भगताद्भिरुदकुम्भधरो लाजवापः पतिश्च तां प्रोक्षयेयुः ॥

ad p. 22, l. 10—11. विवाहोत्सवे प्रेक्षकाः ॥

ad p. 22, l. 12—15. प्रागेव तथा प्रतिज्ञाप्य तथा प्रतिज्ञा कुर्वतीं तां ध्रुवादीन्यदा प्रथममेते दृश्यन्ते तदा प्रेक्षयेत् । तान्दर्शयित्वा पश्येति प्रेरयेत् । सापि ध्रुवं दृष्ट्वा ॥

द्वाविंशः खण्डः ॥

ad p. 22, l. 18—21. स्वं कुलं भर्तृगृहं प्राप्तां तां वधूं सुशीलाः सुप्रजाः समवजीर्णाः जीवत्पतयो जरत्यः प्रत्यवरोपयन्ति शिबिकादिभ्यः स्वाङ्के अनेन मन्त्रेणावरोपयन्ति। एना एनेन। अजीव्री अजीर्णा सती। शिष्टं स्पष्टम् ॥

ad p. 22, l. 21—p. 23, l. 1. अथ तां पतिर्जरतीनामङ्कात्प्रत्यवरोप्य वृषभस्य चर्मण्यास्तीर्णे अनया ऋचा उपवेशयेत्। पुरस्तन्त्रान्तकृत्यमेतत् ॥

ad p. 23, l. 1. तस्या अङ्के कुमारं निवेश्य तस्य हस्ते मोदकान् फलानि वा दद्यात् ॥

ad p. 23, l. 4. (...रमस्वेति) ततश्चोत्तरतन्त्रम् ॥

ad p. 23, l. 4—5. अथ संवेशिनौ अखट्वाशायिनौ। असंवर्तमानौ अपरिष्वजन्तौ ॥

ad p. 23, l. 5—6. (ऊर्ध्वं...संभवः) त्रिरात्रादूर्ध्वं संनिहिते पुण्यदिने संभवः संयोगः स्यात्। चतुर्थस्याह्न अपुण्यत्वे यावत्पुण्यदिनं अपरिष्वजन्तौ सह शयातामेव ॥

ad p. 23, l. 6. (निशायां...°कर्मण्यं) ऊर्ध्वं त्रिरात्रान्निशायां चतुर्थ्यां रात्रावित्यर्थः। जाया च पतिश्च जायापतिकर्मण्यं गृहस्थकर्मार्हं सायंप्रातर्होमादि तदाप्रभृति कार्यमित्यर्थः ॥

ad p. 23, l. 6—16. औपासनाग्नौ पुरस्तन्त्रान्तकृत्यमेतत्। संवेशनाङ्गो ऽयं होमः प्रत्याहुति संपातं च सिञ्चेत् ॥

ad p. 23, l. 16—17. प्रायश्चित्ताहुत्यनन्तरं चरोरवदायाग्नये स्वाहा प्रजापतये स्वाहेति ससंपातं हुत्वा। एतासां सप्ताहुतीनां संपातान्पात्रे समानीय भार्याहस्ते दत्त्वा सनाभिनवरन्ध्राणि समालिम्पेति तां ब्रूयात् ॥

ad p. 23, l. 17. (नाभिं प्रथमं) प्रेषिता सा मिश्रितैः संपातैर्नाभिं प्रथममञ्जीत ॥

ad p. 23, l. 17—18. (ततो यान्यूर्ध्वं) तत ऊर्ध्वं यानि चक्षुर्घ्राणकर्णास्यानि तान्यञ्जीत ॥

ad p. 23, l. 18. (ततो यान्यर्वाञ्चि) ततो यान्यर्वाञ्चि नाभियोनिपाय्वस्तान्यञ्जीत। ततः स्विष्टकृदाद्युत्तरतन्त्रं। आज्ये चरौ च क्रमात् प्रस्तरमूलाञ्जनं भवति ॥

ad p. 23, l. 18—19. (ऊर्ध्वमर्ध°...तृचेन) संवेशनं मैथुनं। तृचस्यान्ते संयोगः ॥

ad p. 23, l. 19—p. 24, l. 1. भार्यां प्रत्यभिमन्त्रणं ।...इयं स्त्री हिरण्ययी अरणी पुत्रारणी एनामश्विनौ देवौ निर्मन्थतां निर्मथ्नीतां सूतवै प्रसवाय । शिष्टं स्पष्टम् ॥

ad p. 24, l. 1. [ऋतावृतावेवमेव] एवमेवार्धरात्रादूर्ध्वमेतेन तन्त्रेण कुर्यादित्यर्थः ॥

ad p. 24, l. 1—2. [संवेशने...दद्यात्] अग्ने प्रायश्चित्तेत्यादि संवेशनहोमानन्तरमाचार्याय विवाहहोमप्रवेशहोमसंवेशनहोमानामङ्गभूतां दक्षिणां गां दद्यात् ॥

ad p. 24, l. 2. आचार्यस्यादर्शने उपद्रष्टृभ्यो ब्राह्मणेभ्यो दक्षिणां गां दद्यात् । विवाहः समाप्तः ॥

त्रयोविंशः खण्डः ॥

ad p. 24, l. 3. [सायंप्रातर्होमे] विधिं वक्ष्याम इति शेषः ॥

ad p. 24, l. 3—4. [अग्नय...उत्तरां] सायमिति शेषः । आज्यं पयो व्रीहिर्वा होमद्रव्यम् ॥

ad p. 24, l. 4. [एवं...सूर्यः] अयं विशेष इत्यर्थः । अस्य चौपासनस्य विच्छेदे ऽपि सायमुपक्रम एवायं भवति ॥

ad p. 24, l. 4--7. सायं प्रातश्च सिद्धस्यान्नस्य बली द्वौ उद्धारौ वर्धयित्वाखण्ड्य गृहीत्वा तयोः पूर्वस्मात्खण्डादग्नावेतः सप्ताहुतीर्जुहोति औपासनाग्नौ तदभावे पचनाग्नौ ॥

ad p. 24, l. 7. [मनसोत्तरां] उत्तरां प्रजापतय इत्येतां मनसा जुहोति ॥

ad p. 24, l. 7--9 ततो होमार्थमुद्धृतादेवेत्यर्थः । सिद्धमाचारात् गन्धपुष्पमुभयतश्चोदकं बलिहरणेषु । ये देवा हर्षणाः हर्षकराः । वेपनाः भीतिकराः । स्फातिमाहराः भुक्तिमिच्छन्तः । वातस्य भ्राजमन्तरिक्षमनुसंचरन्ति । तेभ्य इत्यादि स्पष्टम् ॥

ad p. 24, l. 9—10. [एवमशनायति] अशनायति अन्नकामे सति पुरुषे एवमेव पूर्ववदेव बलिं भूयो हरेदित्यर्थः ॥

ad p. 24, l. 10. (आयस्थाने...स्वाहेति) तत्रावशिष्टं सर्वं आयस्थाने लभस्थाने संवत्सराहाराय (°सराभाराय B) लभ्यमानस्य व्रीह्यादेः संग्रहस्थाने मृत्योरधिष्ठानाय स्वाहा इति मन्त्रेण बलिं हरेत् ॥

ad p. 24, l. 10—14. शेषस्य द्वितीयस्य उद्धृतान्नस्य बलिहरणमेतेषु सप्तसु आयतनेषु । ततः प्रदक्षिणमावृतं कुर्यात् । उदधाने इत्यादीनामुदपात्रसमीपे । गृहमध्ये नवसु वास्तुभागेषु उत्तरपूर्वस्मिन्भागे खट्वा-

देः स्थाने द्वारबाह्यशिलायां द्वारपिधानफलकायां वास्तुमध्ये इति क्रमादर्थः गृह्याभ्य इत्यादि स्पष्टम् ॥

ad p. 24, l. 14. (शेषं...निनयेत्) शेषं सर्वं ब्रह्मायतने एव धन्वन्तरये हरेत् ॥

ad p. 24, l. 14. [सदा...°वाचनं] यथा प्रसन्ना ब्राह्मणाः स्वस्त्यस्त्विति वदन्ति तथा तेषां प्रेरणं स्वास्तिवाचनं । ब्राह्मणान्भोजनादिभिः सत्कुर्यादित्यर्थः । सो ऽयं मनुष्ययज्ञः ॥

ad p. 24, l. 14—15. यद्ब्राह्मणैः सत्कृतैः स्वस्तिवाचनं सा महती सर्वारिष्टानां शान्तिरित्याचक्षते वदन्त्याचार्याः । वैश्वदेवं समाप्तम् ॥

चतुर्विंशः खण्डः ॥

ad p. 24, l. 16. नवविकारेण चरुणा यक्ष्यमाणस्तज्जातीयेनैव पुराणविकारेण चरुणाग्रे ऽग्निधन्वन्तरी प्रजापतिमिन्द्रं च यजेत ॥

ad p. 24, l. 17. [तिस्रश्च नवाहुतीः] तदनन्तरं तिस्रो नवाहुतीर्वक्ष्यमाणा जुहुयात् । एकेनैव तन्त्रेणेति भावः ॥

ad p. 24, l. 17. (नवेन यजेत) वक्ष्यमाणविधिरेव सिद्धावयं विधिर्नियमार्थः । नवेन द्रव्येण यजेतैव नान्यत्र पूर्वं तद्विनियोग इति शरदि संबध्यते ॥

ad p. 24, l. 17. (शरदि व्रीहीणां) ऐन्द्राग्नो वैश्वदेवो द्यावापृथिव्यश्चरव इति प्रतिवाक्यं संबध्यते शरदि व्रीहीणां विकारेण ऐन्द्राग्नश्च वैश्वदेवश्च द्यावापृथिव्यश्च त्रयश्चरवः पृथक् पात्रपक्वाः स्युः ॥

ad p. 24, l. 18—19. (एकचरुर्वा) एकपात्रपक्वचरुर्वा ऐन्द्राग्नो वैश्वदेवो द्यावापृथिव्यश्च स्यात् । तदेवं पुरस्तन्त्रान्ते पुराणेनैकेनैव चरुणाग्निधन्वन्तरिभ्यां स्वाहा प्रजापतये स्वाहा इन्द्राय स्वाहा इति तिस्रो हुत्वानन्तरं त्रिभिर्वा चरुभिरेकचरुणा वा इन्द्राग्निभ्यां स्वाहा विश्वेभ्यो देवेभ्यः स्वाहा द्यावापृथिवीभ्यां स्वाहा इति तिस्र आहुतीर्जुहुयात् । अथ स्विष्टकृत् । तत्र प्रतिहविः सकृदवदानं पञ्चावत्तिनः द्विर्द्विरेकैकस्मात् । ऋतुभेदेन तु द्रव्यभेदः ॥

ad p. 24, l. 19. (उक्ते...°घारणे) प्राशनाय होम इव उपस्तरणाभिघारणे कुर्यात् ॥

ad p. 24, l. 19. (द्विर्हविषो ऽवद्यति) प्राशनाय नवात् हविषः द्विरवद्यति ॥

ad p. 25, l. 3—5. प्राश्याचम्य परतन्त्रं समापयेत् । विश्वचर्षणीः सर्वप्रजास्वरूपिणी (sic) । वाक्यावृत्तिः समाप्तिज्ञापनार्था ॥

श्रीनिवासाध्वरिकृता टीकेयमतिलघ्व्यपि[१] ।
सुमतीनां भवेन्नित्यं संतोषाय सुबोधिनी ॥
इति जैमिनिसूत्रं पूर्वम् ॥
जैमिनिसूत्रमुत्तरम्[२] ।
प्रथमः खण्डः ॥

ad p. 25, l. 6—8. शुचिवाससः शुक्लवाससः । वास्तु गृहं । सव्यमाचरन्तः अप्रादक्षिण्येन क्रियाः कुर्वन्तः । हविष्यैस्तिलैरुपसिच्य संसृज्य अन्नमुपसाधयेरन् पचेरन् ॥

ad p. 25, l. 9—11. (पाद्यमानीय etc.) सर्वस्मात् (सवस्मात् B, व्यध्वस्मात् M) तदहरुद्धारात्प्रागुद्धृतं पाद्यं स्नातवद्भ्यस्तेभ्यः समानीय दत्त्वा तान्ब्राह्मणांस्त्र्यवदातान् त्रिभिर्विद्याजन्मवृत्तैरवदातान् शुद्धान् आ मे गच्छन्त्वित्यादिना उपवेशयेत् ॥

ad p. 25, l. 11—13. मूलसमीपे छित्त्वा समाहृतान्दर्भान्प्रसव्यान् अप्रदक्षिणं बद्धान्विष्टरान् कृत्वा मन्त्रैर्ब्राह्मणेभ्यः प्रदद्यात् ॥

ad p. 25, l. 13—14. (हविष्यो°...दद्यात्) हविष्यैस्तिलैः सहितमुदकं तिर्यङ् न्यस्तपवित्रं गन्धान्सुमनसश्च तूष्णीं दद्यात् ॥

ad p. 25, l. 14—17. अवत्त्वा अवदाय । परिस्तरणीयानीति (sic B en M) इतिशब्दः प्रभृतिपर्यायः इध्मपरिधिमेक्षणानां ग्रहणार्थः । तत्सर्वमादायाग्नौ करिष्यामीत्युक्ते कुर्विति तैरनुज्ञातः । प्राग्दक्षिणामुखः आग्नेयाभिमुखः । त्रिर्धून्वन् ह्रस्वतृणानि ॥

ad p. 26, l. 5—6. क्षीरं घृतं वासिञ्चति । वर्धयित्वा प्रभूतं परिवेष्य (परिवेष्ट्य the MSS.) । मया प्रत्तं दत्तं हविः । आमासु पक्वमाममपि अपक्वमपि असुपक्वमपि दुस्वादुपक्वमपि तस्मिन्निदमाज्यममृतं निविष्टं तस्य त् हे पितरः यूयं स्वधया मदध्वमित्यर्थः ॥

ad p. 26, l. 6—17. वर्धितानि एतद्व इत्यादिभिरादिशति संकल्पयति । ... (ad अमृता etc. l. 8): हे अग्ने त्वं एकधामापि अद्वितीयस्वरूपो ऽपि त्रिवृता त्रिविधयावृत्त्या पश्यन्ती मध्यमा वैखर्यात्मना वर्तमानो ऽसि । तस्माद् द्वे वाचो ऽमृतवाचः सरस्वत्याः अमृतपरमार्थस्वरूप तेजोमयी वागिति हि श्रूयते । त्वदनुग्रहेण वाक् ऋङ्मयी अत्र या प्रयुज्य-

[१] °लघ्वपि B, M.

[२] This indication not in the MSS.

माना साप्यमृता भवतु । पितॄणां श्रवणीया भवतु । वाचः वाक्यमध्यश्च अमृता भवन्तु । एभिरित्यादि स्पष्टं । हे देवा इहलोके अस्मभ्यं वसीयः सुखमस्तु । (ad l. 10 sq.): अयं यज्ञ इत्यादिपूर्वार्धं स्पष्टं । पितृदैवत्यं पात्रदेयमिदं हविरपि परमं भवत्वित्यर्थः । नो अस्माकं वाक्च मनश्च पितर इति प्रतिजानीम पितृस्वरूपमित्येव संकल्पयामः । तस्मात्तदुभयं शुद्धं । अश्विभ्यां प्रत्तं अश्विनोर्बाहुभ्यां दत्तं तस्माद्धविरपि शुद्धमिति भावः । (ad l. 12 sq.): य इह पितर इत्यादि स्पष्टं । ये पितरः वाचं वाचः श्रुत्या रहस्यं वस्त्वाप्त्वा ब्रह्म विदित्वेत्यर्थः (ब्रह्मविदेत्येत्यर्थः B) अमृता बभूवुः । शिष्टं स्पष्टं ॥

ad p. 26, l. 18. अनुदिशति निर्दिशति ॥

ad p. 26, l. 19—p. 27, l. 2. मे मया संपादिता भोज्यादयः । यद्यदि । अप्रकामा अरमणीयाः । प्रकामा रमणीया वा । ब्राह्मणे भोक्तरि । समृद्धे श्रोत्रिये । यद्यपि सति । अब्राह्मणे वा अश्रोत्रिये । यद्यपि वा सति । यो वात उग्रां निर्ऋतिं श्राद्धघ्नं रक्षो यथा स्कन्दति निगृह्णाति । नः पितरः येन प्रकारेण प्रीयन्ते तथा तत्सर्वं स वायुः शुन्धतु शुद्धं करोतु । तेनेत्यादि स्पष्टम् ॥

ad p. 27, l. 4—6. यन्मे मया दत्तं मन्त्रकृतं हविः रामा शकुनिः श्वापद इति तिर्यग्योनयः एवमादिरशुचिर्जन्तुः । प्राशत् प्राश्नाति स्म । वैश्वानर इत्यादि स्पष्टम् ॥

द्वितीयः खण्डः ॥

ad p. 27, l. 7—11. शेषमनुज्ञाप्य अन्नशेषैः किं क्रियतामिति प्रश्नेन इष्टैः सह भुज्यतामिति प्रत्यनुज्ञां लब्ध्वा । उल्मुकं संनिहितादेव पितृकार्याग्नेः कंचिदुल्मुकमाकर्मसमाप्ति अनिर्वास्यदग्निकं (sic) निदध्यात् ॥

ad p. 27, l. 13. अपहस्तेन पितृतीर्थेन ॥

ad p. 27, l. 15—17. मात्रादीनामविचारेण (°नां विचारेण B) पित्रादीनविवेचयतः इदं पितृभ्य इत्यादयो मन्त्राः ॥

ad p. 27, l. 19 sq. पित्रे नमः पितामहाय नमः प्रपितामहाय नम इति नमस्कृत्य । एतद्व इत्यादिना क्षौमपुच्छं वा वस्त्रपुच्छं वाच्छिद्य वस्त्राण्यतिसृजति ॥

तृतीयः खण्डः ॥

ad p. 28, l. 15—16. मार्गशीर्षमासे या पौर्णमासी सा आग्रहायणी । ततः परं ये त्रयो ऽपरपक्षास्तेषामपरपक्षाणां मध्ये एकैकस्मिन्नपरपक्षे एकैकाष्टका कर्तव्या भवति । अष्टम्यां कर्तव्या श्राद्धक्रिया अष्टकेत्युच्यते ।

ताश्च तिस्रो ऽष्टकाः क्रमात् शाकाष्टका मांस ष्टका अपूपाष्टकेति च अभिधीयन्ते ॥

ad p. 28, l. 16—p. 29, l. 2. तेषां हविषां तैर्हविर्भिः ओदनेन च पृथक्पृथक्पठितैश्चतुर्भिर्मन्त्रैश्चतस्र आहुतीः स्थालीपाकावृता रेखन दि- पूर्णपात्रदक्षिणान्तक्रमेण जुहुयात्। अष्टकादयस्तिस्रो देवताः संवत्सरादि पञ्च प्रकारभिन्नः (°न्नं B)कालात्मा भगवान् चतुर्थी देवता। तस्मै भगवते नमोभिर्हविर्भिः कृणुता तृप्तिं कुरुत हे सखायः।कृणुता इति सांहितो दीर्घः। तेषां संवत्सरादीनां पञ्चानां यज्ञियानां यजनीयानां सुमतौ सुमत्या अनुग्रहेण वयं सकुटुम्बाः ज्योक् चिरमजीता अजीर्णाः अहताः अविच्छिन्नायुषश्च स्याम भवेम ॥

ad p. 29, l. 2—3. अष्टभ्य आहुतिभ्यः परमेहि भगेति त्रिरुक्त्वा अग्निमुपस्थाय स्विष्टकृतं हुत्वा प्रस्तरादानाद्युत्तरतन्त्रं समापयेत्। स्विष्टकृदवदानं तु हविर्द्वयात्पृथक्पृथक्सकृत्सकृद्भवति ॥

ad p. 29, l. 4.[तस्या°…श्रोणीमिति] तस्या गोः सव्यं पार्श्वं सव्यं जघनं सव्यमुरु [l. °मूरुं] च हविरर्थमुद्धरति ॥

ad p. 29, l. 4—5. यस्मिन्दिने अयं होमः ततः परस्मिन्दिवसे अन्वष्टक्यं नाम श्राद्धं कर्तव्यं होमदिवसे वा ॥

ad p. 29, l. 5—7. ब्राह्मणान्हविरर्हान् दत्तदन्तधावनस्नानीयादिकान् स्नातांश्च दत्तपाद्यान् आ मे गच्छन्त्वित्यादिनोपवेश्य नांस्तर्पयित्वा आसनादिशेषानुज्ञापनपर्यन्तं यथाविधि कृत्वा प्रत्येत्य यावत्पिण्डनिधानकर्म। प्राग्दक्षिणायत चतुरश्रं गोमयेनोपलिप्य तस्मात्पितृहोमाग्नेर्दक्षिणतः षडग्नीनित्युपलक्षण यावत्पिण्डसंख्यानग्नीनित्यर्थः प्रणीय ये रूपाणीत्यादिना प्रागुक्तेन प्रतिष्ठाप्य ये समाना इति प्रदक्षिणपर्यन्तं यथा न नश्येत्तथा कृत्वा तेषामग्नीनामेकैकस्मिन्नग्नावेकैकस्याग्नेरुत्तरपश्चादेकैकां कर्षूमवटमायामेन प्राग्दक्षिणेन प्रादेशमात्रीं पार्थिवेन पृथुत्वेन विस्तरेण त्र्यङ्गुलामवाग्वा। वाशब्दश्चार्थः। अधस्ताच्च निम्नतयेत्यर्थः। एकाङ्गुलां खानयेत्त्रिखनेत् ॥

ad p. 29, l. 8. (तासु… हस्तेन) तासु कर्षूषु अपहता इति पृथक् रेखा लिखित्वा अनुलेखं दर्भानास्तीर्याचमनादि क्रमेण यथाविधि षट् पिण्डान्मिलितेन हविर्द्वयेन निदध्यात्। पिण्डभाजस्त्वत्र मन्त्राः पितृभ्यः पार्श्वानि स्त्रीणामिति वचनात्पितृमातृपितामहपितामहीप्रपितामहप्रपितामह्य इति गम्यन्ते। जीवतो विना मृतानामेव पिण्डदानमिति ग्राह्यं। अनुनामापहस्तेनेति वध्वंशकथनस्योपलक्षणत्वात् (वध्वांश° M, विध्यंश° B) पूर्वखण्डोक्तः सर्वो ऽपि विधिरत्र प्राप्नोति ॥

ad p. 29, l. 8—9. मांसाष्टकायामुद्धृतस्य सव्याङ्गत्रयस्य अन्तरं सारभूतं मज्जांशं पितृभ्यः पितृपितामहप्रपितामहेभ्य उपकर्षति पार्श्वानि बाह्यांशानि स्त्रीभ्यः मातृपितामहीप्रपितामहीभ्यः प्रददातीत्यर्थः ॥

ad p. 29, l. 9—11. तत्रामयावी पिण्डान्प्राश्नीयादित्याद्युक्तपिण्डविनियोगे केचिदध्वर्यवः कर्मतन्त्रकर्तारः पूर्वाचार्याः प्रजाकामस्य पत्नी मध्यमं पिण्डं प्राश्नीयात्। श्राद्धस्य सर्वस्यापि स्थालीपाकं हुतशेषमन्नं वा पत्नी प्राश्नीयादिति ब्राह्मणेष्वधीयते ॥

चतुर्थः खण्डः ॥

ad p. 29, l. 12—13. अथ दहनादिसंस्कारपटलमुपक्रमिष्यमाण आहिताग्निसंस्कारस्य प्रधानत्वात्तमेव प्रथमं विधित्सुः सतिशरीर (sic, cp. p. 29, l. 17) इत्यादिना अनष्टशरीरस्य विशेषं विधास्यन्नष्टशरीरस्याहिताग्नेः कर्तव्यं विदधाति। आहिताग्नेः शरीरनाशे पलाशतरूणां पलाशपत्त्रनालानां त्रीणि षष्टिशतानि षष्ट्युत्तरशतत्रयमाहृत्य तैरस्थ्नां प्रतिनिधिभूतैः कृष्णाजिने त्वक्स्थानापन्ने कृष्णाजिने नाडिस्थानापन्नैः कुशैर्बन्धनसाधनैस्तानितान्यङ्गानि बद्ध्वा प्रतिकृतिं कुर्यात्। तत्र प्रत्यङ्गमियत्तापरिच्छेदे (sic) ब्राह्मणमेवोदाहरति अशीत्यर्धमित्यादि विज्ञायत इत्यन्तेन ॥

ad p. 29, l. 13—17...इत्येवंप्रकारेण एतावन्ति एतावत्संख्यानि इहलोके पुरुषस्य मध्ये शरीरं शरीरमध्ये शरीराणि शरीराङ्गभूतान्यस्थीनि भवन्तीति विज्ञायते श्रुतौ दृश्यत इत्यर्थः। अथ आहिताग्नेः क्रमसंस्कार उच्यते. Now follows immediately the text (with commentary) of Jaim. brāhm. (cp. Journ. of the American Oriental Society, XIX, p. 103 sqq.) I. 46; I. 47; I. 48. After the comm. on Jaim. br. I. 48. 5 the text continues: इत ऊर्ध्वं संस्तरणीं नाम गां हत्वा तस्यास्तत्तदङ्गानि परेतस्य तत्तदङ्गेषु विन्यसनादिविधिः कलावनुपयुक्तत्वान्न व्याख्यातः; then follows the sūtra (cp. Jaim. gṛhs. p. 30, l. 3): आस्ये हिरण्यशकलमादाय (sic) उपरि काष्ठानि संस्तीर्य यथास्थितमग्नीन्प्रोह्य उपदीपयन्ति (cp. Jaim. br. I. 49. 5); then follows Jaim. br. I. 49. 6, first sentence (unto देवलोकः प्रत्यागच्छति) and then Jaim. gṛhs. p. 30, l. 4 (अथ सामभिरुपतिष्ठते) unto l. 6 (...इति ब्राह्मणं). Colophon of this part: इत्याहिताग्निदहनपटलः ॥

ad p. 29, l. 17—18. वक्ष्यति (viz. p. 30, l. 7) आहिताग्नेश्चेत्पूर्वं जाया म्रियेत तां निर्मन्थ्येन दहेदित्यादि तस्यायं पुरस्तादपवादः निरान्त्रकरणनिष्पुरीषकरणाहुतीनां निवृत्त्यर्थश्च । अन्यत्सर्वमाहिताग्निवदेव ।

सतीशरीरं पतिव्रताशरीरमित्यर्थः । उपरिष्टाद्वक्ष्यमाणनिर्मन्थ्येन दहनं तु अपतिव्रताया इति गम्यते ॥

ad p. 29, l. 18—p. 30. l. 2. (अत्र पात्राणि...इत्येतेनानुवाकेन) अत्र सतीशरीरदहने तस्यामित्याद्यनुवाकविहितं यज्ञपात्रनिधानमपि आहिताग्निवदेव कुर्यादित्यर्थः । वचनेनापि सिद्धे सत्यारम्भो ऽयं नियमार्थः । अत्रैव पात्राण्यपचिनोति (sic) नान्यत्रेति । तस्मान्निर्मन्थ्येन दहने पात्राणामग्नीनां च उत्सर्ग एव न तु चितासंयोगः उभयत्रापि भार्याभावात् आहिताग्नेः श्रौतकर्मलोपस्तुल्यः ॥

ad p. 30 l. 2. (य एवंवित्...पूर्वमेव) स यदोपतापी स्यादित्यादिना पूर्वोक्तः । जीवत एव श्मशानप्रवेशविधिः पूर्वमेव कृतादियुगेष्वेव नाधुना प्राकृतैस्तथा कर्तुं शक्यमित्यर्थः ॥

ad p. 30, l. 3. (चतुर्गृ°...°संभवं) अन्यमाहिताग्नीतरमौपासनाग्निमन्तं समिदाधानाग्निमन्तं वा । आहिताग्निसंस्कारोक्तप्रकारेषु यथा यावता प्रकारेण संभाव्यते तथा संस्कुर्यात् । चतुर्गृहीतं गृहीत्वा । होमस्तु सर्वेषामग्निमतां कार्य इत्यर्थः ॥

ad p. 30, l. 4—6. (सामभिरुप° etc.) सामभिरेतैर्वक्ष्यमाणैरग्निमुपतिष्ठते । नाके सुपर्णमिति ऋचो (ऋच M) ग्राम्ये गेयमरण्ये गेयमिति च द्वे सामनी । तत्र ग्राम्यं सामात्र गेयं भवति । चिताग्निसंयोगेन धूम उदिते सति त्वेषस्ते धूम ऋण्वतीति साम गेयं । अग्नौ समारूढे परेतं स्पृष्टवति अग्ने मृड महं असीति अस्यामृचि द्वे सामनी । तयोरन्यतरेणोपतिष्ठते । असौ लोकः पराग्वै भवति असंनिहितो वै भवति । तस्मात्पराग्भिरेतैः सामभिरुपतिष्ठेत अनावृत्तैरित्यर्थः । इति हि ब्राह्मणं इति प्ररोचनार्थः ॥

पञ्चमः खण्डः ।

ad p. 30, l. 6—7. निर्मन्थ्येनापूर्वारणिमन्थनजनितेन । सांतपनेन श्रौताग्निसंतप्तकपालोद्भूतेनाग्निना वा तां दहेत् । अत्र वक्तव्यसतीशरीरमित्यादि सूत्रव्याख्यानावसर एव उक्तम् ॥

ad p. 30, l. 7—9. श्मशानकृतं श्मशानार्थस्थलं । अनिरिणं ऊषरवर्जितं । अपसलवक्रोदकं अपसव्यावृत्तोदकं च । स्वकृतं स्वत एव तथाविधं । तदलाभे यत्नतस्तथा कृत्वा वा यत्र वा ओषधयो जायन्ते तस्मिन्स्थले वा शरीरं निःशेषं दग्ध्वा दग्धमनवेक्षमाणा उदककरणाय यान्ति ॥

ad p. 30, l. 9—10. (न वाहिनीषु कुर्वन्ति) वाहिनीषु नदीषु प्रवाहजलेष्वित्यर्थः उदकदानं न कुर्यात् किंतु स्थावरजलेषु वाप्यादिष्वेव कुर्यादित्यर्थः ॥

ad p. 30, l. 10. (तेषां योयः...ऽग्रं) तेषामुदकदायिनां मध्ये योयः पश्चाज्जातः वयसन्यूनः स्यात्सो ऽग्रमुदकदानमाचरेत्। तदनन्तरं वयोज्येष्ठ इत्यर्थः॥

ad p. 30, l. 10—11. (कुर्यदुपकूलं) जलमध्ये उदकदानं न कुर्यात् किंतु उपकूलं कूलसमीपे कुर्यात्। यथा कूले क्षिप्यमाणं जलं पुनर्वाप्यादौ संनिपतेत् तथा कुर्यादिति गम्यते॥

ad p. 30, l. 11. [अकूले...खात्वा] वाप्यादिजलस्य कूलादतिविप्रकृष्टत्वादिनिमित्तेन जलाशयकूले उदकदानं कर्तुं अलाभे सति क्वचित्कूपं खात्वा घटाद्याहृतजलेन तस्मिन्कूपे कुर्यात्॥

ad p. 30, l. 11—12. एतत्त उदकं गोविन्दशर्मन्नित्येवमादिप्रकारेणेत्यर्थः॥

ad p. 30, l. 12. (वाहिनीषु...केशान्) स्थावरजलालाभेन प्रवाहजलेष्वेवोदकदाने केशानुच्चैर्बद्ध्वा उदकं दद्यादित्यर्थः। अन्यत्र मुक्तकेशेनैव उदकदानमिति गम्यते॥

ad p. 30, l. 12—14. (निमज्य etc.) उक्तप्रकारेण निमज्य एकाञ्जलिं दत्त्वा लम्बमानान् केशान् करनिष्पीडितजलानुपनिबध्य जलाशयतीरं (रा MS.) नीतस्य दीप्ताङ्गारकरस्य उल्मुकस्याग्निमनेन मन्त्रेण स्पृशेत्। शूकाहिर्नाम कश्चिदग्निः। अपहतेति व्यत्ययात् बहुवचनं अपजहीत्यर्थः॥

ad p. 30, l. 16—17. कल्याणीभिर्दीर्घायुषो भवन्त इत्यादिभिः शोकापनोदिनीभिर्वाग्भिरित्यर्थः॥

ad p. 30, l. 17. माषो नाम प्रमाणविशेषः। माषप्रमाणपरिमितस्वर्णं विक्रीतद्रव्येण सर्वे क्षुद्यावृत्तिं कुर्वन्ति। अल्पमश्नन्तीत्यर्थः॥

ad p. 30, l. 18. (शान्त्या वा) किंचिदप्यभक्षित्वा वेत्यर्थः। इत्युदकदानविधिः। अथ संचयनविधिः॥

ad p. 30, l. 18—19. क्षीरोदके समे संसृज्य शरीराण्यस्थीनि मृण्मयेन कोशेन औचित्यात् गोशृङ्गाकारनिर्मितेनेत्यर्थः॥

ad p. 30, l. 20. (असंह्लादयन्) असंह्लादयन् कटकटाशब्दमकारयन्॥

ad p. 31, l. 1. तदाहृत्य गच्छन् कंचन चतुष्पथं महावृक्षं नदीं वा अतीत्य गत्वा तीर्थेषु पुण्येषु निखनेत्॥

ad p. 31, l. 2. प्रेतस्य तृतीये ऽहनि संचयनानन्तरं संस्कर्तारं श्रोत्रिया अपामार्गपिष्टेन मृदा गोमयेन च स्वकरदत्तेन स्नापयन्ति॥

ad p. 31, l. 2—3. (वासांसि...आसते) सर्वेऽप्यघिन इति शेषः॥

ad p. 31, l. 3. [चतुर्थ्यां...°वर्तयेरन्] चतुर्थदिवसमारभ्य अघिनः सर्वे भिक्षाशनेन जीवेयुः तस्यां भिक्षायां श्रोत्रियगृहे नीतायां वैश्वदेवादेः सिद्धत्वाद्यज्ञशेषासिततया पूता ह्यघिनो भवन्तीति भावः ॥

ad p. 31, l. 4. (कालं च...संतरेयुः) यावत्कालं च ये (वयं MS) अग्नौकरणादिकारिणो भवेयुस्तावत्कालं भिक्षाशिनश्च स्युरित्यर्थः ॥

ad p. 31, l. 4—5. (ऊर्ध्वं etc.) एकोद्दिष्टश्राद्धप्रदानपर्यन्तं दशाहमध्ये विहितादन्यत् न किंचित्कस्मैचिद्दद्युः ॥

ad p. 31, l. 5. (नक्षत्रेषु नियमः) एकोद्दिष्टश्राद्धस्य नक्षत्रनियम उच्यते ॥

ad p. 31, l. 5—6. (मघासु...°समयेषु) एकतारेषु आर्द्राचित्रास्वातीषु पूर्वसमयेषु पूर्वफल्गुनीपूर्वाषाढापूर्वप्रोष्ठपदासु ॥

ad p. 31, l. 6. (न रोहिण्यामुत्तरेषु ध्रुवेषु) उत्तरेषु उत्तरफल्गुणीउत्तराषाढोत्तरप्रोष्ठपदासु एतान्येव प्रतिषिद्धानि नक्षत्राणि ध्रुवाणीत्यभिधीयन्ते। विहिताभे [sic] प्रतिषिद्धेतरेषु नक्षत्रेष्वपि कुर्यादिति भावः ॥

ad p. 31, l. 6—9. सामान्यश्राद्धापेक्षया एकोद्दिष्टश्राद्धे विशेषविधिरुच्यते। एकवत् यथाश्राद्धं पिण्डप्रदानं च क्रियमाणं मृतमेकं प्राप्नोति। तथा मन्त्रवाक्येषु पितामहादिनिर्देशवर्जं पदविन्यासः कर्तव्यः। ये च त्वात्रान्वित्यादि च न ब्रूयात्। मृतस्य एकस्यैवार्थे त्र्यवरा ब्राह्मणा भोजनीयाः। ते च वस्त्रादि (l. वस्त्रादिभिः) सर्वकामैश्च तर्पणीयाः। पिण्डदानानन्तरं च गच्छतोऽनुमन्त्रणं शेषस्याप्राशनं (sic) स्वस्तिवाचनानन्तरं भोजनं चेति ॥

षष्ठः खण्डः ॥

ad p. 31, l. 10—11. गृहकर्माणि गृहस्थाश्रमधर्मस्य सिद्ध्यर्थं गृहवृद्धिं गृहस्य धनधान्यैर्द्विपद्भिश्चतुष्पद्भिश्च समृद्धिमिच्छन्नुक्तकाले गृहशान्त्याख्यं कर्म आरभेत ॥

ad p. 31, l. 11—15. अपामार्गादयोऽष्टौ। सदाभद्रा शिशुपूला। अमृताः पूर्वा [l. दूर्वाः]। तृणं कुशाः। परिसमूह्य संमृष्टधूल्यादिकं क्वचित्समूहीकृत्य। सिद्धार्थकान् सर्षपान्। वास्तुबलिं कृत्वा गृहमध्ये प्रदेशमीश्व[व]ल्लीगन्धपुष्पादिभिरलंकृत्येत्यर्थः। अलंकृतवास्तुस्थले पुरस्तन्त्रान्ते वास्तोष्पतये स्वाहेत्याज्येन हुत्वा सावित्र्या सहस्रं चाज्येन जुहुयात् ॥

ad p. 31, l. 15—16. उक्तप्रकारेण चतसृषु विदिक्षु होतव्यं वास्तुमध्ये मांत्रं वेत्यर्थः ॥

ad p. 31, l. 16. [गौर्वा°...दक्षिणा] अयमिदं समुदितं दक्षिणात्वेन देयं न तु विकल्पः ॥

ad p. 31, l. 16—17. परिविष्य तर्पयित्वा । पुण्याहं भवन्तो ब्रुवन्त्वित्यादि तैः पुण्याहं वाचयित्वा समापयेत् ॥

ad p. 32, l. 1—3. अश्वादिकं वा उपतप्येत सर्वेषां द्विपदां चतुष्पदामन्यतरद्वा उपतप्येत तदाप्येवं जुहुयादित्यर्थः ॥

अष्टमः खण्डः ॥ [1]

ad p. 32, l. 12. अथातः अनश्नता प्रयोक्तव्या संहिता अनश्नत्संहिता तत्प्रयोगं तत्प्रयोगविधिं व्याख्यास्याम इत्यर्थः ॥

ad p. 32, l. 12—13. अनश्नत्संहितायाः प्रयोक्ता शुक्लवासाश्चीरवासा वा स्यात् ॥

ad p. 32, l. 13—14. ब्राह्मण एव अनश्नत्संहितां प्रयुञ्ज्यान्न तु क्षत्रियवैश्यौ ॥

ad p. 32, l. 21—p. 33, l. 1. सामसावित्रीं तत्सवितुर्वरेण्यमिति साम । सोमं राजानमिति साम । ब्रह्म जज्ञानमित्यृचि सामद्वयं च मनसाधीत्य वेदादिमारभेत ॥

ad p. 33, l. 1. [संतत°...मौनी] संततमविच्छिन्नधारं यथा भवति तथा मौनी व्यवहारान्तररहितः ॥

ad p. 33, l. 1. [न चान्तरा विरमेत्] संहितासमाप्तिपर्यन्तं मध्ये विरतो न भवेत् ॥

ad p. 33, l. 1—3. (अथान्तरा...आरभेत) अथ मध्ये व्यवहरेत् विरतो वा भवेच्चेत् आतम्य यावद्दानि [l. यावद्दानं] निरुद्धप्राणो भूत्वा वृत्तान्तात्प्रागधीताच्छेशमारभेत ॥

ad p. 33, l. 3—4. अप्रतिभायां मध्ये कतिपयवेदांशस्य स्फुरणे यावता कालेन अस्फुरितांशं वेदमधीयीत तावत्कालं ऋग्वेदाद्यजुर्वेदात्सामवेदाद्वा यज्ञानीयात् यावतीर्ऋचः यावन्ति यजूंषि यावन्ति वा सामानि जानीयात्तान्यधीयीत[2] । एवं चेत् अस्फुरितांशाध्ययनफलमाप्नुयादित्यर्थः ॥

ad p. 33, l. 4—5. अस्फुरितांशवेदतुल्यच्छन्दोदैवतब्राह्मणं साम वा तावत्कालमधीत्य तत्फलमाप्नुयात् ॥

---

१ The Comm. on the 7th. kh. is missing.

२ Here M² breaks off.

ad p. 33, l. 5. (अकानि°...°भ्ययेत्) अकानित्यृचि यत्साम तदेकमेव वा अस्फुरितवेदांशाध्ययनतुल्यकालमावर्त्य अस्फुरितवेदांशाध्ययनफलमाप्नुयात् ॥

ad p. 33, l. 5—6. अस्य संहितां प्रयुञ्जानस्य सर्वाभीष्टसमृद्धिर्भवत्येव [सर्वाहीष्टसमृद्धिर्भवतेव MS.] ॥

ad p. 33, l. 6—7. (आद्यं...जैमिनिः) आद्यं त्रिवर्गं अग्न आयाहीत्यृचि यत्सामत्रयं तदेव वा सहस्रकृत्व आवर्त्य संहिताप्रयोगफलं लभेतेति जैमिनेर्मतमिति । आचार्यग्रहणं पूजार्थं ॥

ad p. 33, l. 7. [च वार्यमन्तं वा] यत्तियासि च वार्यमित्यन्तं यानि सामानि तानि मात्रमधीत्य वा संहिताध्ययनफलमाप्नुयात् ॥

ad p. 33, l. 7. [यथाकामी वा] स्वेक्षया यत्र क्वचित् यानि कानि च सामानि यथाशक्ति वाधीत्य संहिताध्ययनफलमश्नुयादित्यर्थः ॥

ad p. 33, l. 7—9. [द्वादश संहिता...ब्रह्म भवति] अनश्नत्संहिता द्वादशधावर्त्य यदनेनाधयित्रा (l °ध्येत्रा ?) अनध्यायेषु अष्टम्यादिषु अधीतं गुरवो वा अशुश्रूषया कोपिता वेति यत् यानि वा अकार्याणि विहितभिक्षाशनादि व्रतानुष्ठानप्रतिषिद्धपर्युषितभोजनादीनि कृतानि ताभिर्दुश्चर्याभिः पवते अपवित्रतां न प्राप्नोति । अस्य ब्रह्म अधीनो वेदश्च शुद्धस्तेजस्वी भवति ॥

ad p. 33, l. 9—10. द्वादशसंहितावृत्त्यनन्तरं पुनर्द्वादशधावर्त्य शुक्रस्य लोकं प्राप्नोति ॥

ad p. 33, l. 12—13. [चक्षुर्लभते] चक्षुरतीन्द्रियज्ञानमित्यर्थः ॥

ad p. 33, l. 13—14. यावकः यवविकारः । उदकमिलिताः सक्तवः उदकसक्तवः । सक्तवो लाजचूर्णाः । एवं संहितां प्रयुञ्जानः क्षिप्रमन्तर्धानशक्तिं लभते ॥

ad p. 33, l. 14—15. (ज्ञातीन्पुनाति) बन्धून्निष्पापान् करोति ॥

ad p. 33, l. 15. तारयते कर्मबन्धादुद्धरति ॥

ad p. 33, l. 15—16. (तामेतां...आचक्षते) तामेतामनश्नत्संहितां देवलोकमारोढुं सोपानपरं परेत्याचक्षते पूर्वाचार्याः ॥

ad p. 33, l. 16. एतया वा अनश्नत्संहितया बहुधावृत्तया देवत्वं देवा ऋषित्वमृषयश्च प्राप्नवन्तः ॥

ad p. 33, l. 16—19. अस्य अनश्नत्संहिताध्ययनस्य प्रातर्मध्याह्ने ब्राह्मे मुहूर्ते वा आरम्भकालः न तु पुण्यदिनान्वेषणम् ॥

ad p. *33*, l. 19—20. (तद्वा एतत् etc.) एतदनश्नत्संहिताध्ययनविधानं । ब्राह्मणेभ्य इति द्विरावृत्तिः प्रश्नसमाप्तिद्योतका । इत्यनश्नत्संहितापटलः ॥ १

यस्यात्मा कमलाक्षपादजलजे भृङ्गायते सर्वदा यद्बुद्धिर्निगमार्थबोधसरणौ नाभ्येति वक्राध्वनि ।

विश्वामित्रकुलाब्धिपार्विकशाशि² स श्रीनिवासाध्वरी चक्रे जैमिनिगृह्यकर्मविवृतिं बालात्मबोधक्षमाम् ॥

इति जैमिनिसूत्रव्याख्यानं संपूर्णम् ॥

---

१ Text and Comm. of khaṇḍa 9 are not given in our Subodhinī.

२ l. °शशी

LIST OF MANTRAS.

The parallels only from the Mantrabrāhmaṇa are given completely ; for those mantras, that are not found in any printed text, parallels from other unpublished texts are given, if possible. After a pratīka the fat figure refers to the page of the Jaim. gṛhya, the second figure to the line. Before a pratīka the figure

1, indicates, that the mantra is cited pratīkena in the Jaim. gṛhs. and that it occurs in the Jaiminīyasaṃhitā ;

2, indicates, that the mantra is cited sakalapāṭhena in the Jaim. gṛhs. and notwithstanding is found in the Jaiminīyasaṃhitā ;

3, indicates, that the mantra sakalapāṭhena is found in the Agniṣṭomasūtra of the Jaiminīyas ;

4, indicates, that the mantra has nowhere an exact parallel ;

5, indicates, that the mantra agrees exactly with the Mantrabrāhmaṇa and that it occurs only in this text.

The mantras occuring in II. 9 are not registrated in this list.

More parallels than those that are indicated by me, can easily be found by means of the "Spruchverzeichniss" to the Mānavagṛhya (ed. Knauer) and by means of the Mantrapāṭha.

The Sāmaveda (Jaiminīya recension) is cited as JS, according to the text published by me.

The Mantrabrāhmaṇa (MBr.) is cited acc. to the edition of Satyavrata in the "Uṣā".

The Gobhilagṛhya (Gobh.) according to the edition of Knauer.

The Mantrapāṭha according to the edition of Winternitz.

Wherever the single name of an author is given, the Gṛhyasūtra attributed to this author is meant.

1 **अक्रान्त्समुद्रः 27**, 2 ; **33**, 5 : JS. I. 3. 6. 5 ; III. 49. 1.

अग्नय इन्द्राग्निभ्याम् 4, 3.

अग्नये कव्यवाहनाय स्वधा 26, 1 : MBr. II. 3. 2 (var.).

अग्नये ऽग्नीषोमाभ्याम् 4, 3.

अग्नये त्वा परिददामि 11, 17.

अग्नये ऽनुमतये स्वाहा 4, 13.

अग्नये समिधमहार्षम् 11, 21 : MBr. I. 6. 32 (var.).

अग्नये सोमाय प्रजापतये 6, 13.

अग्नये सोमाय रुद्राय 32, 16.

अग्नये स्वाहा 4, 1.

अग्नये स्वाहा सोमाय स्वाहा 24, 5.

अग्निः प्रथमः प्राश्नातु 25, 3 : MBr. II. 1. 15 (var.).

अग्निरैतु प्रथमः 19, 15 : MBr. I. 7. 10 (var.).

1 **अग्ने त्वं नो अन्तमः 13**, 20 : JS. I. 2. 4. 9. 2 ; III. 34. 15.

अग्ने प्रायश्चित्ते 23, 6 : MBr. I. 4. 1 [var.].

1 **अग्ने मृड 30**, 5 : JS. I. 1. 3. 3.

अग्ने वायो सूर्य 23, 14 : MBr. I. 4. 5 (var.).

अग्ने व्रतपते 13, 4, 9 : MBr. I. 6. 9 [varr.].

4 **अग्ने शूकाहे 30**, 13.

अघोरचक्षुः 21, 7 : MBr. I. 2. 17 (var.).

अङ्गादङ्गात् 7, 10 : MBr. I. 5. 16 (varr.).

अत्र पितरः 27, 17 : MBr. II. 3. 6.

अदिते ऽनुमन्यस्व 3, 14 (**5**, 18): Gobh. I. 3. 1.

1 **अधायामुत** (?) **32**, 8 : JS ?

4 **अधिगन्तरधिगच्छ 11**, 4.

अनुमते ऽनुमन्यस्व 3, 14 (**5**, 18): Gobh. I. 3. 2.

अनृक्षरा ऋजवः 19, 12.

4 **अन्तरिक्षे ऽङ्क्ष्व 4**, 12.

अन्नपते ऽन्नस्य 8, 14.

अन्वद्य नः 20, 12 : MBr. II. 2. 19 (varr.), cp. AV. VII. 20. 1 ; Maitr. S. III, p. 189, l. 10 ; Kauś. sū. 45. 16.

अपहतो मे पाप्मा **17**, 11.

अपहता असुराः **27**, 7 : MBr. II. 3. 3 (varr.).

4 अपो ऽभिवीक्षे **16**, 2 : cp. Khād. II. 5. 31.

अप्रजस्ताम् **20**, 16 : MBr. I. 1. 14 (var.).

अप्सरासु या मेधा **12**, 4 : Taitt. ār. X. 41 ; Mantrap. II. 4. 6 ; Hir. I. 8. 4.

अभिरमन्तां भवन्तः **27**, 3.

अभ्यङ्क्ष्वासौ **28**, 1.

अमीमदन्त पितरः **27**, 18 : MBr. II. 3. 7.

अमुष्मै स्वधा **26**, 18.

4 अमृता वाक् **26**, 8 : cp. Kāṭh. (altind. ahnenk. p. 255).

अमो ऽहमस्मि **21**, 12 : cp. Mantrap. I. 3. 14 ; differing in Jaim. up. brāhm. I. 54. 6.

4 अयं यज्ञः **26**, 10 : cp. Kāṭh. (altind. ahnenk. p. 256).

अयं त इध्म आत्मा **3**, 18 : Āśv. I. 10. 12 ; Bhār. I. 4 ; Hir. I. 2. 11.

अरुन्धत्यरुद्धा **22**, 14 : cp. Gobh. II. 3. 11.

4 अर्कवानन्नादः **18**, 1.

अर्यम्णं नु **22**, 2 : MBr. I. 2. 3 (var.).

अश्मा भव **7**, 17 : MBr. I. 5. 18. a and 19.

4 अश्मासि **30**, 14.

अष्टकायै सुराधसे स्वाहा **28**, 18.

अष्टकायै स्वाहा **28**, 17.

अह्ने त्वा परिददामि **7**, 12 : MBr. I. 5. 15 (var.).

आकूत्यै स्वाहा **4**, 17.

आङ्क्ष्वासौ **28**, 1.

आचाम पितः **27**, 11.

4 आदर्शो ऽसि **16**, 19.

आदित्य व्रतपते **13**, 6 : MBr. I. 6. 11 (varr.).

आ नः प्रजाम् **21**, 9 : MBr. I. 2. 18 (var.).

आप उन्दन्तु **9**, 6 : MBr. I. 6. 3 (Jaim. longer).

आप ओषधयः **5**, 11.

1 **आपोहिष्ठीयास्तिस्रः 13**, 16 ; **22**, 10 : (do not seem to occur in Jaim. Saṃh.).

4 **आमासु पक्कम् 26**, 5—6 : cp. Kāṭh. (altind. ahnenk. p. 256).

4 **आ मे गच्छन्तु पितरः 25**, 9 : cp. Kāṭh. (l. c. p. 255).

आयमगात्सविता 9, 2—4 : MBr. I. 6. 1 (Jaim. much longer).

आयुषे त्वा 4, 13.

आलिखन्विलिखन् 8, 1 : cp. Pārask. I. 16. 23.

4 **इदमन्नमयं रसः 7**, 8.

इदं पितृभ्यः 27, 15.

इदं भूमेर्भजामहे 2, 2 : MBr. II. 4. 1 (cp. Jaim. gṛhs. p. 2, l. 3).

इन्द्रस्ते हस्तम् 11, 10 : Hir. I. 5. 19 ; MBr. I. 6. 15 (varr.).

इन्द्राय स्वाहा 3, 21.

इमंस्तोम्यं तृचम् 2, 3 : JS. III. 32. 4—6.

इममश्मानम् 10, 17 : MBr. I. 2. 1 [var.].

इमामग्निस्त्रायताम् 19, 17 : MBr. I. 1. 11 [var.].

इयं दुरुक्तात् 12, 6 : MBr. I. 6. 27 [slight var.].

इयं नारी 21, 20 : MBr. I. 2. 2 [longer].

इह गावः 22, 21 = Bhāradv.; MBr. I. 3. 13 [var.].

इह धृतिः 23, 2 : MBr. I. 3 14.

इह प्रियम् 22, 19 : Mantrap. I. 9. 4.

4 **ईर्त्वमसि** (!) **21**, 16.

1 **उदुत्तमम् 17**, 8 : JS. II. 5. 1.

2 **उदु त्यम् 4**, 19 : JS. I. 1. 3. 11 ; IV. 1. 10.

उद्वयं तमसस्परि 4, 21 ; **13**, 21.

उष्णेन वायो 9, 4—6 : MBr. I. 6. 2 (var.).

ऊर्जं वहन्तीः 28, 5 : MBr. II. 3. 15.

1 **ऋचं साम 14**, 9 : JS. I. 2. 3. 6. 10.

ऋचा स्तोमम् 4, 18.

ऋतस्य गोप्त्री 12, 8 : MBr. I. 6. 28 (var.).

एकमिषे 22, 6 : MBr. I. 2, 9—12 [varr.].

एकाष्टकायै स्वाहा 28, 18.

4 **एतत्ते पितरसौ 25**, 12.

एतत्ते पितरसौ 27, 13.

एतद्वः पितरः 26, 7 : cp. Kāṭh. [altind. ahnenk. p. 256].

एतद्वः पितरः 27, 20 : MBr. II, 3, 14, 12, 16 [the last with var.].

एवमु त्यम् 25, 1 : MBr. II. 1. 16 (slight var.).

4 **एषा व ऊर्क् 26**, 14 : cp. Kāṭh. (altind. ahnenk. p. 256).

एहि भग 29, 3.

ओं तपश्च तेजश्च 2, 17 : MBr. II. 4, 5 and 6 (several varr.).

ओषधयो वनस्पतयः 5, 11.

कन्यला 21, 19 : MBr. I. 2. 5 [slight var.].

कामाय स्वाहा 4, 17 : cp. Mān. II. 13. 6.

को नामासि 11, 7 : MBr. I. 6. 17.

को ऽसि कतमो ऽसि 7, 16 : MBr. I. 5. 14. a.

4 **गन्धर्वो ऽसि 18**, 1.

गर्भं धेहि 23, 20 : MBr. I. 4. 7.

गृहाः पशवः 5, 10.

गृह्णामि ते 21, 1 : MBr. I. 2. 16 [slight var.].

गृह्याभ्यो देवताभ्यः 24, 11 : Mān. II. 12. 6; Kauś. sū. 74. 10.

3 **गौर्धेनुर्हव्या 19**, 3—7.

चन्द्र प्रायश्चित्ते 23, 12 : MBr. I. 4. 3 (var.).

2 **चित्रं देवानाम् 4**, 20 : JS. II. 4. 6.

जीवा स्थ 12, 19—20: cp. Śaṅkh. II. 6. 1.

4 **ज्योतिरभिवीत्ते 16**, 3: cp. khād. II. 5. 31.

1 **तरत्स मन्दी (चतस्रः) 13**, 16 : JS, III. 31. 27.

तां पूषन् 21, 11.

त्रियायुषम् 10, 1 = Mantrap. 11. 7. 2 : MBr. I. 6. 8 (varr.) Jaim. up. brāhm. IV. 3. I (first half).

1 **त्वं वरुण 13**, 20 : JS. III. 54. 6.

1 **त्वेषस्ते धूमः 30**, 5 : JS. I. 1. 9. 3.

1 **दधिक्राव्णः 14**, 13 : JS. I. 2. 3. 5. 7.

4 **दिव्यङ्गत्व 4**, 11.

देव सवितः प्रसुव 3, 15—17 (**5**, 18): MBr. I. 1. 1.

देवस्त्वा सविता 2, 13 : Gobh. I. 7. 25.

देवस्य त्वा सवितुः 1, 7 ; **18**, 19.

देवा ऋत्विजः 5, 8.

4 **देवाश्च पितरश्च 28**, 9.

देहि भित्तां भवति 12, 18 : Kauś. sū. 57. 18.

द्यौस्ते पृष्ठम् 20, 13 : MBr. I. 1. 12 ; Hir. I. 19. 7.

5 द्विषन्तं मे ऽभिधेहि **4**, 14 : MBr. II. 8 13. b.
द्विषतां वज्रो ऽसि **17**, 7.
1 धानावन्तम् **14**, 13 : JS. I. 2. 1. 10. 7.
धारयतु प्रजापतिः **9**, 8 : Mān. I. 21. 3.
ध्रुवो ऽसि **22**, 12—13 : cp. Gobh. II. 3. 9.
नमो वः पितरः **28**, 2 : MBr. II. 3. 8—11 (varr).
नमो वाताय **11**, 2.
1 नाके सुपर्णम् **30**, 4 : JS. I. 2. 3. 1. 3.
नान्दीमुखाः पितरः **6**. 18.
नेत्रे स्थः **18**, 3 : MBr. I. 11. 12 (var.).
परीममिन्द्र }
परीमं पोष } **10**, 8—14 ; **17**, 19 : Hir. I. 4. 8 ; Kāṭh. 41 ; AV. XIX. 2. 42.
परीमं सोम }
पवित्रे स्थः **2**, 8 : Gobh. I. 7. 22.
4 पशुमभिवीक्षे **16**, 3 : cp. Khād. II. 5. 31.
पितरेतत्ते **27**, 15.
1 पुरुषसूक्तम् **6**, 4 : JS. II. 3. 6—4. 2.
पूषा त्वेतः **22**, 16.
4 पृथिव्यामङ्गुष्व. **4**, 21.
प्रजापतये स्वाहा **3**, 21.
4 प्रजापतिः पुरुषः **6**, 5.
प्रजापते न त्वत् **5**, 2; **6**, 22; **20**, 19; **32**, 10: MBr. II. 5. 9.
प्रजां पशून् **7**. 5.
1 प्रत्यग्ने **32**, 9 : JS. I. 1. 10. 6.
4 प्रदातः प्रयच्छ **11**, 4.
1 प्र मित्राय **14**, 1 : JS. I. 2. 2. 3. 3.
5 प्र मे पतियानः **20**, 4 : MBr. I. 1. 8. a.
प्राणानां ग्रन्थिरसि **11**, 13 : MBr. I. 6. 20 (differing).
प्राणाय त्वापानाय **7**, 2.
5 प्रास्याः (पतियानः etc.) **20**, 5 : MBr. I. 1. 9. a.
ब्रह्मचर्यमगाम् **11**, 7 : MBr. I. 6. 16.
ब्रह्मचार्यसि **11**, 20 : MBr. I. 6. 25 (var.), 26 (var.).
ब्रह्मचार्याचार्याधीनः **13**, 10.
1 ब्रह्मजज्ञानीये (उभे) **32**, 21 : to JS. I. 2. 3. 1. 9.
ब्रह्मवर्चसी भूयासम् **17**, 21.
भद्रान्नः श्रेयः **31**, 19 : MBr. II. 1. 13 (slight varr.).
भवति भिक्षां देहि **12**, 16 : Kauś. sû. 57. 16.
भिक्षां भवति देहि **12**, 17 : Kauś. sû. 57. 17.
भूर्भुवः स्वाहा **10**, 20—**11**, 1.

भूः स्वाहा भुवः स्वाहा **4**, 1 ; **5**, 4 ; **12**, 5.
मनः समाधीयताम् **6**, 17.
मयि पद्या विराट् **18**, 15.
मयि व्रते **11**, 14—17 : MBr. I. 2. 21 (varr.).

1,3 मयि वर्चः **18**, 16 : JS. II. 1. 4.
मयि श्रीः श्रयताम् **18**, 15 : Āśv. I. 24. 29 ; Mān. I. 9. 16.

1 महानाम्नी **15**, 11 : JS. II. 7.
महाव्याहृति **6**, 22 ; **8**, 19 ; **10**, 19 ; **20**, 7 ; **32**, 10.
मह्यं त्वा यशसे **18**, 20.
मा ते गृहे **20**, 10: MBr. I. 1. 13 (varr.).

4 मा मे क्षेष्ट 28, 7 : cp. Kāṭh. (altind. ahnenk. p. 258.)
मासाः पितरः **5**, 9.

4 मृत्योरधिष्ठानाय स्वाहा **24**, 10.

1 मेधाकारम् **14**, 10: JS. III. 28. 6.

4 य इह पितरः **26**, 12: cp. Kāṭh. (altind. ahnenk. p.255–256)

1 यं रक्षन्ति **32**, 9: JS. I. 2. 1. 8. 1.

1 यज्ञः संवत्सरः **5**, 12.

1 यत इन्द्र **32**, 8; JS. I. 2. 2. 5. 2; III. 55. 12.
यत्क्षुरेण **9**, 16—18: Mān. I. 21. 7; Aśv. I. 17. 16; Pār. II. 1. 19. Mantrap. II. 1. 7; Hir. I. 9. 16.
यदप्सु ते सरस्वति **5** 15—17; TBr. II. 5. 8. 6.

1 यद्व उ विश्पतिः **32**, 9: JS. I. 1. 12. 8.

4 यन्मे प्रकामः **26**, 18 sqq. : cp. Kāṭh. (altind. ahnenk. p. 256—257).

4 यन्मे रामः **27** , 4: cp. Kāth. (altind. ahnenk. p. 258).
यमायाङ्गिरस्वते **26**, 3.

1 यशसा मे **17**, 19: JS. II. 2. 2.
या अकृन्तन् **20**, 2 : MBr. I. 1. 5 (varr.).
या तिरश्ची **20**, 7—9 : MBr. I. 5. 6 (varr.).
यानि कानि च पापानि **20**, 17: MBr. I. 3. 6 (var.).
येन तत्प्रजापतिः **9**, 11.
येन धाता **9**, 9—11: Āśv. I. 17. 12; MBr. I. 6. 7 (many varr.).
येन भूयश्चरात्ययम् **9**, 13: Āśv. I. 17. 13 (text of Bibl. Ind.).
ये रूपाणि **27**, 9: MBr. II. 3. 4 (var.).
ये समानाः **28**, 10.—12.

4 येह पितरः **26**. 16: cp. kāth. (altind. ahnenk. p, 256).

4 ये हर्षणाः **24**, 8.

4 वनस्पतीनां गन्धः **16**, 14—16.

4 वनस्पतीनां पुष्पम् **16**, 17.

4 वनस्पतेस्त्वक् **16**, 13.

1 वामदेव्यम् **5**, 17; **13**, 16: to JS. III. 4. 5.
वायो प्रायश्चित्ते **23**, 8: MBr. I. 4. 2 (var.).
वायो व्रतपते **13**, 5: MBr. I. 6. 10 (differing.).
विरूपाक्षो ऽसि **2**, 17(20); **9**, 1: MBr. II. 4. 6 (many differences).
विश्वा उत त्वया **22**, 3: MBr. I. 2. 5. b (var.)
विष्णोर्मनसा पूते **2**, 9: Gobh. 1. 7. 23.
विष्णुर्योनिम् **23**, 18—20: MBr. I. 4. 6.

4 वेदेषु यथास्वम् **15**, 1.
वेदोऽसि **7**, 17.
व्याहृति **13**, 13; **32**, 20.
व्रतानां व्रतपते **13**, 7: MBr. I. 6. 13 (differing.).
शण्डाय मर्काय **7**, 20: cp. Pār. I. 16. 23.

4 शम्यासि **30**, 14.
शिवा नः शंतमा **17**, 12: cp. Taitt. ār. I. 3 (9).
संवत्सराय परिवत्सराय **28**, 18: MBr. I. 1. 12 (var.).

1 सदसस्पतिमद्भुतम् **14**, 9; **32**, 8: JS. I. 2. 1. 6. 7.
सदसि सन्मे भूयाः **5**, 6: cp. Kauś. sū. 136. 3.

1 सनादग्ने **32**, 9: JS. I. 1. 8. 8.

1 समन्या यन्ति **16**, 3: JS. II. 1. 6.
सं मासं प्रविश (!) **7**, 16: cp. MBr. I. 5. 14. b.

3 समुद्रं वः प्रहिणोमि **5**, 12—15.
समृद्ध्यै स्वाहा **4**, 15; 17: Mān. II. 13. 6.
सरस्वतेऽनुमन्यस्व **3**, 14: Khād. I. 2. 19; Gobh. I. 3. 3 (var.).
सह नो ऽस्तु **14**, 5: Pār. II. 10. 22 (var.).
सामसावित्री **14**. 7; **32**, 21.

1 सावित्री **13**, 19; **14**, 2, 7; **31**, 14; **32**, 18: JS. IV. 3. 8.
सुमङ्गलीरियम् **22**, 10: MBr. I. 2. 14.
सूर्य प्रायश्चित्ते **23**, 10: MBr. I. 4. 4 (var.).
सोमः प्रथमः **21**, 4.

1 सोमं राजानम् **14**, 8; **32**, 21: JS. I. 1. 10. 1.
सोमाय पितृमते **26**, 2: MBr. II. 2. 1 (var.).
सोमाय स्वाहा **4**, 1.
सोमो ऽददत् **21**, 3: MBr. I. 1. 17.

4 स्वराभिवीक्षे **16**, 2: cp. Khād. II. 5. 31.
स्वस्त्ययनो ऽसि **12**, 13; **17**, 21.
हिं भूर्भुवः स्वः। किं पश्यसि **7**, 4: MBr. I. 5. 5 (slight var.).
हिं भूर्भुवः स्वरागन्त्रा **11**, 8: MBr. I. 6. 14.
हिरण्ययी अरणी **23**, 22.

———